A Guide to the Book of EXODUS

A Guide to the Book of EXODUS

John H. Dobson

Judson Press® Valley Forge

A GUIDE TO THE BOOK OF EXODUS

First published in 1977 by the S.P.C.K.
Holy Trinity Church, Marylebone Road, London NW1 4DU
Published in 1978 by Judson Press, Valley Forge, PA 19481

This book is one of a series sponsored and subsidized by the Theological Education Fund in response to requests from Africa, Asia, the Caribbean, and the Pacific. Special attention is given to problems of interpretation and application arising there as well as in the West, and to the particular needs of students using English as a second language.

Library of Congress Cataloging in Publication Data

Dobson, John H.
A guide to Exodus.

Includes index
1. Bible. O.T. Exodus—Commentaries.
I. Title.
BS1245.3.D62 1978 222'.12'07 78-17530
ISBN 0-8170-0766-0

Contents

Illustrations, Map, Diagram

ACKNOWLEDGEMENTS

The photographs in this book are reproduced by courtesy of the British Museum (p. 115), Lee/Dennis, Methodist Information, Singapore (pp. 144 and 171), the Mansell Collection, London (pp. 86 and 183), and Camera Press Ltd.

The map is based, by kind permission of the Lutterworth Press, on one of the maps in their Students' Bible Atlas by H. H. Rowley.

Preface

When I was asked to write *A Guide to Exodus* I hoped to finish the work in two or three years. It has taken five or six. It began in Uganda, at Bishop Tucker Theological College. It stopped for some months in 1972–3 as I moved back to England and looked for a job. It has been completed while I have worked in a busy parish.

I wish to thank the students and staff of Bishop Tucker College. They encouraged me in the first stages of the work. I also wish to thank Miss Daphne Terry of the TEF for her many helpful suggestions, and her patience as the months have gone by. My thanks also to my family and to people in St Andrew's Parish, Gorleston: they have had to cope with someone who has often been buried in books and papers.

In the past many different scholars have put forward ideas about the Book of Exodus. In a small book such as this Study Guide it is not possible to discuss many of their views. I cannot hope to please everyone who reads this Guide, but I hope that those who disagree with some of the things I say will nevertheless be helped to think clearly and prayerfully about the meaning of the Book of Exodus for us today.

Gorleston, UK JOHN H. DOBSON

Using this Guide

The plan of this book follows the same sort of pattern as other biblical Guides in the series.

In his Introduction the author discusses some of the reasons why the Book of Exodus is important to us today, suggests a useful way to begin our study of it, and shows how Exodus is related to the other books of the Pentateuch and to the Bible as a whole.

Then the commentary is in three main parts, covering Exodus 1.1—15.21 (God brought the Israelites out of Egypt), 15.22—18.27 (God led the Israelites to Sinai), and 19.1—40.38 (God made His Covenant with the Israelites), respectively. The Bible text itself is divided for convenience into fairly short sections, the treatment of each consisting of:

1. An *Outline* of the passage and summary of its context within the book;
2. *Interpretation and Comment* on the passage as a whole and on its teaching and relevance for Christians—and others—today;
3. *Notes* on particular words and points of possible difficulty, especially as relating to the history of the time, and to comparable passages and references in other parts of the Bible.

SPECIAL NOTES

Separate Special Notes deal in greater detail with the historical and literary background, including certain matters on which the opinion of experts is still divided. Readers should find these helpful in sorting out some of the puzzles which may confront them in their study of Exodus. However, the commentary itself does deal with these matters, though more briefly, and readers with limited time need not regard the Special Notes as essential to a general understanding of the book of Exodus.

STUDY SUGGESTIONS AND QUESTIONS

Suggestions for review and further study are provided at the end of each section. Besides enabling students who are working alone to check their own progress, they provide subjects for individual and group research, and topics for discussion. They are divided into two main sorts:

1. *Review of Content* These will help readers to ensure they have fully grasped the ideas and points of teaching studied, and to check their understanding of specific words and phrases;
2. *Bible Study and Reflection* Some of these relate the content and teaching in Exodus to that in other parts of the Bible, and will enable

students to complete their study of particular biblical themes. Others will help readers to clarify their own thinking and beliefs on the themes studied, and to relate the teaching of Exodus to their own lives and situation.

The best way to use these Study Suggestions is: first, re-read the Bible passage; second, read the appropriate section of the Guide once or twice, and then do the work suggested, either in writing or in group discussion, without looking at the Guide again except where instructed to do so.

The *Key* on p. 195 will enable you to check your work on those questions which can be checked in this way. In most cases the Key does not give the answer to a question: it shows where an answer is to be found.

Please note that all these are only suggestions. Some readers may not wish to use the study material at all; and some teachers may wish to select only those questions which are most relevant to the needs of their particular students, or to substitute questions relating more directly to their own situation.

INDEX

The Index (p. 199) includes only the more important proper names and the main subjects which appear in Exodus or which are discussed in the Guide.

BIBLE VERSION

The English translation of the Bible used in the Guide is the Revised Standard Version (RSV). Reference is also made to the New English Bible (NEB) or the Jerusalem Bible (JB) where these help to show the meaning more clearly.

Further Reading

EXODUS

SHORTER COMMENTARIES

Exodus: An Introduction and Commentary, Alan Cole. Inter-Varsity Press

Exodus: Introduction and Commentary, G. Henton Davies. Allenson

LONGER COMMENTARIES

Century Bible, New Series: Exodus, J. P. Hyatt. Thomas Nelson, Inc.
Exodus, B. S. Childs. SCM Press

MOSES

Moses, G. von Rad. Lutterworth (WCB Series)

Moses, Martin Buber. OUP

BACKGROUND

The Student's Bible Atlas, H. H. Rowley. Lutterworth

The Bible and Archaeology, R. J. Thompson. Wm. B. Eerdmans Publishing Company

A History of Israel, John Bright. The Westminster Press

The Old Testament Against Its Environment, G. E. Wright. SCM Press

Ancient Orient and Old Testament, K. A. Kitchen. Inter-Varsity Press

The articles in your Bible dictionary on: Aaron, Commandments, Covenant, Egypt, Exodus, Law, Moses, Passover, Pentateuch, Plagues, Redemption, Sacrifice, Tabernacle.

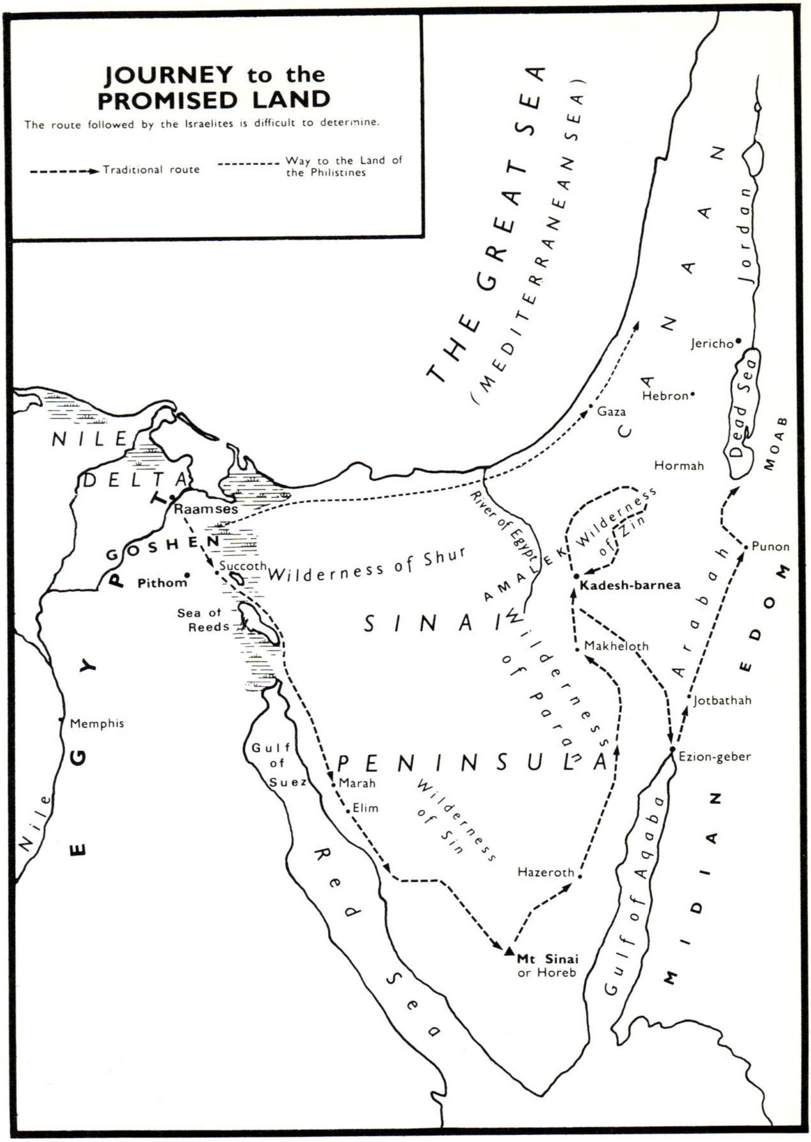
JOURNEY to the PROMISED LAND
The route followed by the Israelites is difficult to determine.
Traditional route
Way to the Land of the Philistines
THE GREAT SEA
(MEDITERRANEAN SEA)
NILE DELTA
Raamses
GOSHEN
Pithom
Succoth
Wilderness of Shur
Sea of Reeds
EGYPT
Memphis
Nile
Gulf of Suez
Red Sea
SINAI PENINSULA
Marah
Elim
Wilderness of Sin
Mt Sinai or Horeb
Hazeroth
Wilderness of Paran
AMALEK
River of Egypt
Wilderness of Zin
Kadesh-barnea
Makheloth
Gaza
Hebron
Hormah
Jericho
CANAAN
Jordan
Dead Sea
MOAB
Punon
EDOM
Arabah
Jotbathah
Ezion-geber
Gulf of Aqaba
MIDIAN

INTRODUCTION
EXODUS AND US

1
Why we study the Book of Exodus

All round the world there are people who know that Moses led the Israelites out of Egypt. People have heard of the Ten Commandments. Millions of Jews, Christians, and Muslims believe that there is only one God and that He is the source of everything that exists in the universe. They believe that God cares for people, that He helps them, that He calls us to know Him and to serve Him and to worship Him. Many of the roots from which their faith has grown are to be found in the Book of Exodus. It is one of the world's greatest books. It is worth studying.

We may study Exodus for many reasons. Here are some of them:

(a) Because we are interested and want to understand it better.
(b) Because we have to pass an examination on it.
(c) Because we want to preach or teach about it.
(d) Because we believe we shall learn about God and the way He wants people to live today.

This study guide is meant to help you to enjoy studying Exodus whatever reasons you have for doing so.

2
What the Book of Exodus is about

Exodus tells the story of a people who were slaves, who were set free, and who set out to go to a new land. It tells a story of what God did for them, and of what He demanded from them.

(a) THE ISRAELITES WERE SET FREE FROM SLAVERY

The Israelites were living in Egypt. The Egyptian rulers oppressed them, and forced them to work as slaves (Exod. 1—2). The writer of the book of Exodus tells how God set them free (Exod. 3—15).

Whenever one group of people, or a tribe or race, is hated or oppressed or exploited by another, they can find in the book of Exodus a message of hope and a challenge. The message of hope is for those who suffer. The challenge and warning is first of all for those who oppress them. But as we study the book we shall find that there are also warnings for those who wish to be liberated.

People who have been oppressed and forced to work for others have found the message of the book of Exodus full of meaning. Africans taken to America remembered Moses in many of their songs. They sang, 'Go down, Moses, tell old Pharaoh, "Let my people go"'. They knew that God wants people to be free.

People still oppress and enslave and hate one another. Rulers are still afraid or unwilling to give freedom and equality to people they rule. The book of Exodus has a message that people need to hear.

(b) THEY SET OUT TO GO TO A NEW LAND

Exodus is also the story of the beginning of a new nation. The writer tells how the Israelites left Egypt, where they had been slaves, to go to the land of Canaan (Palestine). They hoped that they would be free, independent, and prosperous in the land that God had promised to give them.

When people set out to journey to a new place, Exodus is a book of encouragement. As we read it, we are encouraged to hope that what lies ahead of us may be better than what we have left behind.

As African tribes have moved from place to place, as people from Europe moved westwards across North America, as Russians have moved eastwards to the 'virgin lands' of Siberia, so people have always hoped to find a land where they can be free and prosperous. As new nations become independent, their people rejoice in freedom and work for prosperity. But often they find after a time that they are not truly free.

The book of Exodus shows that if the Israelites wanted to prosper and to be truly free in the new land to which they were going, they had to be ready to live a certain kind of life. They must give God the first place in their lives. They must also treat each other justly and fairly. Chapters 19—40 are mainly about the laws which God gave to the people whom He had already set free. If they kept them, they would continue to enjoy God's presence and His blessing.

Today also people look forward. They hope for a new age in which they may be free and prosperous and live in brotherhood. As we read the book of Exodus we are reminded that those who wish to be truly free must be ready to treat other people justly. There is no place for violent action to destroy other people and their property. True freedom is God's gift. We must use it to worship and serve God, and to serve our fellow men and women.

(c) GOD, THE WORLD AND OUR LIVES

When the book of Exodus was written, there were many people who thought that there were a large number of gods and goddesses. Others thought that there might be one creator-god, but that he was too far away to be concerned with the everyday affairs of people's lives. The writer of the book of Exodus, as he tells his story, makes it clear that he believes there is only one true God. He is a God who comes near to people. He makes Himself known. He has a purpose for men's lives, and He makes it known to them. He is active in the world that He has made. He is God of the past, of the present, and of the future.

In the world today there are people who ask, 'Is there only one God, or are there many gods?' There are those who believe in a Creator, but who pray to other gods because they think the Creator is too important, or too far away, to be troubled about human beings and about their problems. But there are many others who say, 'We live in a wonderful world, but we do not think there is any God who made it. We want to be free, to be loving, and not to hurt anyone, but we do not think that this has anything to do with faith in God.' A study of the book of Exodus may not answer the questions that such people have in their minds, but it may help us to think again whether we live in a world that belongs to God or not.

(d) THE PURPOSE OF THE WRITER

The writer of the book of Exodus told a story about the people of Israel and what God did for them and said to them. He told the story because he believed it was true. But this was not the only reason why he wrote the story in a book. He wrote it down in a book because he thought it was important that other people should be able to go on telling the story and telling it accurately. He wanted people to hear the story because he believed that it would help them to trust in God and know the right way to live.

Two men are talking together. They both have young boys to bring up.

Yofesi: 'Hello, Petero, how are you and your two boys?'
Petero: 'We are all well, thank you. The boys have just left our village. They have gone to the school in the town. We heard it has the best teachers. They send many boys to university. So all of us in our family have saved up money to send the boys to school there.'
Yofesi: 'Thank you for telling me about the school.'

When Yofesi has heard about the school, he probably thinks, 'Is this true?' If he considers that it is true, he must make a decision. He must decide whether to try to send his own sons to that school. If he decides to do this, then he must act. He and his family must save the necessary money.

The writer of the book of Exodus wrote a story. He meant the readers and listeners to think, to make decisions, and to act. When we read Exodus, we shall find that we are constantly having to do the same three things:

1. *To think:* Does this book tell us something true about God and about our lives?

2. *To decide:* Do we mean to trust in God and to seek to live as He wants us to do?

3. *To act:* To do what we see to be God's will for us.

The Contents and Context of the Book of Exodus

We begin our study of the Book of Exodus by thinking about its title, outline, and context.

THE TITLE OF THE BOOK

Exodus was written in the Hebrew language. It had no title. When the Jews wanted to refer to it they used its first words 'And these are the names' (Exod. 1.1) as a title.

When the book was translated into Greek it was given the title *Exodus*. *Exodus* is a Greek word that means 'a going out, a departure, a procession'. It is a useful title for the book, because it reminds us that the book contains the story of how the Israelites went out as free men from slavery in Egypt.

Later on, European translators used the title, *The Second Book of Moses*. So the RSV has the title *The Second Book of Moses, commonly called Exodus*. This might mean either of two things.

(a) It might mean that this is the second of a group of five books in which Moses is the most important person. We may compare it with the title, *The Second Book of Samuel*. The Second Book of Samuel includes many events which happened after Samuel died, but it is 'Part 2' of a story in which Samuel is the central character.

(b) Or it might mean that this is the second of the books which Moses wrote. (We shall consider the question of who wrote the book of Exodus when we reach the end of studying it.)

2. MAKING AN OUTLINE OF EXODUS

When a medical student begins to study the human body, he does not usually begin with a detailed study of the hand or any other small part. He needs first of all to know something about the body as a whole. In our study of Exodus it will be helpful if we can first find out what the book as a whole is about. One way to do this is to make a rough outline of the book.

If you have a Bible with page headings, here is one way that you can make an outline of Exodus. Read through the page headings. Then read them through again and see what the main subjects of the book are. Write down as briefly as you can the main subjects you have found.

If your Bible has no page or section headings, read the first two verses of each chapter of Exodus. When you have done this, write down what you think are the main subjects of the book. When you have done this for yourself, study outlines A and B given below.

OUTLINE A

1. God delivered the Israelites from slavery in Egypt (Exod. 1—18).
2. God gave his commandments to the Israelites at Sinai (Exod. 19—40).

OUTLINE B

1.1—15.21: God delivered the Israelites from Egypt

1. The sufferings of the Israelites in Egypt (1.1–22).
2. The birth and call of Moses (2.1—4.26).
3. The contest with Pharaoh: the Plagues, and the Passover (4.27—12.36).
4. Israel's escape from Egypt: crossing the Sea of Reeds (12.37—15.21).

15.22—18.27: God led the Israelites from Egypt to Mount Sinai

1. God provided water, manna, and quails (15.22—17.7).
2. Israel's victory over the Amalekites (17.8–16).
3. Leaders appointed to help Moses (18.1–27).

19.1—40.38: God made His Covenant with the Israelites at Sinai

1. The Covenant: commandments about daily life (19.1—24.18).
2. Commandments about worship: the ark, the tabernacle, and the priests (25.1—31.18).
3. The breaking and renewing of the Covenant (32.1—35.3).
4. The making of the tabernacle (35.4—40.38).

As you see, Outline A gives emphasis only to the two main themes of the Book of Exodus. It helps us to remember that Exodus is a book about what God did for the people of Israel, and about what He expected them to do as people whom He had set free.

Outline B gives more details. When we are studying a particular part of Exodus, this outline may help us to see how it fits into the whole book. When we have read the whole of Exodus, Outline B may help us to recall its contents.

3. THE CONTEXT OF THE BOOK OF EXODUS

(a) EXODUS IS A PART OF THE PENTATEUCH

The Book of Exodus is part of a longer story. The story is told in the books of Genesis, Exodus, Leviticus, Numbers, and Deuteronomy. These five books are often called the *Pentateuch*, that is 'the five-volume book'. Let us consider briefly the five parts of the book.

1. *The Book of Genesis* begins with God. The writer tells a story of God's work in creating and controlling the world. He shows that God has a plan for people, a good way for them to live (Gen. 1—2). Because God has planned the best way for men, when they refuse to live in God's way they make trouble for themselves, for other people, and for the world. Genesis shows how departing from God's plan and breaking His laws leads to shame, hatred, crime, trouble, and punishment (Gen. 3—11).

Genesis also tells how God chose Abraham and his descendants, so that through them all the nations of the world might be blessed. God also promised to give the land of Canaan to Abraham's descendants (Gen. 12—36). Genesis ends with the story of how the family of Jacob, descendants of Abraham, left Canaan and went to live in the land of Egypt (Gen. 37—50).

2. *Exodus* continues this story. It tells how the Israelites in Egypt, the descendants of Jacob, grew in numbers, and how the Egyptians treated them as slaves; how God called Moses, and reminded the Israelites that He had promised to give them the land of Canaan; how God delivered them from Egypt, led them through the wilderness, and gave them His law at Mount Sinai.

This story of the beginning of the nation of Israel and of God's purposes for them is continued in:

3. *Leviticus:* a book of laws about sacrifice, priesthood, and holiness.
4. *Numbers:* a book about the Israelites' journey from Mount Sinai to Moab, on the borders of Canaan.
5. *Deuteronomy:* a book about how Moses preached to the Israelites in Moab before they crossed the river Jordan into Canaan.

(b) EXODUS IS PART OF THE BIBLE

For the Jews, Exodus is part of the Law of God (*Torah*) which they believe God inspired men to write down. Through many hundreds of years, Jews have remembered how God set their ancestors free from oppression by the Egyptians. Year by year, at the Passover Festival, they still look back and thank God for what He did at the time of the exodus from Egypt. They also look forward hopefully to what God will do for them in the future. They are confident that God will not fail in His love and goodness towards them.

Christians also believe that Exodus is part of the Holy Scriptures, a collection of books written by men of God to help and guide His people

'Exodus tells . . . how God delivered the Israelites from Egypt, led them through the wilderness, and gave them His law at Mount Sinai' (p. 6).

Looking down from the height of Mount Sinai today, we see the sort of desert country through which the Israelites journeyed to reach the Promised Land.

(see 2 Pet. 1.19–21 and 2 Tim. 3.14–17: both these passages refer to the Old Testament). Christians believe that what is shown in the book of Exodus about God's ways of saving and guiding the people of Israel can help us to understand His ways of saving and guiding all who will trust in Him.

When we reach the end of our study of the Book of Exodus we shall be able to consider in more detail its relationship to the other books of the Bible.

STUDY SUGGESTIONS AND QUESTIONS

REVIEW OF CONTENT

1. What is the meaning of the word *Exodus*?
2. What is the meaning of the word *Pentateuch*?
3. In the RSV we find the title 'The Second Book of Moses'. In what two different ways have people understood this title?
4. Into what main sections did we divide the Book of Exodus in Outline A and Outline B (p. 5)?

BIBLE STUDY AND REFLECTION

5. Look again at Outline A on p. 5. Many people who have great problems in their lives say, 'I need the help of God, but I don't deserve it. I think I must first of all make myself good enough for God, and then perhaps He will help me.' What would you say to such a person? Does Outline A help you to think about your answer? If so, in what way?
6. Look again at Outline B on p. 5. What are the three main ways in which it shows that God acted to help the Israelites? Do you think God still helps people in similar ways today? Give reasons for your answer.
7. 'The writer of Exodus meant readers to think, to make decisions, and to act' (p. 3). Read Exod. 19.7–9 and 24.3–8. In what ways do you think the writer of Exodus expected readers of these passages to think, to decide, and to act?
8. Why do you think the writer of Exodus wrote the book? Consider these possible answers:
   (a) To tell people an interesting story,
   (b) To teach people about the history of Israel,
   (c) To help people to trust in God.
   (d) To challenge people to live in a new way.
   Which do you think are the best answers? (Does your answer to question 7 above help you to decide about this question?)
9. 'Christians believe that . . . the book of Exodus . . . can help us to

understand God's ways of saving and guiding all who trust in Him' (p. 3).

(a) Read 1 Cor. 10.1–12. In what ways did Paul think the story told in Exodus could help Christians who believed that, so long as they were baptized and received Holy Communion, God must be pleased with them?

(b) Read Acts 7.17–41. Stephen spoke about the ways in which the Israelites had responded to Moses. In what ways was he suggesting that people were responding similarly to Jesus? What do you think he hoped that his hearers would learn from what he said? What decisions did he want them to make?

(c) Read Hebrews 3.1–6. (i) In what ways does the writer suggest that Jesus was similar to Moses? (ii) In what ways does he say that Jesus was superior to Moses? (iii) He was writing to Christians who had previously been Jews. Because of suffering they were tempted to give up their faith in Jesus and to become Jews again. What decision was the writer of the letter encouraging them to make?

STUDY GUIDE AND COMMENTARY

PART 1 1.1–15.21

GOD BROUGHT THE ISRAELITES OUT OF EGYPT

1.1–22
Oppression in Egypt

OUTLINE AND CONTEXT

1.1–7: The Israelites in Egypt increased in number.
1.8–22: The Egyptian king tried to control them:
  (a) by making the Israelite men work for the Egyptians (1.8–14).
  (b) by having Israelite boys killed when they were born (1.15–22).

The beginning of the Book of Exodus links it to the Book of Genesis. Exodus 1.1 reminds the reader of Genesis 37—50, the story of how Jacob's family went to Egypt and settled there. The account of the troubles suffered by the Israelites (Exod. 1.8–22) introduces the story of how God delivered them (Exod. 2.1—15.21).

INTERPRETATION AND COMMENT

Exodus 1.1–17 covers a period of nearly 400 years (Gen. 15.3; Exod. 12.40). During that time the Israelites grew from a family to a group of tribes. They were few: they became many. The writer of Exodus says that this was because God blessed them (Exod. 1.7, 20–21; compare Gen. 1.28). But the ruler of Egypt, the Pharaoh, considered that the Israelites' increase in numbers was a danger to Egypt (Exod. 1.10). So he tried to control them, first by making them work as slaves, and then also by having their baby boys killed.

This chapter makes us think about two important matters:

1. the oppression of one group of people by another;
2. the growth of populations.

1. OPPRESSION

The Egyptian king forced the Israelites to work as his slaves. This was not something strange or unusual in Egypt. The Egyptians treated in the same way other groups of people who had come into Egypt from neighbouring lands.

The history of the world is full of stories of how people in every continent have made others their slaves. In the present century millions of people have been forced to work in prison camps, in Germany under Hitler, in Russia under Stalin, and in other countries. In many parts of Africa today people are despised or oppressed because they belong to a particular tribe or race or colour. In India many people have been persecuted because they were Muslims, in Pakistan because they were Hindus. Throughout the world there are problems where richer countries have brought in workers from poorer countries.

The book of Exodus shows that the oppression of one group of people by another is evil. It shows that God can help the oppressed and punish the oppressors.

In the laws of Israel special care was shown for immigrants; that is, for foreigners from other lands who came to live in Israel. In the RSV such immigrants are called 'strangers' or 'sojourners'. (Read Exod. 22.21; 23.9; Lev. 19.10; 19.33–34; Num. 15.14–16; Deut. 10.18–19). Immigrants who settled in the land were to be treated fairly. There was to be the same law for them as for the native Israelites. More than that, they were to be given special care and help. The Israelites were to remember how they themselves had been immigrants in Egypt. Their law and their conduct in this respect were to express the principle which Jesus taught later on: 'Treat others as you would like them to treat you.'

2. POPULATION GROWTH

Old Testament writers believed that children are a blessing from God (Gen. 1.28; Exod. 1.20–21; Ps. 127.3–5). But we need to think whether this is so in every situation. In a family where parents love each other, and can provide love and care for their children, it is easy to welcome children as a blessing. But what should we think about a family where the parents are always quarrelling, and have already more children than they can properly care for?

In some areas of the world there are still very few people. But in the world as a whole the population is growing very quickly. Millions of people do not have enough food to eat. There are too few schools, hospitals, houses, and roads. In one country where the national government was spending a quarter of its total income on education, the population was growing so fast that each year a larger proportion of children were unable to go to school. In some countries married women have a baby almost every year. After some years, many of these women become weak or ill, or they die, simply as a result of having too many children. In the world of today, we have to ask ourselves: 'Does God want us to go on having many children? Does He want populations to grow without limit?'

Some Christians say: 'It is God's will for us to have many children. The Bible says that God wants us to be fruitful and multiply.' But this answer

'They set taskmasters over them to afflict them with heavy burdens' (Exod. 1.11). 'History is full of stories of how people in every continent have made others their slaves' (p. 11).

In parts of Latin America even young children are afflicted with 'burdens', like this Peruvian boy carrying a heavy load of stones for making a road. What are the reasons which lead people to make others 'serve with rigour' (1.13)?

seems to be too simple. The command to be fruitful and multiply (Gen. 1.28) was given when the world was empty of people. When a bucket is empty, someone may say, 'Fill this bucket with water.' But he does not mean that we should go on pouring in more and more water after the bucket is full.

NOTES

1.1. Israel . . . Jacob: These are both names of Isaac's younger son (Gen. 25.26; 32.28; 35.10). The name *Jacob* meant 'He took hold of the heel' or 'He wrongly took the place of'. A similar name, *Jacob-el*, meant 'May God protect'.

The name *Israel* probably meant 'God strives' or 'May God strive'. Israel became the most common name in the Old Testament for the whole nation, but the name Jacob was also used (see, for example, Isaiah 49.5).

1.8–14. A new king: The title given to each king of Egypt was *Pharaoh*. Pharaoh Sethos (or Seti) I ruled about 1316–1304 B.C. His son Ramesses II ruled about 1304–1229 B.C. They were the Pharaohs who had a new capital city built in the Nile Delta area. The Egyptians called it *Pi-Ramesse* (the House of Ramesses). In Exodus 1.11 it is called Raamses. An Egyptian inscription from the time of Ramesses II mentions *Apiri* (Semitic people) who 'hauled great stones for the fortress of the city Pi-Ramesse'.

1.10 If war befalls us: That is, if enemies come to attack Egypt. The Egyptians at that time had many enemies. The most powerful were the Hittites who lived in Asia Minor and northern Syria. In 1299 B.C. they defeated a large Egyptian army in Syria.

1.10. Escape from the land: The Hebrew words are 'Go up from the land', which means 'Go to Canaan' (see Gen. 50.5–9).

1.15–20. Shiphrah means 'Beautiful'. **Puah** means 'Splendid'. These are both very ancient names. They have been found in writings dating from the time of Moses and earlier.

1.21. The midwives feared God: To 'fear' God means to respect Him and worship Him, and so to try to please Him in daily life. This verse does not mean that the midwives were afraid of God.

1.21. He gave them families: That is, He gave them children of their own.

STUDY SUGGESTIONS AND QUESTIONS

REVIEW OF CONTENT

1. For about how many years did the Israelites live in Egypt?
2. Why did the Egyptians become afraid of the Israelites?
3. What did the Egyptians do to try to control the Israelites and to reduce their numbers?

4. The Israelites suffered while they were living in a foreign country. How did this experience affect the laws they made about immigrants?

BIBLE STUDY AND REFLECTION

5. The Israelites were immigrants in Egypt, and the Egyptians oppressed them. Think about your own country. Ask yourself:
   (a) How do we treat immigrants?
   (b) Is everyone treated in the same way by the law, or are there some laws which apply only to immigrants or to people of a particular tribe or colour?
   (c) Is everyone treated in the same way by the police and the courts?
   (d) Can you think of any groups of people who are treated unfairly in your country? If so, why do you think this happens?
   (e) If your answers to (a)–(d) show that there are problems and injustices, what do you think can be done about them: by individual Christians? by the Churches working together? by all the people?
6. Someone whose family was leaving one country to live in another said 'You cannot expect us to change our ways.' What kind of problems arise when people with different customs and cultures live together in one country? How far do you think immigrants should: (a) keep their own customs? (b) adopt the customs of the people of the land to which they have moved?
7. Read Genesis 50.22–26. What promise is there in this passage which might have given hope and courage to the Israelites when they suffered in Egypt?
8. The Israelites believed that God had called them to be His people. They suffered very much in Egypt. Christians also believe that God has called them to be His people. Should they expect that their life will be easy? Give reasons for your answer. Refer, if you can, to passages in the New Testament. (You may find it helpful to look up 'suffering', 'hardship', 'tribulation', and 'cross' in a Concordance.)
9. As Christians we pray to God, 'May your will be done'. Are there any ways in which you think God is calling you to work: (a) to help those who suffer, and (b) to prevent more people from suffering.
10. Find out as accurately as you can:
    (a) What the present population of your country is, or what it was at the last census?
    (b) How much it is increasing, or how much it increased between the last census and the one before that.
    (c) What the present population of the world is estimated to be.
    (d) By how many millions the population of the world is likely to be increasing each year.
    What do you think people should do about this situation?
11. 'Children are a blessing from God' (p. 11).

(a) Do you think this is always so?
(b) For what reasons did Pharaoh want to stop the Israelites increasing in numbers?
(c) For what reasons do many modern governments want to limit the growth of population in their countries?
(d) Do you think that parents today should have as many children as they can? Give reasons for your answer. If not, in what ways do you think parents should limit the number of their children?

2.1–25

Moses before his Call

OUTLINE AND CONTEXT

2.1–11: Moses was born. When he was three months old a daughter of Pharaoh found him hidden by the river. She brought him up as her son.
2.12–15a: Moses killed an Egyptian foreman who was beating an Israelite.
2.15b–22: Moses escaped to Midian. He lived with Reuel, the Midianite priest. He married Zipporah, a daughter of Reuel.
2.23–25: God heard the prayer of the Israelites who were suffering in Egypt.

The story in Exodus 2.1–3 follows on from the command in Exodus 1.22 that Israelite boys were to be thrown into the Nile. Exodus 2.23–25 recalls Exodus 1.8–14 and prepares the reader for the story of how God called Moses to deliver the Israelites (3.1—4.17).

INTERPRETATION AND COMMENT

1. THE BIRTH OF MOSES (2.1–3)

The Old Testament contains four stories about the birth of children through whom God intended to work out His plan for His people. They are the stories of the birth of Isaac (Gen. 15–21), Moses (Exod. 2), Samson (Judges 13), and Samuel (1 Sam. 1). In each story we find that the parents had a problem. In the story of Moses there was the danger that the Egyptians might kill the child. In the other three stories the mother had spent many years without being able to have a child: but God was at work to overcome the problem.

When Isaiah wrote his prophecy of the birth of Immanuel ('God with us', Isa. 7.14), he used words similar to those in Exodus 2.2, Judges 13.5a, and Genesis 17.19a. It is as though Isaiah was saying, 'Yes, there are many problems. But God is at work. A special child will be born. Through him

God's promises and purposes will be fulfilled as they were through Isaac and Moses.'

The writers of the Gospels of Matthew and Luke remembered these Old Testament stories and prophecies when they wrote the story of the birth of Jesus. They emphasized the problem Mary had: she was not married. But they showed that God was at work in a special way. So, through the birth of Jesus, God came in a new way to deliver His people.

2. THE ESCAPE OF MOSES TO MIDIAN (2.11–22)

Moses wanted to help the Israelites whom the Egyptians were oppressing, so he killed the Egyptian foreman (2.11–12). Moses also wanted to make people act justly, so he tried to stop Israelites from fighting each other (2.13). But Moses did not manage to succeed by violent action. There is nothing in the story to suggest that God had called Moses to do what he did. Moses acted in his own way. He did not yet know how God wanted him to act.

In Midian, Moses helped the daughters of Reuel (2.16–19). One reason why Moses later became a great leader was that he was so ready to help people who were in need.

3. GOD'S CONCERN FOR HIS PEOPLE (2.23–25)

God was concerned about the suffering of the Israelites. He heard their prayer. He was ready to act to set them free. This is one of the great teachings of the Bible: God hears the prayer of His people when they are in trouble, and He helps them (see also Psalm 9.9–10; 18.61; 31.21–24; 62.8).

But if God cared for the Israelites, we may wonder why they suffered in Egypt for so many years before He took action to deliver them. This is a problem which Christians still face today, as they pray for their fellow Christians in parts of the world where Christians are persecuted. When the Communists gained control in China, it happened that in one university two hundred of the students were Christians. Because they believed in God, they would not say that they were in favour of a government which said there was no God. The Communists set out to destroy their faith. Each day they were teased, bullied, and persecuted. But each night they met secretly to pray together. As none of them would give up their faith they were each isolated from their Christian companions. After weeks of indoctrination they were led out to a public trial. They were given a chance to deny their faith in God. The first student to be questioned was a girl. She said, 'When I was put in prison I believed in Jesus Christ and I thought the Bible was true. Now I still believe in Jesus Christ and I know the Bible is true'. She was killed, and one by one all the rest of the two hundred Christian students after her. It seems that God heard their prayer for courage, but this did not mean that they escaped from suffering.

If we believe in God, we shall often find ourselves asking, 'Why did God allow this or that to happen?' We may not always be able to find an answer to our questions.

NOTES

2.1. The house of Levi: That is, the descendants of Levi, the tribe of Levi. *A daughter of Levi* means a young woman who was a member of the tribe. It seems that among the early Israelites marriage was most commonly between a man and a woman of the same tribe. But the examples of Moses (Exod. 2.21) and of Boaz (Ruth 4.10) show that Israelite men sometimes married women who did not belong to their own tribe or country. (For Levi's birth, see Gen. 29.34).
2.3. A basket made of bulrushes: The Egyptians used papyrus reeds for making baskets, chests, and boats.
2.5. The daughter of Pharaoh: We do not know her name. The Pharaohs of Egypt usually had many concubines as well as their wives. We do not know whether this was a daughter of the Pharaoh's wife, or of a concubine.
2.7. A nurse . . . to nurse the child: That is, a woman to feed the child at the breast.
2.10. She named him Moses: The name Moses is probably an Egyptian word *Mose* meaning originally 'he is born'. Compare the name of the Pharaoh Thutmose, which means 'the god Thoth is born'. But the Hebrew form of his name, *Mosheh*, was also a reminder that he was rescued from the river, for the Hebrew word *Mashah* means 'pull out'.
2.15. Midian: The Midianites were a progressive and powerful group of tribes. They lived chiefly in the region east of the Gulf of Aqaba. It was an area with many small oases and water that could be used for irrigation. Discoveries made by archaeologists since 1969 suggest that at the time of Moses the Midianites were over-lords of Moab and Edom, and also controlled the trade-routes of north-west Arabia.

The story of Moses's friendship with the Midianites belongs to the earliest stages of Israel's history. In the time of the Judges the Midianites were enemies of Israel (Judges 6—7).
2.18. Their father Reuel: Reuel means 'friend of God'. The same name is used in Num. 10.29. But in other passages he is called Jethro (Exod. 3.1; 4.18; 18.1). Why does he have two different names? There are two possible sorts of explanation:

(a) It is natural for people to have two names. An English teacher in Uganda was surprised to find that a man who said his name was Dronyi, had written on his exercise book 'Name: Wani'. The man later explanied, 'Wani is my grandfather's name. I also use it'. In the Old Testament the use of two different names is not uncommon. For example, Jacob was called Israel, Pul was called Tiglath-Pileser, and Daniel was called Belteshazzar.

The use of more than one name for a single person is also common in the ancient writings of Egypt, Canaan, and Mesopotamia. Reuel was probably the clan name of Moses's father-in-law, and Jethro his personal name.

(b) Other scholars believe that there were originally two quite different stories told and written down. In one story Moses's father-in-law was a man called Reuel. In another story he was a man called Jethro. Later on an editor combined both stories together, using both names as if they referred to the same man.

There are many problems like this that we find as we study Exodus. We shall discuss them further in Special Note E on pp. 184–191.

2.21. Zipporah: This name means some kind of bird, perhaps a sparrow. In Judges 7.25 we read of Midianite chiefs with bird or animal names: Oreb (raven) and Zeeb (wolf).

2.24. God remembered his covenant: This means that God began to take action to fulfil the promises He had made to Abraham, Isaac, and Jacob (Gen. 12.7; 26.3–4; 28.13–14) It does not mean that He had for some time forgotten the covenant and then suddenly remembered it.

2.24–25. God heard ... remembered ... saw ... knew: The Old Testament writers believed that God is personal. They believed that human beings are made in some ways like God (Gen. 1.27). So when they wrote and spoke about God they naturally used words to describe His activity, words which we also use to describe the activity of people. But they did not believe that God was exactly like a man, or limited as we are by our human bodies.

STUDY SUGGESTIONS AND QUESTIONS

REVIEW OF CONTENT

1. Why was Moses in danger of being killed when he was born?
2. For how long did his mother keep him at home before she put him in a basket among the reeds?
3. Why did Moses have to escape from Egypt? Where did he go?
4. What did Moses do to help the daughters of Reuel?
5. How can we explain the fact that Reuel is also called Jethro?
6. What did the writer of Exodus mean when he wrote, 'God remembered his covenant with Abraham'?

BIBLE STUDY AND REFLECTION

7. In what ways do you think the experiences of Moses in Egypt and in Midian prepared him for the work which God called him to do in leading the people of Israel?
8. In Egypt Moses lived as a member of a royal family (2.10). In Midian

he was ready to work to help women (2.17–19). What do you think we can learn from this? (Read also Mark 10.42–45; John 13.12–17).

9. Moses killed the Egyptian foreman (2.11), but this did not lead to Moses's being able to help the people of Israel out of their troubles. What would you say to someone who said, 'Christians should be ready to act violently and to kill in order to help or to try to liberate those who are oppressed'? Give reasons for your answer.

3.1–22
The Call of Moses (1)

OUTLINE AND CONTEXT

3.1–6: At Horeb, God revealed Himself to Moses as the God of Abraham, Isaac, and Jacob.
3.7–12: God told Moses that He would deliver the Israelites from their suffering. He called Moses to go and lead them out of Egypt. He promised to be with Moses.
3.13–17: God told Moses to tell the Israelites that Yahweh, the God of Abraham, Isaac, and Jacob, had promised to bring them out of Egypt and into the land of Canaan.
3.18–22: God warned Moses that Pharaoh would refuse to let them go, but that in the end He would compel Pharaoh to do so.

Exodus 3—4 continues the story of Exodus 1—2. The call of Moses while he was pasturing Jethro's flock, follows on from 2.16–22. God's promise to deliver the Israelites continues the theme of chapter 1 and 2.23–25. The announcement in 3.18–20 of what God will do in Egypt prepares the way for the story of the plagues in Exodus 5—12.

INTERPRETATION AND COMMENT

Exodus 3 contains many important ideas about God. Note particularly:

1. GOD MAKES HIMSELF KNOWN TO PEOPLE.

Moses was doing his daily work, looking after sheep. He was not expecting anything unusual to happen. He was not seeking for God. But God was seeking for Moses. God spoke to Moses, and the whole course of Moses's life was changed.

God spoke to Moses about what He was going to do for His people. For God makes Himself known not only by words but also by doing what He has said. It was as Moses went on into the future with God, and found that

God kept His promise, that he came to know God more fully. When God reveals Himself to people, as He did to Moses, it is not to give them information about Himself, but to challenge them to trust Him and to go forward in life with Him. A verse of a Chinese hymn says:

> 'God, during the dark time, you have been with me;
> I do not know what the future holds,
> But I dare to trust you no matter what may come,
> By faith I lean upon you and go forward'.

2. GOD CALLS PEOPLE TO SERVE HIM, AND HE GIVES THEM POWER TO DO SO

When God wanted to set the Israelites free from Egypt, He chose a man to lead them out. He chose Moses. God wanted Moses to work for Him. That meant that Moses must work and suffer in order to help other people (3.10). Moses did not like the idea of having to go to the powerful Pharaoh of Egypt. So he said to God, 'I am the wrong sort of person to do this work' (3.11). But God promised to be with him (3.12). Compare Matthew 28.18–20. It is God's presence and power that can make people able to serve Him and carry out His commands.

We would all like to know exactly how God spoke to Moses. Did He speak in words that Moses could hear with his ears, or through some kind of vision, or by causing thoughts to arise in Moses's mind, or how? We do not know. It may be good that we do not know. Gladys Aylward, who was for more than twenty years a missionary in China, has told the story of her life. On more than one occasion she heard God speaking to her, to tell her what to do. Does this mean that we cannot know what God wants us to do unless we hear a voice? No. God uses many different ways to show us what He wants us to do. If the story of Moses's call explained exactly how it happened, perhaps many people would feel that they could not know God unless they had an experience exactly the same as that of Moses.

3. GOD MAKES PROMISES TO PEOPLE, AND HE DOES WHAT HE HAS PROMISED

In Exodus 3.6, 13–16, God is four times called, 'the God of your fathers'. The word 'fathers' here means 'forefathers' or 'ancestors', and refers to Abraham, Isaac, and Jacob. When God tells Moses that He is the God of Abraham, Isaac, and Jacob this is not only so that Moses may know that He is the same God whom Abraham worshipped. It is particularly to remind Moses of the promises He had made to Abraham (Gen. 12.7) and had renewed to Isaac (Gen. 26.3–4) and to Jacob (Gen. 28.13–14). Moses and the Israelites were to have new hope and courage because God was about to fulfil His promises and give them the land of Canaan.

In many parts of the Bible different writers show that God is a God who has plans for human beings, who makes His plans known through words of promise, and who does what He has promised. See for example 1 Kings 8.15, 24; Matthew 1.22; 2 Peter 1.3–4. It is this movement from promise to fulfilment that makes a unity of the Old Testament and the New Testament. St Mark says that Jesus began His public preaching with the message, 'The time of fulfilment has come' (Mark 1.15a). The faith of Jews and Christians is a hopeful faith because they are looking forward to the fulfilment of God's promises, because He is someone who can be trusted.

In the Old Testament the promises and warnings given by God through the prophets are linked to God's personal activity. Some scholars have suggested that the Israelites thought that when a prophet spoke a 'word of God', then that word which he had spoken helped to cause the events to happen. But the Old Testament writers do not write as if they thought a prophet's word had a kind of magic power to make events come to pass. They say that God, who gave the word to the prophet, Himself acts to do what He has said (see, for examples, 1 Kings 8.15; Amos 3.7; Isa. 44.26; 48.3). It is rather like a man who promises to marry a woman and then after some time does marry her: it is not the word of promise that causes the marriage to take place, but rather it is the man himself, for he made the promise because he intended to act to fulfil it.

4. HE IS THE ONE GOD, WHO IS, AND WHO IS THE CREATOR OF EVERYTHING ELSE

In Exodus 3.13–15 we find that Moses asks a question about the name of God. Why was this important? In Old Testament times the name a person was given often showed the sort of person he was. The name of the prophet who challenged the prophets of Baal on Mount Carmel was Elijah (Hebrew *Eliyahu*) which means 'My God is Yahweh'. His name revealed his character. God's 'name' is important because it reveals his character.

The name of God given in Exodus 3.13–14 is first of all, 'I am who I am'. We might also translate it as 'I will be what I will be', or as, 'I am there, wherever it may be, I am there.' The Hebrew word translated 'I am' is *Ehyeh*, for when God speaks of Himself He says, 'I am'. But when men speak of Him they must say 'He is'. The Hebrew word *Yahweh* probably means, 'He is' or 'He who is'. When the Israelites spoke of God as 'He who is', they thought of Him as the God who had been with them in the past and would be with them in the future to help them. (In English an expression like 'I go to school' often means 'I have been going to school in the past, I go now, and I expect to go in the future.' So also in Hebrew 'He is' can refer to the past, the present, and the future).

Some scholars say that Yahweh does not mean 'He who is' but 'He who causes to be' or 'He who creates what exists'. Whether they are right or not, certainly people in Israel learnt to think of God in both ways: (a) as the one who is with His people to help them (Exod. 3.12), and (b) as the creator of all that exists (Gen. 1). See also Isaiah 40.12–31 where both ideas are found together.

NOTES

3.1. Jethro, the priest of Midian: For Midian, and for Jethro's names see notes on 2.15 and 2.18 (p. 17).

3.1. Horeb, the mountain of God: See map, p. xiv. In Exodus 19.11 this mountain is called Mount Sinai. Why does the writer of Exodus use two different names? We cannot be certain. Here are two possible reasons:

(a) Horeb may have been the name of the mountainous district in which Sinai was a mountain. Such a use of more than one name for a place is found elsewhere in the Old Testament: for example, Jerusalem is also called Zion, and Mount Zion. It is common in the writings of ancient Egypt. It is common in the world today: a man who is travelling from Scotland to the British Houses of Parliament might say 'I am going to London' (the city) or 'I am going to Westminster' (the part of the city).

(b) There may have been two different stories told and written down. One earlier writer may have called the mountain 'Horeb', the other may have called it 'Sinai'. The writer of Exodus may have used both these stories when he wrote the Book of Exodus. See special notes B and E (pp. 43, 44 and 184–191).

3.2. the LORD: In the RSV, when LORD is written in capital letters it stands for the Hebrew name for God: Yahweh. Throughout the period in which the books of the Old Testament were written the Israelites used the name Yahweh. But at a later time the Jews felt that the name Yahweh was so sacred that they should not use it. So, when they read the Scriptures, whenever the readers came to the name Yahweh they said *Adonai* (my Lord, my master) instead of Yahweh. When the Old Testament books were translated into Greek, the translators used the Greek word *Kyrios* (Lord, master). This Greek translation, which we call the Septuagint, was used in the early Church. We need to remember this when we read passages like 1 Corinthians 12.3 and Philippians 2.9–11. To say that Jesus is *Kyrios* (Lord) is not only to say that He is our master, it is to say that He shares in the name and nature of God.

3.2. The angel of the LORD: In several passages in the Old Testament, writers tell a story in which 'the angel of the LORD' (or 'messenger of the LORD') speaks, and as the story goes on it is clear that it is the Lord who is speaking. In these stories people see 'the angel of the LORD', and say, 'We have seen God'. So it seems that when these writers wrote about the 'angel of the LORD' they thought of him as in some way being or representing the LORD Himself. See Genesis 16.7–13; 21.17–20; 22.11–18; Judges 6.11–24; 13.15–23, and notes on Exodus 14.19 (p. 77), and 23.21 (p. 129). Some Christian scholars see in these stories of the Angel of the

LORD a foreshadowing of Christ who makes God known because He shares the nature and being of God.

3.2. The bush was burning: We naturally ask, 'How did this happen? What kind of bush was it? Was it an acacia tree covered with red blossoms? Or were there real flames? If so, how were they caused? To all these questions we can give no certain answer. It is better to admit that we do not know.

The writer of Exodus was probably more interested in the question, 'What did this mean?' God's revelation of Himself by means of a flame of fire reminds us that He is living, holy, and powerful—able to do what is beyond our natural power.

3.5. Put off your shoes: A sign of respect for a holy place. Compare the way in which Muslims take off their shoes before going into a mosque, or Hindus into a temple. For the meaning of the word 'holy', see note on 28.36–38 on p. 145.

3.6, 15, 16. The God of your fathers: See p. 20 section 3 for the meaning of these words. For the use of them, see also Exodus 13.4, 11 and Deuteronomy 1.8; 4.1; 6.10, 23; 26.3, 15. In Exodus and Deuteronomy the words always refer to Abraham, Isaac, and Jacob. But in later Old Testament books the meaning of 'your fathers' changes, to mean 'your ancestors who came out of Egypt'. See, for examples, Judges 2.20; 1 Kings 8.21; Jeremiah 11.4.

3.8. Flowing with milk and honey: That is, a land providing plenty of food. An Egyptian nobleman called Sinuhe lived in Northern Canaan for many years about 1950 B.C. On his return to Egypt he had his story written down. He said of the land: 'There were figs and vines and more wine than water. There was plenty of honey and oil and every kind of fruit . . . There was corn and barley and all kinds of sheep and cattle . . . There was milk in every shape and form.'

3.8. Canaanites, Hittites, Amorites, Perizzites, Hivites, and Jebusites: Canaan (Palestine) was a land that lay between the great Empires and civilizations of Egypt, Asia Minor, and Mesopotamia. Important trade routes passed through it. It was a route for migrating peoples, and a battleground for opposing armies. Long before the time of Moses, Palestine had a very mixed population as a result of migrations, trade, and wars.

After the Israelites had settled in Canaan their chief enemy, in the time of Samson, Samuel, Saul, and David, was the powerful tribe of the Philistines. They had entered Canaan soon after the Israelites. The fact that this list in Exodus 3.8 does not mention the Philistines suggests that it is a list that was written down long before the time of David.

3.12. You shall serve God: That is, you shall worship God. In the Old Testament a servant of God is not simply someone who does what God wants him to do, but someone who obeys God and does his work because he respects and honours and worships God.

3.21–22. You shall not go out empty . . . you shall despoil the Egyptians: To 'go out empty' means to be sent away without a proper reward for work done (compare Gen. 31.41–42). In Israelite custom, when a slave was set free he was not to be sent away empty-handed (Deut. 15.13–14). The Israelites were slaves being set free from Egypt. When the writer of Exodus wrote this part of his story he did not describe the Israelites as being like thieves who steal other people's possessions: they were like slaves receiving the proper gifts due to them when leaving a master.

STUDY SUGGESTIONS AND QUESTIONS

REVIEW OF CONTENT

1. In what place and by what different means did God reveal Himself to Moses?
2. To what two groups of people did God say that He wanted to send Moses?
3. (a) What were the questions Moses asked God?
   (b) Why do you think Moses asked these questions?
   (c) How did God answer them?
4. (a) State briefly what main ideas about God were discussed in the section 'Interpretation and Comment' (pp. 19–21).

BIBLE STUDY AND REFLECTION

4. (b) What other ideas about God can you find in this chapter?
5. Are there any difficulties or problems in the chapter that you cannot find an answer to? If so, what are they?
6. 'God calls people to serve Him' (p. 20).
   (a) In what ways do you think God speaks to people and calls them to serve Him today?
   (b) Do you think God only calls people to be missionaries and leaders in the Church? Or do you think He calls people to be farmers and politicians and teachers and factory workers? Give reasons for your answers.
   (c) Do you think there are some kinds of work to which God does *not* call people? If so, what are they? Why do you think this?
   (d) The people of Israel were praying in Egypt when God called Moses to help them. Do you know of any other stories of men or women who were called to serve God in a particular way while other people were praying about that need?
7. '*God makes promises to people*' (p. 20).
   In 2 Corinthians 1.20 Paul wrote that 'all promises of God find their "yes" in Jesus Christ'. What promises do you think Paul meant? How did they find fulfilment in Jesus?

Special Note A: The Revelation of the Name Yahweh

Scholars do not agree about the right way to understand the story in Exodus 3 of the revelation of the name Yahweh to Moses. There are two main views.

1. WHAT WAS REVEALED TO MOSES WAS A NEW NAME FOR GOD

According to scholars who hold this view,

(a) The name Yahweh had never been known or used by the Israelites until the time of Moses.

(b) The name was revealed to Moses at Horeb as an entirely new name, so that Moses would be accepted as a leader truly called by God.

(c) The form of the story as we have it in Exodus 3.1–22 is not the original or first form of the story, since the writer uses the name Yahweh before it had been revealed to Moses (3.2, 4, 7).

(d) The use of the name Yahweh in many of the stories in Genesis, and in Exodus 3.2–7, shows that in early Israel there were at least two different groups of storytellers and writers: (i) a group of storytellers and writers who thought that Abraham did not know the name Yahweh: it was revealed first to Moses; and (ii) a group of storytellers and writers who believed that the name Yahweh was known to Abraham.

(e) The story in Exodus 3.13–15 presents the name as something new, a name unknown to Moses until that moment. (It is the story as told by the first group of people mentioned in section (d)).

2. WHAT WAS REVEALED TO MOSES WAS THE MEANING OF GOD'S NAME

As we have seen, in the Old Testament a person's name often expresses his character or nature. According to scholars who hold this view:

(a) What the people of Israel in Egypt needed was not a new name for God but encouragement to believe that He would be with them and deliver them from Egypt. They were given this encouragement by the assurance that their God was (i) the One who is present, and (ii) the One ready to keep His promise made to Abraham. (For the name as it is unfolded in 3.16 is not simply 'Yahweh', but 'Yahweh the God of your fathers . . . Abraham . . . Isaac and . . . Jacob').

(b) If Moses had announced a new and unknown name to the people of Israel they would have had no reason to accept Him as their God.

Some of the scholars who hold this view, that in Exodus 3 we have the

explanation of the inner meaning of a name already known to Moses (compare Exod. 34.6–7), go on to argue:
(c) The idea that the first tellers of the stories about Abraham and his descendants can be divided into two groups who used different words or names for God is not likely to be correct.

These are the two main views that scholars have put forward. When equally learned scholars disagree, it is difficult for the rest of us to know what to think: 'When elephants fight it is the grass that suffers.' We shall return to some of these problems later in our course of study, but meanwhile it is wise to recognize that, whichever view we accept, there will be other serious and honest students who will not agree with us.

4.1–31
The Call of Moses (2)

OUTLINE AND CONTEXT

4.1–17: *Moses made more excuses:*
(a) 'The Israelites will not believe you have sent me' (4.1).
(b) 'I am no good at speaking' (4.10).
(c) 'Please send someone else' (4.13).
God answered, and He encouraged Moses:
(a) 'I will help you to convince the Israelites' (4.2–9).
(b) 'I can make you speak well' (4.11–12).
(c) 'Your brother Aaron will speak for you' (4.14–16).
4.18–31: *Moses returned to Egypt:*
He said goodbye to Jethro (4.18–20). God warned Moses that Pharaoh would not want the Israelites to leave Egypt (4.21–23). Moses's son was circumcised (4.24–26). Moses and Aaron told the Israelites that God was going to set them free (4.27–31).

Exodus 4.1–17 continues the story of Moses's call. The return of Moses to Egypt (Exod. 4.18–31) brings to an end the story of Moses's call and begins the story of his contest with Pharaoh (Exod. 4.27—12.36).

INTERPRETATION AND COMMENT

1. MOSES'S EXCUSES AND GOD'S ANSWERS (4.1–17)

God was calling Moses to a great work. It was a work that would make

Moses a famous man. But Moses said, 'No. I don't want to go. I might fail. People might not be willing to follow me.'

People often react as Moses did when they are asked to do difficult tasks. They are afraid that they may fail. They find many reasons why they cannot do the work. All these reasons sound better than saying, 'I don't want to do it.' Then perhaps someone says to them, rather angrily, 'Don't make excuses. Go and do the work!'

But notice how kind God was to Moses. He did not say, 'Go and do the work!' He said, 'Do not be afraid. I will be with you to help you.' Then God gave Moses three ways in which he might persuade the Israelites (Exod. 4.2–9).

When Moses said, 'I am no good at public speaking,' God answered, 'That does not matter. I made man's mouth: I can make you able to speak well enough.' When Moses was still unwilling, and asked God to send someone else (Exod. 4.13), God was angry. But even so, He promised to help Moses by sending his brother Aaron to speak for him.

The story of Moses's excuses shows that God understands our fears. He knows that we often feel unable to do the work He is calling us to do. But patiently and firmly He goes on calling us. He wants us to learn not to be afraid, but to step out into the future trusting in Him. One Christian leader used often to say, 'Attempt great things for God: expect great things from God.'

2. MOSES AND MAGIC (4.1–9)

Moses's rod, his shepherd's staff, was used in the first sign which he was to show the Israelites (Exod. 4.2–5). In every age and in every part of the world there have been people believing that certain objects have special magic powers. In ancient Egypt almost everyone believed in magic. They even thought that their gods needed magic rods, and that these rods gave the gods power to do certain things that without the rods they could not have done. Some of the stories about Moses seem to suggest that he was like the Egyptian magicians with their rods.

However, there are some important differences. Most Egyptian stories of magicians and magic rods emphasize the cleverness of the magician and the power of the rod. But when Moses or Aaron stretched out his hand or his rod, the writer of Exodus tells us that it was the Lord who acted. The power was from God; it was not a magic power in the rod, nor was it a result of Moses's own ability (see Exod. 9.23; 10.13; 14.21). The signs which God gave Moses to perform were not signs that Moses was a clever magician. They were signs that God had sent him, and that through Moses He would do his work.

Other writers in the Old and New Testaments give us warning;

(a) that those who trust in God should avoid all kinds of magic, witchcraft, and divination, and

'God was calling Moses to do a great work, but Moses said, "I don't want to go. I might fail." People often react as Moses did when they are called to do difficult tasks. But God understands our fears' (pp. 26, 27).

During the recent war these Vietnamese farmers were called to volunteer for the difficult task of defending their village and its people. Do you think they believed God was calling them to the work? Do you think their reaction would have been different if they had believed so?

(b) that the ability to do unusual things is not by itself any proof that a person has been sent by God: what he does must also be tested by what he says, and whether he encourages people to be faithful to the God who has revealed Himself through His word (see Deut. 13.1–5; 18.9–12; Mark 13.22; 2 Thess. 2.9; 1 John 4.1–3).

3. MOSES AND THE CIRCUMCISION OF HIS SON (4.24–26)

This is a difficult passage to understand. When we read it we may wonder why 'the Lord sought to kill Moses.' Our main clue for solving the problem is the words in Exodus 4.26: 'because of circumcision.' What saved Moses was the circumcision of his son. So it seems likely that the threat to Moses's life was because he had not circumcised his son.

God had commanded the Israelites to circumcise their sons while they were still children (Gen. 17.12). Circumcision was a sign of God's covenant with Abraham and his descendants. It was a sign: (a) of God's love and of His readiness to keep the promises He had made to Abraham and his descendants, and (b) of their willingness to obey God. Moses had not circumcised his son. He had to learn that a man who will not obey God's commands is not able to serve Him.

Moses's son had been born in Midian. It is probable that the Midianites used circumcision as a puberty rite, as many tribes do today, to show that a boy is a full member of the tribe and ready for marriage. Perhaps Moses had been content to follow Midianite custom in not having his son circumcised as a child. Now, at this time of crisis, Zipporah circumcised him. In doing this she was breaking the custom of her own people. When people become followers of Christ they often find that there are customs in their own tribe or nation that they can no longer keep.

NOTES

4.3. It became a serpent . . .: When we read this story many of us ask, 'Did this really happen? Or is it a story that is not true?' We may also say, 'We do not live in a world in which sticks can be turned into snakes.' These questions are not easy to answer. But let us notice:

(a) the writer of the story of Exodus did not believe that sticks can normally be turned into snakes; his story makes clear that this is something unusual.

(b) the writer of Exodus believed that this happened because God had a special and important purpose.

We have to ask ourselves, 'Do we live in a world in which God is at work? Is He a God who can bring about changes that are beyond the normal power of human beings?'

4.6. His hand was leprous: The Hebrew word which the RSV translates as 'leprous' was used for several kinds of skin disease. It did not refer to the disease which we call leprosy. NEB translates; 'The skin was diseased.'

4.9 . . . blood . . .: Notice that this story in vv. 1–9 mentions a snake (serpent), skin-disease, and blood. These are all things that people fear. In most countries we find taboos and superstitions connected with them. The story suggests that all these things are under the control of God. He is great. Those who trust Him need have no fear.

4.10. I am not eloquent . . .: This means, 'I have never been able to speak well in public. You have spoken to me now, but that makes no difference, I am still a poor speaker.'

4.14. The anger of the Lord: God had been very patient with Moses (Exod. 3.11–4.12). But God is not soft or weak. He cares deeply for what is good. He is therefore opposed to all that is evil, to all that prevents people from doing His will.

4.16. He shall be a mouth for you . . .: In Egypt the 'chief mouth' was a title used for an official next in authority to Pharaoh. So God was telling Moses: (a) that Aaron would be his spokesman, and (b) that Aaron would be second in authority to Moses.

The Pharaoh, who gave authority to his 'chief mouth', was considered by the Egyptians to be a god. So when God said to Moses, 'You shall be to him as god,' He meant, 'Aaron will accept your authority. He will do as you say.' He did not mean that Aaron would worship Moses.

4.20. Moses took his wife and sons: In Exodus 18.1–5 we find that Zipporah and the boys were with Jethro when the Israelites left Egypt. So either: (a) Moses sent his family back to Jethro's home after he had returned to Egypt, as the writer of Exodus 18.2 states; or (b) there were once two different stories in one of which Moses's family never went to Egypt, as many scholars believe.

4.25. A bridegroom of blood: The Hebrew is *hathan dammim*. No one is certain what this means. Hathan means either: (a) a person in the son-in-law relationship, (b) a husband or bridegroom where there is reference to his wife's relatives. Nor is it clear whether Zipporah touched the feet (perhaps a polite reference to the genital organ or penis) of Moses (RSV) or of Gershom with the bloody foreskin.

4.27. And kissed him: Embracing with the arms and kissing on the neck was a normal way of greeting a relative or close friend (see Luke 15.20; Mark 14.44–45).

4.29. The elders: The heads of families.

4.30. And did the signs: We should translate, 'And he did the signs' (compare NEB and JB). It was Moses who was commissioned to do the signs (Exod. 4.1–9, 28). In any case Aaron would not have placed Moses's hand into the fold of his cloak. The RSV translation states that Aaron did the signs: this also is a possible translation, but it does not make good sense. It is a normal rule for translating that where two ways of translation seem possible, we should prefer one that makes sense in its context to one that does not.

4.31. The Lord had visited the people: In the Bible the word 'visit' often means 'to go and give help to' (Ruth 1.6; Matt. 25.36; Luke 1.68). It does not mean, 'to go and stay with'.

STUDY SUGGESTIONS AND QUESTIONS

REVIEW OF CONTENT

1. What excuses did Moses make, and how did God answer them?
2. What were the three signs which Moses was to do? Why was he to do them?
3. What lessons do you think the writer of Exodus meant people to learn: (a) From the story of the signs Moses was given to do? (b) From the story of the circumcision of Moses's son?

BIBLE STUDY AND REFLECTION

4. Compare with the story of how God called Moses (Exod. 3.1–4.17):
   (a) The call of Isaiah (Isa. 6.1–13),
   (b) The call of Jeremiah (Jer. 1.1–19),
   (c) The call of Peter (Luke 5.1–11).
   In what ways are all these stories similar? What do you think we can learn from this? In what ways are they different? What can we learn from the differences?
5. 'He did the signs in the sight of the people, and the people believed' (Exod. 4.30–31). Not long afterwards the people were discouraged and angry with Moses (Exod. 5.21). What dangers, if any, do you think there may be if we encourage people to trust in God because of unusual things that we, or other people, are able to do? Give reasons for your answer, and see also Mark 13.22; 2 Thessalonians 2.9; 1 Corinthians 1.22–23; 2.1–4; Matthew 12.38–39.
6. In John's Gospel the miracles done by Jesus are often called 'signs' (John 2.11; 2.23–25; 3.2; 6.25–34; 20.30). What was the purpose of these signs? (See John 2.11; 20.30–31.) In what ways were they different from the sort of signs that Moses did?
7. Moses said that he was not good at speaking in public. Why do you think God chose him to be a leader, a teacher, and a prophet? (See also 1 Cor. 1.26–31; 4.7; 2 Cor. 3.4–6; 12.9.)
8. It seems likely that Moses had not circumcised his son because he (Moses) was living in Midian and married to a Midianite. Consider: (a) Are there ways that Christians in your country fail to follow Christ because they are influenced by the ideas and customs of the people with whom they live? If so, what are these ways?

(b) Are there some customs of your country or tribe which need to be changed? If so, what are they? How do you think they could be changed?
(c) If you are a member of a Church, do you think there are any customs in your Church which need to be changed so that Christians can obey Christ more fully, and can make Him better known in the world? If so, what are they? How do you think they might be changed?

5.1–23

'I will not let Israel go'

OUTLINE AND CONTEXT

5.1–5: Pharaoh told Moses that he would not let the Israelites go and sacrifice in the wilderness.
5.6–14: The Israelites were made to collect their own straw for making bricks.
5.15–19: The Israelite foreman complained to Pharaoh.
5.20–23: The Israelites accused Moses of getting them into trouble. Moses prayed.

Exodus 5 begins the story of how Moses tried to persuade Pharaoh to let the Israelites go. Moses's failure leads in to the story in Exodus 6.1–7.7 of how God encouraged him.

INTERPRETATION AND COMMENT

1. THE SUFFERINGS OF THE ISRAELITES BECAME WORSE

Sometimes when things go wrong, we say to people, 'I told you so! I warned you, but you would not listen.' When God called Moses to go to Egypt to set Israel free, Moses said, 'I can't do it. Please send someone else' (Exod. 3.11; 4.13). As a result of Moses's request to Pharaoh that he should let the Israelites go, the Egyptians inflicted worse sufferings on the Israelites (Exod. 5.1–21). Then Moses said to God, 'Why did you send me?' (Exod. 5.22). He was saying to God, 'I told you so! I told you I wouldn't be any good'.

Of course, God could have said, 'I told you so!' to Moses. (Read Exod. 3.19 and 4.21.) God had warned Moses. But it seems that Moses had not really listened. It is always easier to listen to God's promises than to listen to His warnings.

Christians are often like Moses. Jesus warned His disciples that it would not be easy for them to be His followers; they would have to be ready to suffer and even to die (Mark 8.34–35; Matt. 10.38–39; Luke 14.27; John 12.24–25). He warned them that they would have to face difficulties and persecutions (Mark 13.9–13; compare Paul's teaching in Acts 14.21–22 and 2 Tim. 3.12). If Christians do not understand that life may be very hard for them, they may quickly become discouraged and disappointed, like the Israelites and Moses.

2. DESPAIR AND LOSS OF FAITH

The Israelites seem to have been crushed by the extra load of work and punishment that was put upon them. We do not read in this chapter that the people or their foremen prayed to God. There is no repeating of the cry for help (Exod. 2.23, 37); there is only a complaint that it is all the fault of Moses. Anyone who is a leader is likely to be blamed when things are difficult, as Moses was. But Moses seems to have understood the people's broken spirits. He did not blame them; he prayed. He poured out his anger and distress to God. And God seems to have understood too. He didn't blame Moses; He encouraged him to go on (Exod. 6.1–8).

When someone is suffering greatly, or is deeply distressed because they have lost a loved relative or been badly treated by friends, it is not always easy for them to go on trusting in God and praying to Him. At such a time most people do not need to be rebuked. It does not help them when someone says, 'It is a sin to stop praying.' What they need is love and help and encouragement. When Job was crushed by his suffering, he said, 'Should not faithful love be shown by friends to one who despairs, who loses his faith in the Almighty?' (Job 6.14).

3. POWER

Pharaoh was powerful. He had a well organized system of government. His own officers kept careful control over the Israelite slaves. They had made some of the Hebrews work as foremen. These unfortunate men were beaten by the Egyptian task masters if enough work was not done, and no doubt were hated by their fellow Hebrews if they drove them to work hard. They seemed quite helpless before the power of Pharaoh and his organized system of oppression.

There are many people in the world today who feel helpless before the power of an organized system of oppression. Some are workers in factories where those in charge have all the power and little kindness. Some are managers in factories where the workers are so organized that they can force others to do what they want. Some are people living in lands where they have no freedom to vote for the political party which they really want. Some are groups who are not allowed freedom to practise their religion. Once in North Korea a small group of Christian children were found meeting to pray and to talk about the Gospel of Christ: the communist authorities pushed chopsticks into their ears to destroy their hearing so that they could never hear the Good News of Christ again.

The story in Exodus 5—15 is the story of a conflict of power. A greater power than Pharaoh's is at work. In the end it is the weak and helpless ones who are delivered, and who rejoice. This is a theme that is often repeated: 'He has cast down kings from their thrones, but the humble have been lifted high' (Luke 1.52).

NOTES

5.1. Thus says the Lord, the God of Israel: This phrase occurs very often in the prophetic writings of Israel (history and prophecy) up to the time of the Exile in Babylonia. The words 'Thus says Yahweh' emphasized two ideas:

(a) That the prophet considered that the message he declared was not his own word, but was God's word.

(b) That the message was serious and important; it was a command that must be obeyed, or a statement about an event that would certainly take place.

5.1. A feast: This means a religious festival at a place to which people must travel. The Hebrew word for such a festival is *hag*: compare the title *Hajji* given to Moslems who have been on a pilgrimage to Mecca.

5.1. In the wilderness: The wilderness, or desert, was a safe place for the Israelites to make their sacrifices. Some of the animals they killed in their sacrifices were animals which the Egyptians considered to be sacred (see note on 8.26 p. 55).

5.2. Who is the Lord? That is, 'Who is Yahweh?' Pharaoh was not wanting to know who Yahweh was. He meant, 'Yahweh is not important!' As we say in English, 'Who does he think he is?'

5.5. The people . . . are many: A change of one letter in the Hebrew would give the meaning, 'The people are idle.' This would make better sense.

5.7. Straw to make bricks: The Egyptians used straw in making bricks. In one ancient Egyptian report an official wrote, 'There are neither men for making bricks nor straw in the neighbourhood.'

5.13. 'Complete ... your daily task': Egyptian officials fixed certain amounts to be done each day. One Egyptian official included in a report about his workmen, 'They are making their quota of bricks daily.'

5.17. 'You are idle': In the picture on p. 86 one of the Egyptian foremen is saying, 'The rod is in my hand. Do not be idle'. Ancient Egyptian records of work show that workers were often absent from work for festivals, and for other reasons. One record tells about workmen working on a royal tomb who were idle for 30 days out of 48.

5.19. When they said: This should be translated, 'When they were told' (NEB).

5.22–23. Thou hast not delivered thy people: The writer of Exodus often mentions the doubts, failures, and complaints of Moses and the Israelites. He emphasizes that their escape from Egypt was not a result of their own goodness or faith, but a result of God's faithfulness, love, and power. See also Deuteronomy 4.37–39; 7.7; 8.11–18.

STUDY SUGGESTIONS AND QUESTIONS

REVIEW OF CONTENT

1. What did Pharaoh do when Moses asked Pharaoh to let the Israelites go away for a festival?
2. (a) Whom did the Israelite foremen blame for the extra work and trouble?
   (b) Whom did Moses blame?
3. What warnings did Jesus give his followers about suffering?
4. When people lose their faith in God because they suffer, what kind of counsel do they usually need?

BIBLE STUDY AND REFLECTION

5. The Egyptians treated their Israelite workmen badly. In your country:
   (a) How are workmen treated?
   (b) How do workmen treat those who employ them?
   (c) If there is trouble between employers and workmen, what do you think are the reasons for it?
   (d) Do you think there is any way in which you, or your Church, could improve the situation?
6. Read Leviticus 19.13 and Deuteronomy 24.14–22.
   (a) What was the purpose of these laws?
   (b) What reason was given why the Israelites should keep them?
   (c) What laws are there in your country about wages and conditions of work?
   (d) Do you think they are satisfactory? If not, in what ways would you like them to be changed?
7. Read Exodus 5.20–23. Someone has said, 'We cannot expect people to be faithful to God if we teach them that following God brings happiness and success.' What is your opinion?
8. Study Exodus 5.20–23; Ecclesiastes 4.1–3; Romans 8.31–39.
   (a) What differences do you find in people's attitude to suffering?
   (b) What do you think are the reasons for these differences?
9. Moses was angry with God (Exod. 5.22–23). Read also Job 16.7–9; 23.1–2; Jonah 3.10—4.11.
   (a) For what reasons were Moses, Job, and Jonah angry with God?
   (b) What can we learn from God's kindness in encouraging Moses, and His patience in teaching Jonah?

10. Moses doubted that God was good (Exod. 5.22). Thomas doubted that Jesus had risen from the dead (John 20.24–29). It has been said, 'If we think seriously, we will also sometimes doubt. The only way not to have doubts is not to think.' What is your opinion?

6.1–27

God encouraged Moses

OUTLINE AND CONTEXT

6.1–9: The Lord encouraged Moses. He told Moses that He would act to set Israel free and to do as He had promised.
6.10–13: The Lord commanded Moses to tell Pharaoh to let the Israelites leave Egypt.
6.14–27: The tribe, clan, and family of Aaron and Moses.

Exodus 6.1–13 continues the story of Moses's first attempt and failure to persuade Pharaoh to let the Israelites go. The Lord encourages Moses and repeats his command to Moses and Aaron that they should go to Pharaoh. The dramatic story of the Plagues is about to begin. It is introduced by Exodus 6.14–27, a section which shows who Moses and Aaron were.

INTERPRETATION AND COMMENT

1. 'I AM THE LORD' (6.2, 6, 8)

This important statement 'I am the Lord', that is, 'I am Yahweh', occurs many times in the Pentateuch (Genesis—Deuteronomy). If we study Genesis 15.7; 28.13; Exodus 12.12; 15.26; 20.2; Leviticus 18.2–6; Deuteronomy 5.6, we shall notice these points:

(a) Each time these words occur they are placed at the beginning or at the end of an important statement.
(b) The words 'I am the Lord' ('I am Yahweh') are used to emphasize either a command or a promise given by God. We may compare this to the way in which we emphasize written words by underlining them.
(c) When used with a command, the words 'I am the Lord' mean: 'You must be sure to do this, because I am Yahweh your God.'
(d) When used with a promise, the words 'I am the Lord' mean: 'You can be sure that I will do this because I am Yahweh your God.' Compare the Jerusalem Bible translation in Exodus 6.8; 'I, Yahweh, will do this.'

In Exodus 6.2–8 the words 'I am Yahweh' are repeated three times. This

'The Lord spoke to Moses and Aaron and gave them a charge. . . . It was they who spoke to Pharaoh about bringing the people of Israel out of Egypt' (Exod. 6.13, 27).

Industrial workers' representatives in Britain vote to continue a strike for better wages and improved conditions of employment. Do you think that all those who protest against what they believe to be injustice and exploitation are guided by God to do so?

gives the strongest possible emphasis to the message which God is giving to Moses. It is as if God said to Moses, 'You can be absolutely certain that I will do what I have promised, for I am God and I always do what I have said.'

And what promise was God emphasizing that He would fulfil? It was the promise to give the land of Canaan to Abraham's descendants. It is in connection with this promise that the words 'I am Yahweh' are found on the only two occasions that they are used in the Book of Genesis (Gen. 15.7; 28.13). So they are fittingly repeated here, in a passage which says that the covenant-promise of the gift of the land of Canaan is now to be fulfilled (Exod. 6.4, 5, 8).

We have looked at these words, 'I am the Lord', carefully because:

(a) They remind us that the idea that God makes promises and keeps them is one of the central ideas of the faith of Israel (see also section 2 below).

(b) Many scholars have argued that these words show that Exodus 6.2–8 is a story of how God revealed His name, *Yahweh*, to Moses. Such an idea is not supported by our study of the usage of the words 'I am Yahweh': they are not the revealing of an unknown name; they are the use of a known name to give emphasis to a promise.

2. GOD ENCOURAGED MOSES (6.2–5)

Moses had been very angry with God (Exod. 5.23). In reply, God encouraged him. In order to give Moses confidence and hope, God reminded him of three things. He said:

1. 'I am the God who revealed myself to Abraham, Isaac, and Jacob' (Exod. 6.3).
2. 'I also made a covenant-promise to them, that I would give them the land of Canaan' (Exod. 6.4).
3. 'I have also heard the groaning of the people of Israel, and I am about to fulfil my covenant-promise for them' (Exod. 6.5).

Many of the writers of the Bible similarly reminded their readers that God has given promises to men, and can be trusted to do what He has said. See pp. 20, 21, and also Numbers 23.19; Psalm 119.41; Isaiah 38.7; 42.9; 44.26; John 14.1–3; 2 Cor. 1.20. When we suffer, when we are sad, when we fear what may happen to ourselves and to the world in future days, we can take courage by remembering that God has made promises to us, and that He will not fail to keep them.

3. DELIVERANCE, REDEMPTION, AND JUDGEMENT (6.6)

God told Moses to pass on the message of encouragement to the Israelites. He must tell them, 'God will *deliver* and *redeem* you with great acts of *judgement.*' These words 'deliver', 'redeem', and 'judgement' are all important words in the Old Testament. What do they mean?

The words 'deliver' and 'redeem' both mean to 'set free' or to 'rescue' from some kind of trouble, slavery, or danger. But each also emphasizes a particular aspect of the act of rescue. The word 'deliver' emphasizes the idea of the oppression or danger from which a person is set free. The Israelites were slaves: God would set them free.

The word 'redeem' emphasizes that the person rescuing someone is in a close relationship to them. In the Book of Ruth, it is Naomi's close relative, Boaz, who can act as redeemer. In Exodus 6.6 the word emphasizes God's personal care for the Israelites: He would help them because He loved them. The word 'redeem' usually also includes the idea of rescuing at a cost to oneself (see also p. 73). Here perhaps the idea of cost is found in the fact that God will exert Himself and use His power in acts of judgement.

We may wonder why the setting of people free should be by 'acts of judgement'. We shall understand this if we think of the two important tasks of a judge in ancient Israel. A judge was expected; (a) to help and deliver people who had suffered wrong, and (b) to punish people who had done wrong. In setting Israel free God was acting as judge, both (a) in helping the Israelites who had been wrongfully made slaves, and (b) in punishing the Egyptians who had wrongfully enslaved them. It is because of this first aspect of judgement that so many of the Psalms call people to rejoice that God is coming to judge the earth.

In all countries laws are made so that judges can punish people who have done wrong. But often a judge has little power either to help the person who has suffered wrong, or to force the criminal to pay compensation. In some countries lawyers and politicians are now seeking to revise their laws, so as to make sure that more help is given to those who have suffered as a result of crimes which other people have committed.

4. 'I WILL TAKE YOU FOR MY PEOPLE' (6.7)

When God delivered the Israelites from Israel, it was not so that they could be free to live as they liked; it was so that they could live as the people of God. We shall see, when we study chapters 20—40, that this meant that they must live a life of love, loyalty, obedience, and worship. If people wish to live together in a community in freedom, they must accept some form of discipline. Children who are left to do as they like, do not usually enjoy such freedom. They become insecure and unhappy. They need some control. They feel that a parent who never disciplines them is a parent who does not care whether they are good or bad; and a parent who does not care is a parent who does not truly love them.

We may notice also that to be the people of God, meant for Israel that the people must be united, they must worship and work together. One of the greatest blessings of being a Christian is that people are brought into unity with each other in the family of God (see Eph. 2.11–22). God does not mean us to be lonely or isolated in our lives. He calls us to be part of His people. That means that we shall seek to join others in work and worship and witness.

The Israelites were often tempted to think: 'God has chosen us to be his people: this means that we are better than other people.' Notice how this idea is opposed in Deuteronomy 7.7; Isaiah 1.2–4, Amos 9.7. To be chosen by God means, not that we are better than other people, but that although we are sinful God has chosen us to be His servants, to bring help and blessing to other people throughout the world (Gen. 12.2–3).

NOTES

6.1. What I will do: Throughout chapters 6—14, notice how the writer emphasizes that it was God, not Moses, who set Israel free. God is the central person in the story. It is His words and acts that the writer proclaims.

6.2–3. I am the LORD: See note on 3.2 (p. 22). Notice also:

1. This brief phrase (in Hebrew: 'I am Yahweh') is not used by Old Testament writers in this way to give emphasis except: (a) in the Pentateuch, and (b) in Ezekiel 20.5–7, 19, where the prophet is referring to the Exodus story. Ezekiel's own way of giving emphasis to a word of God was by saying, '"As I live" says the Lord . . .' (Ezek. 5.11; 33.11).

2. Older English translations used the form 'Jehovah' for 'Yahweh'. The word Jehovah was made up by combining together (a) the consonants of *Jahveh* (a form of *Yahweh*), (b) the vowels of *Edonay* (a form of *Adonai*—my Lord).

It is rather strange that the group of people called Jehovah's Witnesses say that it is very important to make known God's name Jehovah, when the form Jehovah does not occur anywhere in the Hebrew text of the Old Testament.

6.3. I appeared . . .: The writer of Exodus shows that the Israelites knew God because He was continually revealing Himself to them. They did not invent an idea of God for themselves. They did not have an idea of God as a result of their own thinking. Throughout the Bible God is shown as the One who takes the first steps in making Himself known—He seeks men before they seek Him.

6.3. As God Almighty: See Genesis 17.1–2. The words 'God Almighty' are a translation of the Hebrew words *El Shaddai. El* means God. The meaning of *Shaddai* is not known. Scholars suggest that it may have meant 'the mountain one' or 'the destroyer'. In the Book of Job the name *Shaddai* is used to emphasize the power and majesty of God. The first translators of the Old Testament into Greek translated *Shaddai* as 'Almighty' (or 'Controller of all').

6.3. But by my name the LORD I was not known to them: The exact meaning of this sentence in Hebrew is not clear. Here are some of the translations scholars have suggested:

(a) By my name Yahweh I was not known to them.

(b) But in my nature as Yahweh I was not known to them.

(c) And was I not known to them by my name Yahweh?—a question to which the expected answer is, 'Yes, you were known to them'.

(d) And by my name Yahweh, behold, I was known to them.

Notice that translations (a) and (c) are opposite in meaning. This may seem strange, but let us consider this question and answer:

Q. 'Do you know Kipchoge Keino?'

A. 'Isn't he a fast runner'

The answer has no punctuation. It could be (a) an exclamation or statement by someone who knows that Keino runs fast: 'Isn't he a fast runner!' Or it could be (b) a question by someone who is uncertain, 'Isn't he a fast runner?'

The Hebrew Old Testament was written with no punctuation marks. So this kind of difficulty sometimes occurs. How can we decide whether translation (a) is a better translation than translation (b) or (d)? Look again at Special Note A (pp. 25, 26). If we take the first view, we shall accept translation (a). If we take the second view (that Yahweh was not revealed as an entirely new name) then we shall prefer translation (b), (c), or (d). Those who prefer translations (c) or (d) will also point out that in Exodus 6.2–5 there are three reasons given why Moses should be encouraged. The second and third reasons, in Exod. 6.4 and 6.5, are both introduced in the Hebrew text by the words 'And also'. We should therefore expect that Exod. 6.3 would end with an encouraging statement; for to say 'I loved you, and also I helped you' makes sense: but to say, 'I did not love you, and also I helped you' does not make sense. Thus if we choose translation (c) or even (d)—though that is less likely to be correct, we have a translation that makes sense in the context, explains the use of Yahweh as a name for God in Genesis, and explains how the mother of Moses could have a name that means 'Yahweh is glory'.

6.4. My covenant: The covenant with Abraham was God's covenant, not Abraham's (Gen. 17.7–10). The covenant was not an agreement made between Abraham and God, but (a) a promise given by God to Abraham (Gen. 17.7–8), and (b) a command which Abraham must obey (Gen. 17.9–10).

6.7. You shall know . . .: In the Old Testament, to 'know' God often means to have personal experience of Him. For the Israelites, to know God as Yahweh was to find out, in the experience of their own lives, that He is the promise-keeping deliverer of His people.

6.8. Which I swore to give: That is, which I solemnly promised to give. In swearing an oath, or making a solemn promise, it was customary to raise the right hand. The Hebrew of this verse says, 'Which I raised my hand to give'. (Compare Ps. 144.8; Rev. 10.5–6.)

6.9. They did not listen: The Israelites believed Moses at first (Exod. 4.31), but the result was trouble (Exod. 5.1–21). So now they would not take any notice of what Moses said. An English proverb says: 'A burnt child fears the fire.'

6.12. Uncircumcised lips: Moses meant that he was not able to speak well enough. (Compare Jer. 6.10.)

6.13. He gave them a charge to the people: That is, He commanded them to go to the people.

6.14–22. These are the heads . . .: The writer of Exodus probably placed the genealogy of Aaron and Moses at this point in his story to mark the fact that they were about to begin the most important stage of their work. Compare the genealogy in Luke 3.23–38; it is placed at the point in Luke's story when Jesus was about to begin his ministry of preaching and teaching.

The genealogy gives: (a) their tribe: Levi (Exod. 6.14–17), (b) their clan: Kohath (6.16–19), and (c) their family (6.20). This genealogy is sometimes taken to mean that there were only three generations from Levi to Moses. But this conflicts with the statement in Exodus 12.40 that the Israelites were in Egypt for 430 years. But if the writer wished only to show the tribe, clan, and family of Moses, he did not need to include all Moses's ancestors in the list. Genealogies in the Old Testament and in ancient Egyptian records often left out some names.

6.20. Amram took to wife Jochebed his father's sister: Jochebed means 'Yahweh is glory'. It is strange to find a statement that Amram married his aunt. This was not allowed by Israelite law (Lev. 20.19–20). There may be an error in the text or translation. The Greek translation known as the Septuagint says Jochebed was Amram's cousin: the daughter of his father's brother.

6.26. By their hosts: That is, organized in their tribal groups.

STUDY SUGGESTIONS AND QUESTIONS

REVIEW OF CONTENT

1. (a) Why was Moses discouraged?
   (b) What encouragement did God give him?
2. (a) What is the meaning of the words, 'I am the Lord'?
   (b) Why are these words repeated three times in Exodus 6.2–8?
3. What is the meaning of the following words?
   (a) deliver (b) redeem (c) acts of judgement

BIBLE STUDY AND REFLECTION

4. The promise of the land of Canaan (Exod. 6.4) was one of several promises made by God to Abraham, Isaac, and Jacob. Read Genesis 12.1–3, 7; 15.4; 17.4–8; 26.23–24; 28.13–14.
   (a) Make a list of the promises which God made.
   (b) In what ways do you think each promise was fulfilled?
5. God encouraged Moses by reminding him of what He had promised to do for the Israelites (Exod. 6.2–8).
   (a) What problems and difficulties do you face in your own life?
   (b) What promises of God mentioned in the Bible give you hope as you face these problems and difficulties?
6. I will take you for my people (Exod. 6.7).
   (a) What can you learn about what God does for His people, from Luke 1.68,77; 2.10,32?
   (b) What do the following verses teach about the conduct, mission, and hope of the people of God?
   2 Cor. 6.14–18   1 Pet. 2.9–10   Rev. 21.1–4
7. 'A judge was expected to help and deliver people who had suffered wrong' (p. 39).
   (a) What sort of penalty do you think is suitable if a man steals a month's wages from someone else?
   (b) Find out what penalties the laws of your country lay down for a man who has stolen money.
   Do you think that the laws of your country allow enough help and compensation to be given to those who suffer as a result of crimes? If not, how do you think the laws should be changed? If the changes you suggest would mean the payment of more money, from whom would the money come?

Special Note B: The Writer of the Book of Exodus

When we look at the cover of this Study Guide to Exodus, we see on it the name of the writer. When we read the Book of Exodus, we do not find anywhere the name of the person who wrote it. If someone asks us, 'Who wrote the book of Exodus?' the only honest answer we can give is, 'We do not know.' Nor are we sure at what date the Book of Exodus was written, nor in what way.

There are many ways of writing books. For example, if a person is writing the story of his own life, he may be able to write a book without using other books. But if a writer is writing a book about the history of his people, he will, if he is wise, use (a) any books and other documents that other people have written about the history, and (b) any stories he can collect from older people.

Most scholars believe that the writer of Exodus used earlier writings and earlier stories told by other people, when he composed the Book of Exodus. We have already seen that they think that the writer sometimes puts together stories that were originally separate: for example a story in which Moses's father-in-law was called Reuel and a quite different story in which he was called Jethro. We shall come back to this question after we have studied the whole Book of Exodus.

In the meanwhile, we have the Book of Exodus. Someone wrote it, or arranged its stories in the order that we now have them. This is the book which the Jews have accepted, and which they read as part of their sacred Scriptures. This is the book which the Church accepts in its Canon of Scripture. This is the book we are studying. So when we refer to 'the writer of the Book of Exodus', we mean the person who wrote the book in the form that we have it now. We will leave till later a fuller discussion of the question of when the Book of Exodus was written (see Special Note E, pp. 184–191).

6.28—8.19

The first three Plagues

OUTLINE AND CONTEXT

6.28–7.13: *Introduction to the story of the plagues:*

(a) The Lord sent Moses and Aaron to Pharaoh (6.28—7.9).

(b) Aaron's rod became a serpent (7.10).

(c) The rods of the Egyptian magicians became serpents, and Pharaoh refused to let the Israelites go (7.11–13).

7.14–24: *The first plague—the Nile water was turned red and foul:*

(a) Moses was sent to warn Pharaoh (7.14–18).

(b) The Nile water was turned red and foul, the fish died (7.19–21).

(c) The Egyptian magicians turned water red, and Pharaoh refused to let the Israelites go (7.22–24).

7.25–8.15: *The second plague—frogs:*

(a) Moses was sent to warn Pharaoh (7.25–8.4).

(b) The frogs came (8.5–6).

(c) The Egyptian magicians also caused frogs to come (8.6).

(d) The frogs were taken away in answer to Moses's prayer, but again Pharaoh refused to let the Israelites go (8.8–15).

8.16–19: *The third plague—mosquitoes:*

(a) The Lord told Moses what Aaron should do (8.16).

(b) The mosquitoes came (8.17).

(c) The Egyptian magicians failed to make the mosquitoes come, but still Pharaoh would not let the Israelites go (8.18–19).

Exodus 6.28—7.7 links the story of the plagues, which begins in this passage, to the story of Moses's call and his unwillingness to go. Exodus 7.14—8.19 tells the story of the first three plagues, and sets a pattern for the telling of the story of the remaining six: in each group of three plagues the first two plagues are announced to Pharaoh, but the third happens without warning.

INTERPRETATION AND COMMENT

1. POWER BELONGS TO GOD

In Egypt the Pharaoh was considered to be a god, 'the One who protects Egypt and subdues the foreign lands'. He was thought to be the child of Amun, the supreme god, and to be the incarnation of the god Horus and the heir of the god Osiris. He carried a sceptre bearing the head of Seth, a god 'rich in magical lore'. Wealth, power, and worship belonged to the Pharaoh. Anyone who approached him had to prostrate himself on the ground, 'smelling the earth, crawling on the ground', and 'calling upon this Perfect God and exalting his beauty'.

In the story of the plagues, God sends Moses to Pharaoh. Moses does not even feel able to speak to Pharaoh (6.30). Again and again the result of all that Moses and Aaron do is only this: 'Pharaoh would not listen to them' (for example, 7.13; 8.15). At first the magic power available to Pharaoh seems to be a match for the power available to Moses. But by the time we reach the third plague we see the beginning of a change, when Pharaoh has to ask Moses to pray to the Lord that He will take away the plague of frogs.

This theme of the power of the Lord as the only true God is linked with two other important ideas:

(a) that through their experience of His power the Egyptians will come to recognize that Yahweh is God (see 7.5,17; 8.10), and

(b) that His power is used for and through those who obey Him (7.6), but against those who refuse to obey (7.16; 8.2).

2. THE HARDENING OF PHARAOH'S HEART (7.3,13–14; 8.15–19)

In Exodus 7.3 we read, 'God said, "I will harden Pharaoh's heart."' When we read this, we may ask, 'Did the writer of Exodus think that God intentionally prevented Pharaoh from letting the Israelites go?' or, 'Did God make Pharaoh refuse simply because He wanted an excuse to send more plagues on the Egyptians?' To answer these questions we need to read through the whole story of the nine plagues. When we do this, we find that in the first five plagues Pharaoh hardened his own heart (Exod. 8.15,32), or simply that his heart was hard (Exod. 7.13; 14,22; 8.19; 9.7). Then from the sixth to the ninth plague, we find more often that the Lord hardened Pharaoh's heart (Exod. 9.12; 10.1,20,27; 11.10).

The story emphasizes first of all what Pharaoh was like. He was obstinate and defiant. He did not want to let the Israelites leave Egypt. He wanted their cheap labour for his building and other works.

But when Pharaoh refused to let them go, he was refusing to do what God had told him to do. Each time a man refuses to listen to God's commands, his conscience seems to grow harder, and it becomes more difficult for him to obey the next call or command of God. The more often we do what is wrong, the more difficult it becomes for us to change and to do what is right. It seems that this is how God has made us. This is part of God's judgement on sin: that when we sin we remove ourselves from Him and make it harder to respond to Him.

So it was with Pharaoh. He began by being obstinate: he hardened his own heart. The more he chose to refuse God the more he settled into this habit. As he refused God so he condemned himself. This was God's judgement. So when the writer of Exodus says, 'God hardened Pharaoh's heart', he does not mean that God was forcing Pharaoh to do something which Pharaoh did not want to do.

God did not make Pharaoh sin in order that He might punish him. God allowed Pharaoh to do as he wanted to do. But when a person uses his freedom in order to disobey God and to go on refusing Him, part of the penalty is to have a hardened heart or a blunted conscience.

Some Christian pastors have a special ministry to people who are involved in magic, sorcery, spiritualism, and other forms of secret or hidden practices. They say that sometimes a person reaches a stage when he has so constantly submitted himself to the influence of spirits or demonic powers that he seems totally shut off from the love and grace of God.

3. THE EGYPTIAN MAGICIANS

In the story of the first two plagues we find that the Egyptian magicians were able to copy some of the things which God enabled Moses and Aaron to do (Exod. 7.22; 8.7). Egypt has always been famous for its magicians and conjurors. Travellers today are still amazed by their cleverness. Both snakes and young crocodiles have been seen to be made rigid so that the conjuror could hold them up by the tip of their tails like rods.

We do not know what the 'secret arts' of the Egyptian magicians were.

We do not know whether they did turn rods into snakes, or whether (like some more recent conjurors) they were able to make snakes appear to be rods. But we do know that we live in an amazing world in which many strange things happen. In the earlier years of this century many people in Europe would not think seriously about magic and witchcraft: they thought it could all be explained as deception or suggestion. In recent years there has been a great increase in the practice of witchcraft and sorcery. An English witch who recently became a Christian has spoken of the things she did when she was a witch, including rites to bring about healing and to make people invisible. She said that the power which controlled her was definitely evil. Amongst the Eskimos one of the most powerful sorcerers was the Shaman Alualuk. He was eventually converted. When he was asked whose power he had used in his sorcery, he replied, 'The devil's, of course.' We cannot expect to understand how such powers work, but we should notice:

(a) that magic and similar practices either destroy the Christian faith of those who habitually take part in them, or prevent the proper development of their faith, and

(b) that deliverance is possible through Jesus Christ.

4. THE FIRST THREE PLAGUES

Every year heavy rains in East Africa and Ethiopia make the waters of the river Nile rise. Before the recent building of the Aswan Dam, every July or August the Egyptian fields along the riverside were flooded. The water was brown with mud, and the mud made the fields fertile so that good crops could grow.

In the first plague the Nile turned red in colour. This may have been caused by heavy rains in Ethiopia washing down fine red soil into the river. Heavy rains and a high flood might also bring down a lot of bacteria, which could kill the fish and make the water bad to drink (Exod. 7.17–21).

Because of dead and decaying fish in the Nile, the frogs might leave the river, causing the plague of frogs on the land (Exod. 8.6). The dead fish might also have infected the frogs with disease which would eventually cause the frogs to die (Exod. 8.13–14). The flooding of the land would make everywhere wet and provide breeding places for the mosquitoes of the third plague. We shall notice that all the first nine plagues are in some way connected with natural events in Egypt (see pp. 54 and 58).

5. GOD AND THE PLAGUES

The writer of Exodus told the story of the plagues because he believed that they showed that God is at work in the world to help His people. He wanted those who read or heard the story to know that they too could know God as the One who controls the world, and helps those who trust in Him and obey Him.

Some readers of the story may have one of the following ideas:
(a) If God was at work, then everything must have happened in some amazing way that has nothing to do with what usually happens in the world.
(b) The story of the plagues refers to some natural events which often took place in Egypt. Like floods and diseases they were natural events, they had nothing to do with God.

In this study guide we shall consider some of the natural events which often took place in Egypt (as we did in sections 3 and 4 above). Beside the ideas:

(1) that if an event is a miracle it has nothing to do with natural causes, and

(2) that if an event has natural causes, it has nothing to do with God, we shall set a *third* idea:

(3) that God uses and controls natural events in the world which He has made.

Let us think for a moment of some of the world's great buildings (for example the Taj Mahal in India, St Peter's Cathedral in Rome, the great new buildings in Brasilia). They have been built with ordinary materials: bricks, stone, concrete, steel. They are great buildings because the architects and builders used these materials with knowledge, skill, and imagination. No one would say: (1) a great architect never uses ordinary building materials, nor (2) if a building is made of ordinary materials it has nothing to do with an architect.

When we consider the natural events connected with the plagues in Egypt, it is as if we are looking at building materials which God used in His work. Christians believe that God shapes the events of this world to fulfil His purposes. One of His greatest miracles is to take people like us, to give us a new life, to shape us so that in character and action we may become more like Jesus, and to use us in the world to do His will.

In the story of the plagues we shall also notice that there is often mention of the time at which a plague will begin or end. The plagues happened at the times which God had revealed to Moses. It was partly because Moses had already announced them beforehand, that people realized that God was at work in these events.

God is still the Lord of time. A Chinese woman tells the story of a 'small miracle' in her experience. Mary was a medical student. During one university holiday she was kept in her university rooms for fourteen days. With her all day and all night, even when she went to wash, there was an older communist woman. No one else was allowed to approach her or speak to her. For fourteen days the communist tried to persuade her to give up her Christian faith. Then on the last day, on the evening before the student was to be taken for trial before a mass meeting, the communist woman suddenly left the room. She was away for only two minutes.

During those two minutes one of the few Christian students in the university came to the window, and said, 'Mary, I am praying for you.' Of course, it was not a miracle that a student should walk past a window, but what was wonderful was that he went past in the only two minutes when Mary was alone. Later on he was able to tell her: 'Mary, I was compelled by the Spirit—God sent me to walk past the window just then.'

NOTES

7.1–2. Aaron shall be your prophet: Aaron was to pass on to Pharaoh whatever messages Moses gave him. This passage helps us to understand how the Israelities thought about their prophets: a true prophet was a man who passed on a message which God had given him.

7.7. Moses was eighty years old: See also Deuteronomy 34.7, which gives Moses's age at his death. Since 40 years seems to have been a figure used to represent a generation, we cannot tell whether the figure of 80 years here: (a) indicates the true age of Moses, or (b) represents two generations—which in fact would be about 50 years.

7.9–12. A serpent: The Hebrew word is *tannin*, which usually means 'crocodile'. It is not the same as the word used for serpent in Exodus 4.3.

7.15. The river's brink: That is, the bank of the Nile.

8.3. Kneading bowls: Shallow wooden bowls. Women mixed flour and water in them to make bread.

8.8. I will let the people go: Pharaoh did not mean to keep his promise; it died with the frogs.

8.10. No one like the Lord our God: Compare Exodus 9.14; 15.11; Isaiah 40.18; 44.6–8; 46.5,9.

8.16. Gnats: Gnats are biting insects. They are smaller than mosquitoes. JB translates: 'mosquitoes'.

8.17. All the dust became gnats: It would be foolish to understand this literally. It does not mean that there was no dust or soil left in Egypt. Anyone who has lived in countries where insects can be seen rising in clouds like smoke will understand what this verse means.

8.19. This is the finger of God: This was a phrase which Egyptians often used. They used it particularly of their gods Thoth and Seth, whose actions they considered to be dangerous to men. Muslims today use the phrase *Mashallah*, 'this is what God wills', in rather the same way, to describe situations over which they have no control.

STUDY SUGGESTIONS AND QUESTIONS

REVIEW OF CONTENT

1. What were the first three plagues?

2. Why did similar events often happen in Egypt?
3. What was it that made people think that these three plagues showed that God was at work?
4. (a) What did Pharaoh say he would do if the frogs were taken away?
   (b) What did Pharaoh actually do?
5. What lessons do you think the writer of Exodus wanted his readers to learn from the story of the first three plagues?

BIBLE STUDY AND REFLECTION

6. Read Exodus 7.1—8.19. Scholars sometimes say that God is presented in the Old Testament as being: (a) 'The God who speaks', or (b) 'The God who acts'. Which description do you think best suits the story in Exodus 7.1—8.19? Give reasons for your answer.
7. 'There is no one like the Lord' (Exod. 8.10). The Israelites knew that their belief in God was different from the beliefs of the Egyptians. In what important ways do you think the ideas of God found in the Bible are different:
   (a) from the ideas of God which people in your country have today?
   (b) from the ideas of God which your ancestors had?
8. Read Exodus 7.6,10,20; 8.5–6, 16–17. These verses emphasize that Moses and Aaron did what the Lord commanded them. Read also John 14.15,21.
   (a) How can a Christian show that he loves Jesus?
   (b) What are the commands which Jesus gave to His followers?
   (You may find a Concordance helpful in answering this question.)
9. Pharaoh hardened his heart. See also Mark 8.17 and Hebrews 3.13. (a) What do you learn from these verses? (b) A Christian poet has written:

   Who is this Pharaoh, who is he?
   Who is the man that I should now condemn
   Who knows God's ways and will not walk in them?
   Is there a chance he might be me?

   What is your answer to these questions which the poet asks?

8.20—9.12

The Fourth, Fifth, and Sixth Plagues

OUTLINE AND CONTEXT

8.20–32: *The fourth plague—flies*

(a) Moses was sent to warn Pharaoh, and to say that the land of Goshen would not be affected by the plague (8.20–23).

(b) The Lord caused flies to fill the houses of the Egyptians (8.24).
(c) Pharaoh agreed that if the flies were taken away, he would let the Israelites go and sacrifice to the Lord (8.25–29).
(d) Moses prayed and the flies were taken away, but then Pharaoh refused to let the Israelites go (8.30–31).

9.1–7: *The fifth plague—cattle disease*
(a) Moses was sent to warn Pharaoh, and to say that the cattle of the Israelites would not be affected by the plague (9.1–3).
(b) The Lord caused the cattle of the Egyptians to die of the disease (9.6).
(c) Yet Pharaoh would not let the Israelities go (9.7).

9.8–12: *The sixth plague—boils*
(a) The Lord told Moses and Aaron what Moses should do (9.8–9).
(b) The boils afflicted men and animals (9.10–11).
(c) But Pharaoh would not let the Israelites go (9.12).

Exodus 8.20—9.12 continues the story of the plagues.

INTERPRETATION AND COMMENT

1. THE DISTINCTION BETWEEN THE ISRAELITES AND THE EGYPTIANS

The writer of Exodus shows that in the fourth, fifth, and sixth plagues, God made a difference between the Israelites and the Egyptians. He did this so that people might learn, (a) that Yahweh is the true God who controls all the world, including the land of Egypt, and (b) that the Israelites were the people of God and not the people of Pharaoh.

(a) *Yahweh is the true God who controls the land of Egypt:* The Egyptians believed in many gods. Perhaps at an earlier period they had believed that the power of each god was limited to the town or land where he was worshipped. But certainly in the period 1500–1200 BC there were many Egyptians who considered that the power of their chief God covered the whole world. For example, an Egyptian hymn written in the fifteenth century BC calls the god Amun 'creator of all that exists'. It also includes the words: '"Hail to thee", says every land.' But the writer of Exodus wanted his readers to understand that the true God is not any of the Egyptian gods; the true God is Yahweh, who made Himself known to Moses and to the people of Israel (Exod. 8.22).

Yahweh showed His power 'in the midst of the earth' (Exod. 8.22), that is, in the land of Egypt. His presence and power were not limited to Sinai or to Canaan or to any other place. The distinction between the Israelites and the Egyptians was meant as a sign, to show the presence and activity of Yahweh in Egypt, in the very land where polytheism and magic seemed to be supreme.

(b) *The Israelites were a people who belonged to God:* All through the story of the plagues, God demands, 'Let my people go'. In Exod. 8.23 we find this idea that Israel is the people of God emphasized in a different way: 'I will put a division between my people and your people'.

Pharaoh had treated the Israelites as if he owned them. He forced them to work for him as slaves. The story of the plagues shows that Pharaoh needed to learn that the Israelites belonged to a greater King, and that they must serve that King.

In the history of the Christian Church, there have been many times when national leaders or governments have tried to prevent people from serving God. Many of the early English colonists in North America left their homes in England because they were not free to worship God in the way they believed they should. A Christian from a communist country described the doctrine she was told to accept: 'The individual is nothing. All his personal beliefs are nothing. The party is all: its acts are good and what it says is correct.' In the central African country of Chad in recent years many Christians have been killed because they have refused to take part in traditional tribal religious rites. While a Christian is commanded to be loyal to his government as far as he can (to render to Caesar what is Caesar's), his first loyalty must always be to God.

2. YOU SHALL NOT GO VERY FAR AWAY (8.28)

Pharaoh realized that Moses was not asking only for freedom to go for a three-day journey to offer sacrifices to Yahweh. He knew that Moses was really asking for permanent freedom from the service of Pharaoh. But Pharaoh tried to set limits to the freedom he would allow the Israelites, so as to make sure that they would return to their labour in Egypt: they must worship Yahweh in Egypt (Exod. 8.25), they must not go far (Exod. 8.28), only the men must go (Exod. 10.11), the flocks and herds must be left behind (Exod. 10.24). Each time, Moses refused to accept what Pharaoh offered; he knew that God demanded the total freedom of the Israelites and their possessions. They must be ready to serve Him in any way that He might demand (Exod. 10.26). They must put themselves and their possessions entirely at God's disposal.

Here is a challenge for people in every age. There are many people who would like to know the presence and blessing of God in their lives, but they will not give up a particular habit they know to be bad. Some are willing to serve God if He does not call them to leave home, others want to worship God and at the same time continue to belong to a group of people whose practices are not consistent with the Gospel of Christ. An Australian aborigine chief said, 'Many of my people who become Christians do not make any progress in their Christian lives because they have not renounced before God the various magical practices of their tribe.'

'Pharaoh was refusing to do what God had told him to do.... He was treating the Israelites as if he owned them' (pp. 46, 52). 'If people refuse to do what God tells them to do, they bring trouble upon themselves and upon others' (p. 60).

Black citizens of the USA rally to demand civil and political rights. These rights have been theirs by law for more than 100 years, but are denied to many of them by the 'hard hearts' of their fellow citizens of different race. What sort of 'plagues' are likely to result from that hardness of heart?

3. THE PLAGUES OF FLIES, CATTLE DISEASE, AND BOILS

These troubles and diseases mentioned in the story of the plagues are things that happened naturally in Egypt from time to time. They are connected with the climate and conditions of Egypt.

The flood waters of the Nile drained off the land in November each year, leaving the land damp and suitable for flies to breed. The fifth plague harmed only the cattle in the fields (Exod. 9.3). It was probably a disease called anthrax, passed on by the frogs which had died in the fields (Exod. 8.13–14). One form of this cattle disease can be passed on to humans from infected cattle. The disease is carried from the cattle by a certain kind of fly, and in humans it causes boils (the sixth plague).

4. MOSES AND THE PLAGUES

In the story of the plagues we notice that, besides demanding that Pharaoh should let the Israelites go, Moses and Aaron had three important things to do. These were:

1. to announce, on six occasions, the coming of the plague, so that when it came Pharaoh would have no excuse for doubting that God had sent the plague;
2. to do some action on six occasions, with their hands or rods, to mark the beginning of the plague;
3. to pray, on three occasions, for the removal of the plague (Exod. 8.28–31; 9.27–33; 10.15–19).

As we read the story we see that, again and again, the writer emphasizes the fact that it was not Moses or Aaron who caused or removed the plague, but the Lord Himself. Notice, for example:

Exod. 8.30–31: Moses prayed, and the Lord removed the swarms of flies;

Exod. 9.5–6: Moses announced the time, 'and the Lord did this thing'

Exod. 10.13: Moses held out his rod, 'and the Lord brought an east wind . . .'

When we read that Moses prayed and God did as Moses asked, some people ask, 'Did Moses by his prayer change God's mind, or cause Him to do something He was not intending to do?' The answer to this question is, 'No.' When the Spirit of God moves us to pray, it is so that the will of God may be done in the world.

NOTES

8.22. Goshen: Goshen was an area in the east of the Nile Delta. It was suitable for cattle and sheep (Gen. 47.1–6).

8.23. Put a division: Notice the RSV footnote—Hebrew: 'set redemption'. Redemption in Hebrew is *peduth*, division or difference is *peluth*. The earliest translations into Greek and Latin have words for 'division'. It seems likely that the word 'redemption' in our Hebrew texts is a mistake made by a scribe who copied out the book.

8.26. Offerings abominable to the Egyptians: The Egyptians seldom sacrificed whole animals to their gods. They considered many animals to be sacred. In the time of the Persian Empire Egyptian priests were disgusted by the Jews who sacrificed rams to Yahweh in the land of the ram-god Khnum. At a later period a Roman ambassador was torn to pieces by a crowd of Egyptians because he accidentally killed a cat.

9.6. All the cattle: If all the cattle died, what cattle were left to suffer from the boils and the hail (Exod. 9.9, 19–21)? Several different explanations have been suggested by scholars; for example:

1. Originally there were two or three different stories. In one story the cattle were all killed by a disease. In another story they suffered from boils. Later on an editor put both these stories together, and did not notice that one contradicted the other.

2. 'All the cattle' in Exodus 9.6 means 'all the cattle in the pasture land' (Exod. 9.3). Other cattle which had not been driven out to pasture were still alive.

3. 'All' is an exaggeration. The real meaning of the Hebrew is 'very many'. Notice that when a story is told, exaggeration may help to express the situation. When a person says, 'On the day our country became independent everyone was happy and smiling', we know that the person who says this did not inspect everyone in the country to see if they were smiling. No doubt there were people who were sad because of illness or accidents on that day. But the exaggeration in the story helps us to gain a true understanding of the widespread excitement and joy of that day. In the story of the plagues we may think that there is exaggeration: this is not the same as saying that the story is untrue.

9.11. The magicians could not stand before Moses . . . : This is the last mention in Exodus of the Egyptian magicians. Whatever power they had, they were in the end helpless before the power of God.

STUDY SUGGESTIONS AND QUESTIONS

REVIEW OF CONTENT

1. What was the fourth plague, and how may it have been caused?
2. What was the fifth plague, and how may it have been caused?
3. What was the sixth plague, and how may it have been caused?
4. What main differences do you find between the story of the first three plagues and the story of the next three plagues (4th, 5th, and 6th)?

BIBLE STUDY AND REFLECTION

5. The plagues were signs which showed God's presence and activity in Egypt.
   (a) Would they have had this meaning if Moses had not announced them before they happened?
   (b) Does your answer to (a) suggest anything about the relationship of prophecy and miracle in the Bible?
   (c) Why were such special signs needed?
   (d) Do you think there are any special signs of God's presence and activity in the world today? If so, what are they?
6. 'I will put a division between my people and your people' (Exod. 8.23).
   (a) Who do you think are 'the people of God' in the world today?
   (b) In what ways do you expect them to be different from other people?
   (c) In what ways, if any, are they in fact different from other people?
7. The plagues we read about in Exodus 8.20—9.21 did not affect the Israelites.
   (a) Do you think that people who trust in God will usually be able to escape from the sufferings and troubles which other people go through? Give reasons for your answer, and examples from everyday life.
   (b) When people who trust in God suffer severely, what questions are they likely to ask? Give examples, if you can, from everyday life, and also study Job 21 and 24; Malachi 3,14–18; Romans 8.12–39.
8. Pharaoh tried to limit the response he would make to God's demand that he should let Israel go (Exod. 8.25–28; 10.11, 24). In what ways do you think we try to limit our responses to the demands which God makes on us, and the demands he makes on our families and friends?

9.13—10.29

The Seventh, Eighth, and Ninth Plagues

OUTLINE AND CONTEXT

9.13–35: *The seventh plague—hail*

(a) Moses was sent to warn Pharaoh (9.13–21).

(b) The Lord sent hail, thunder, and lightning (9.22–26).

(c) Pharaoh agreed to let the Israelites go if the hail stopped (9.27–32).

(d) The hail stopped, in answer to Moses's prayer; but Pharaoh refused to let the Israelites go (9.33–35).

10.1–20: *The eighth plague—locusts*
(a) Moses was sent to warn Pharaoh, but Pharaoh was unwilling to let the Israelites take their families with them (10.1–11).
(b) The Lord sent locusts on the land of Egypt (10.12–15).
(c) Pharaoh admitted that he had done wrong (10.16–17).
(d) The locusts were removed in answer to Moses's prayer, but Pharaoh still refused to let the Israelites go (10.18–20).
10.21–29: *The ninth plague—darkness*
(a) The Lord told Moses what he must do (10.21).
(b) Darkness covered the land of Egypt for three days (10.22–23).
(c) Pharaoh agreed to let the Israelites go with their families, but not with their flocks and herds (10.24–26).
(d) Pharaoh sent Moses away (10.27–29).

Exodus 9.13—10.29 continues the story of the plagues.

INTERPRETATION AND COMMENT

1. THE PURPOSE OF THE PLAGUES (9.14–17; 10.2–3)

Notice that God sent the plagues for several reasons besides that of trying to persuade Pharaoh to let the Israelites leave Egypt. The plagues were also:

1. To show the power of Yahweh, so that people throughout the land of Egypt might know of Him (Exod. 9.16).

2. To show the foolishness of Pharaoh's pride (Exod. 9.17; 10.3). Pharaoh had no power to avoid the plagues of which Moses had warned him.

3. To show the Israelites that God cared for them, in order that they might tell their descendants what great things God had done for them (Exod. 10.2). Bearing witness, or giving testimony to the way God had saved His people, became an important part of the religious life of the Israelites.

2. THE STORY OF THE FIRST NINE PLAGUES

The writer of Exodus took a great deal of care in telling the story of the first nine plagues. He arranged the story in groups of three plagues, each group beginning with a plague that was announced to Pharaoh 'in the morning', and ending with a plague that was not announced. Within this general pattern the story becomes more and more exciting as Pharaoh appears ready to give way and then hardens his heart. Yet at the end of the nine plagues Pharaoh still refuses to let the Israelites go. We may wonder why the writer took so much trouble to tell the story so carefully. Perhaps it was because he saw in the story so many lessons which he hoped that people might learn as they read the story or listened to someone else reading or re-telling it. Here are some of these lessons:

(a) Yahweh is the one true God who controls the world (Exod. 7.17; 8.10, 22; 9.14–16, 29).

(b) God makes His plans known to men, and He does what He has said He will do. He warns Pharaoh that the plagues will come, and they do come. See also Exodus 7.13; 8.13, 15, 19; 9.12, 20–21, 35.

(c) If people refuse to do what God tells them to do, they bring trouble upon themselves and upon others.

(d) A person's willingness to obey God is more clearly shown by what he does than by what he says he will do (Exod. 8.8, 28–32; 9.27–28, 34).

(e) God is at work in the world to save His people and to fulfil His purposes for them. But we often need to be patient: God's purposes are not always brought to completion quickly.

3. THE HAIL, THE LOCUSTS, AND THE DARKNESS

These plagues also were connected with events that naturally occur in Egypt. Hail does not often occur in Egypt, but, when it does, it usually comes in the months of January and February. By February the barley crop would be nearly ripe and the flax in flower (Exod. 9.31). Wheat and spelt (Exod. 9.32) are sown later than barley. So they would escape the damage done by the hail.

Heavy rains in Ethiopia and the Sudan which cause the Nile to flood also produce good conditions for the breeding and swarming of locusts. Locusts do not breed in Egypt, but they can travel long distances when helped by the wind (notice the mention of wind in Exod. 10.13, 19).

The darkness (Exod. 10.21–23) was probably caused by a strong wind, the *Khamsin*. Such winds stir up dust and sand, and obscure the light of the sun. They are most severe in March, and have been known to last for as long as three days.

The Passover and the tenth plague took place in the month *Abib*, that is in March or April. Thus the story of the plagues covers a period from the beginning of the Nile flood in July or August through to the following March or April. It fits in well with what we know of conditions in Egypt, and the plagues occur in the order that we should expect, when we consider the climate and the diseases known to occur in Egypt.

But when we have learned something about how the plagues happened we have not finished explaining them. If there is a pot of hot porridge we may ask, 'Why is it hot?' The answer may be (a) 'The pot was put on the fire. The heat from the fire made it hot.' But if we ask, 'Why is it hot?' we may also be told (b) 'My wife knows that I like my porridge hot, so she put the pot on the fire.' Answer (a) and answer (b) are both sensible and true answers. Answer (a) tells us about how an event has occurred; answer (b) tells us about a person with a purpose, a person who caused the event to occur. In this section we have considered the question of how the plagues happened. We have given an answer of the same kind as answer (a). But the writer of Exodus was much more interested in the Person who sent the plagues, and His purposes. His answers are like answer (b): he talks about God and His purposes in acting as He did. (See Interpretation and Comment, pp. 57, 58.)

NOTES

9.14. Upon your heart: There seems to be no reason for mentioning Pharaoh's heart. The translators of the Jerusalem Bible have assumed there is a mistake. They have corrected it to 'on you'. To copy out a book accurately by hand is a difficult task. We should not be surprised to find problems and errors in the Biblical text. But note: (a) such errors are few, compared with the errors in many other ancient manuscripts, and (b) where there are errors, they do not alter any of the main teachings that we find in the Bible. For example, in this verse it makes no difference to the meaning of the story of the plagues, whether we translate 'upon your heart', or 'upon you'.

9.18. From the day it was founded: When we hear someone talking about an event which has happened 'since independence', we know that he comes from one of the countries of the world which has become independent in the last thirty years. For such a person 'Independence' is the great event to which he looks back. The Egyptians regarded the foundation of the United Kingdom of Upper and Lower Egypt (about 2850 BC) as the greatest event since the creation of the world. They often referred to it. For example, Tuthmose III (about 1460 BC) wrote that the god Amun rejoiced over him more than over all the kings who had been 'in the land since it was founded'.

9.20. The servants of Pharaoh: That is, his court officials.

9.24. Fire ran down to the earth: A description of lightning.

9.29, 33. Stretch out my hands: Moses would stretch out his hands in prayer. The people of Israel did not pray usually with head bowed and hands together, but with their hands raised (see also 1 Tim. 2.8).

9.35. Through Moses: This is probably a mistake. It is better to follow the Greek (Septuagint) translation: 'to Moses'. Compare Exodus 9.12.

10.2. Now I have made sport of the Egyptians: There is no other suggestion in Exodus that God was mocking the Egyptians. The Hebrew verb 'make sport of' in some passages means 'deal severely with', or 'cause suffering to'. This second meaning seems better in this verse.

10.5, 15. The face of the land: The Hebrew words are 'eye of the land'. The Egyptians sometimes thought of the sun and moon as the two eyes of the god Ra. So in these verses to 'cover the eye of the land' probably means to obscure the light of the sun. In Angola in July 1931 swarms of locusts completely obscured the sun for some hours.

10.10. The Lord be with you if . . . : This means, 'I swear by Yahweh, I will not let you go with your women and children.'

10.10. Look, you have some evil . . . : The meaning is probably 'Take care or you will be in trouble.' The NEB version is 'Beware, there is trouble in store for you.'

10.11. The men among you . . . : In a pilgrimage festival it was usually only men who were required to go (Exod. 23.17; Deut. 16.16).

STUDY SUGGESTIONS AND QUESTIONS

REVIEW OF CONTENTS

1. What was the seventh plague?
2. What was the eighth plague?
3. What was the ninth plague?
4. In what ways can these plagues be connected to natural events in Egypt?
5. What does the writer of Exodus say were the purposes for which God used the plagues?

BIBLE STUDY AND REFLECTION

6. The plagues revealed the power of God and the pride of Pharaoh. Other writers of books in the Bible also mention the pride of rulers and God's judgement on them. Read Job 12.13–25; Ezekiel 28.1–10; Daniel 4; Acts 13.20–23.
   (a) What lessons do you think these passages have for people today?
   (b) Can you think of any rulers or governments who seem to act in a way that is selfish and proud?
   (c) If you have any position of authority in the community, in your Church, at work, at school, or in your family, is there anything you have learned from these passages which suggests that you need to alter the way you speak or act?
7. Giving testimony to God's acts of saving and blessing his people was an important part of the religious life of Israel (Exod. 10.2).
   Read Deuteronomy 6.20–25; 26.1–11; Joshua 4.1–7; Psalm 105.23–45.
   (a) What acts of God are mentioned in these passages?
   (b) To whom were people expected to tell the story of God's goodness?
   (c) What lessons have you learned from these passages?
8. The first followers of Christ were called on to bear witness to Him (John 15.27). Testimony is an important part of Christian life.

(a) To what people do you think a Christian should speak about his or her experience of God's goodness?
(b) Some Christians think that when they give a testimony they must speak in detail about what they have done wrong in the past. What is your opinion? What do you think is the most helpful sort of testimony a person can give?

11.1—12.28
The Passover

OUTLINE AND CONTEXT

11.1–3: God had told Moses that the last plague would soon come.
11.4–8: Moses told Pharaoh that the first-born sons of the Egyptians would die.
11.9–10: In spite of the warning, Pharaoh refused to let the Israelites go.
12.1–20: God gave Moses and Aaron instructions about the Passover.
12.21–28: Moses told the Israelites what they must do.

Exodus 11 completes the story of the first nine plagues, showing that Pharaoh still refused to let the Israelites go (Exod. 11.9–10). Exodus 12 tells the story of the Passover, and so prepares for the story of the Israelites' escape from Egypt (Exod. 12.28—15.21).

INTERPRETATION AND COMMENT

1. INSTRUCTIONS FOR THE PASSOVER (12.1–28)

Before Moses left Pharaoh's palace, he announced that one more plague, worse than all the rest, would strike the Egyptians (Exod. 11.1–10). God then instructed Moses to prepare for: (a) a special sacrifice on the night of the final plague, and (b) the future repetition of such a sacrifice each year. Each family group must select and sacrifice a lamb, put some of the blood on the doorway of their house, and eat the lamb during the night. In the night the first-born sons of the Egyptians would die, but the sons of the Israelites would be safe: God would pass over them and spare them. (The Hebrew word for Passover is *pasach*: it means both 'pass over' and 'spare'. From it we get the English word 'paschal' used in 1 Cor. 5.7.)

From the next year onwards the people of Israel must celebrate a special religious festival each year in remembrance of how God had brought them out of Egypt.

2. THE SACRIFICE OF A LAMB (EXOD. 12.3–8, 21)

We may ask why a lamb was chosen for this sacrifice, and what meaning the sacrifice had. Scholars have tried to answer these questions by finding out about the ancestors of the Israelites and their ways of sacrifice. But we do not know enough about this subject to be able to be sure what the correct answer is.

The ancestors of the Israelites had kept sheep and goats. They had their own customs and laws about sacrifice. It was probably a custom among them to sacrifice a sheep or a goat in the spring and to smear its blood on their tent-poles or door-posts. We cannot be certain that they did so, and if they did so we cannot be certain why they made this sacrifice; but here are some of the reasons that scholars have suggested:

(a) Perhaps they believed that evil spirits threatened their homes and their flocks, and that the blood of a sacrificed lamb would turn away the evil spirits.

(b) Perhaps they believed that the sacrifice of a lamb in the spring would persuade their gods to keep their flocks safe, and to make them produce offspring in the coming year.

(c) Perhaps each spring, when they left their winter pastures in the wilderness and moved to land which they could cultivate during the spring and summer, they offered a sacrifice hoping to gain protection from the dangers of their journey.

(d) Perhaps they ate a sacrificial meal together each year, to show that the whole tribe was united and at peace with one another.

In any case, when Moses told the Israelites to sacrifice a lamb on the fourteenth day of the month Abib, the Israelites probably did not think that this was something very strange or new. But whatever meaning such a sacrifice had had in the past, it was to have a new meaning in the future.

3. THE MEANING OF THE PASSOVER—REMEMBRANCE (12.14, 24–27)

Israelite prophets and teachers believed their lives were controlled by the one true God (Job 12.7–10; Isa. 41.20). They did not think that sacrifices were needed to drive away evil spirits. They believed that their flocks and herds also were under the control of God, and that He did not need the help of magic or of sacrifices in order to bless them (Deut. 28.1–4). The religious festivals of the Israelites became chiefly occasions for rejoicing before God, and for remembering what He had done for them. Notice carefully what is said about memorials and remembering in Exodus 12.14, 24–27; 13.3–9; and Joshua 4.4–7.

But what did this 'remembering' mean? We have seen that for God to 'remember his covenant' (Exod. 2.24) meant not only to think about it, but to begin to act to fulfil it (see note on Exod. 2.24, p. 18). So also for the Israelites, 'remembering' meant more than thinking. In the Passover festival it meant thinking how God had set them free in the past; thanking Him for what He had done, and for all the benefits that they now enjoyed; and committing themselves to go forward into the future, obeying and trusting in God who had already done so much for them.

4. THE MEANING OF THE PASSOVER—OTHER ASPECTS

(a) The Passover was a *family celebration* (Exod. 12.3–4). Israelite families were to take part together. Fathers were to celebrate the feast with their sons, and explain its meaning to them (12.25–27). The Passover was not only for the priests or leaders of Israel. It has always been one of the strong points of the religion of Israel, that so much of it is centred round the family and the responsibility of the father for the instruction of his sons.

(b) The Passover was *a festival for all Israel* (Exod. 12.3–6). Each family group celebrated the Passover at the same time and in the same way. The Passover reminded the Israelites that, although they belonged to different tribes, they were all one people worshipping God together (Exod. 12.47).

(c) The Passover was *a preparation for a journey* (Exod. 12.11). When the Israelites first celebrated the Passover in Egypt they wore their travelling clothes. It was a preparation for their journey out of Egypt. In later years, after they reached the land of Canaan, this custom reminded them that human life is like a journey: we go forward with God to do what He has, in His love, prepared for us to do.

(d) The Passover was *a sacrifice*, offered to God and enjoyed by His people (Exod. 12.27). The way of escape for the people of Israel involved the death of a lamb for each family. When it had been sacrificed, the family ate a meal together. To eat together meant thanksgiving, joy, and unity.

5. THE PASSOVER AND CHRIST

St Paul spoke of Christ as the Passover Lamb (1 Cor. 5.7). Other New Testament writers referred to Him as the Lamb or the Lamb of God (John 1.29; Rev. 5.6; 15.3). They used the language and ideas of the Passover (together with ideas from such passages as Gen. 22.1–14 and Isa. 53.4–9), to help people to understand more about Christ and the Christian life, especially to show:

(a) That through Christ's sacrifice, those who trust in Him are set free from sin, from death, and from bondage to inherited traditions (Matt. 26.26–28; 1 Cor. 11.23–26; Rev. 15.2–3; 1 Pet. 1.18–21).

(b) That Christian living is to be a joyful celebration of our deliverance by Christ, and that since He has died for our sins, we should be living a life of purity, sincerity, and truth (1 Cor. 5.6–8).

(c) That Christ leads His people onwards to a glory that He has prepared, a glory which is not limited to the one nation of Israel, but is for people from 'every tribe and tongue and people and nation' (Rev. 5.6–10).

6. THE PASSOVER AND THE LORD'S SUPPER

If we understand the Passover, we shall also understand some important truths about the Lord's Supper. In the history of the Church we find that Christians have called the Lord's Supper (1 Cor. 11.20) by many names: for example, the Breaking of Bread, the Eucharist, the Holy Communion, the Mass. There have been many different ways of celebrating it: in homes and in churches, with special clothes for the leader, and with ordinary clothes; with long written prayers, or with prayers that are not written down. But in whatever way we take the service, we shall understand its meaning better if we see how it is connected to the Passover.

Christ died on the cross on the day of the Preparation (Mark 15.42; John 19.31). That was the day on which the Passover lambs were killed, ready for people to eat at the feast during the coming night (John 18.28).

Jesus was thinking about the Passover festival and His own sacrifice of Himself, when He sat with His followers for the Last Supper. He took bread and blessed God for it, as is done in the Passover meal. But instead of saying, 'This is the bread of affliction which our fathers ate in Egypt,' He said, 'This is my body which is for you. Do this in remembrance of me.' So the Lord's Supper is linked to the Passover in many ways. Let us note some of them:

(a) The Lord's Supper was at first celebrated at an ordinary meal-time in people's homes. It helped people to feel that they were part of the family of God.

(b) Like the Passover, the Lord's Supper reminds those who take part, of their unity, for all are expected to take part together (see Matt. 26.27, 'Drink of it, all of you', and 1 Cor. 10.17).

(c) In the Lord's Supper we look forward to those blessings which God has promised us, for we proclaim His death 'until He comes' (1 Cor. 11.26).

(d) As the Passover is a festival of remembrance, so is the Lord's Supper. It is in remembrance of Jesus (1 Cor. 11.24–25). Such remembering, as we have seen (pp. 62, 63), means more than thinking. It means thinking how God has set us free, thanking Him for all the blessings which He gives us through Jesus, and committing our lives afresh to Him so that we may go forward together to praise Him and serve Him in the world.

There are of course also differences between the Passover and the Lord's Supper. The Passover festival was once a year; the Lord's Supper was probably celebrated weekly in the early days of the Church. The Passover involved the sacrifice of lambs; the Lord's Supper included no sacrifice of a living animal, for, as the writer of the Epistle to the Hebrews made clear, Christ's sacrifice was a single decisive act which needed no repetition (Heb. 9.24–28; 10.10–14). The Passover was limited to men; the Lord's Supper is for all, for in Christ 'there is neither male nor female; for you are all one

'If we understand the Passover we shall also understand some important truths about the Lord's Supper' (p. 64).

In Palestine today a sect calling themselves Samaritans actually continue to celebrate the Passover by sacrificing lambs each year (right).

A special open-air Mass was celebrated by Polish clergy in 1970, on the 25th anniversary of their liberation from Dachau concentration camp, where they had been prisoners of the Nazis during World War II (below).

Do you see any connection between these two ceremonies? In what ways, if any, does either of them help you to understand the Lord's Supper?

in Christ Jesus' (Gal. 3.28). The Passover directed attention mainly towards an act of God in the past; the Lord's Supper brings us into communion with a risen and living Lord.

7. THE FESTIVAL OF UNLEAVENED BREAD (12.14–20)

These are instructions for a festival to be held each year. It began on the night of the Passover. On the evening of the fourteenth day of the month Abib the Israelites sacrificed the Passover lambs. They ate the lambs during the night. Since they counted each day as beginning at sunset, they in fact ate the lambs on the fifteenth Abib. This was the first day of the Festival of Unleavened Bread.

Leaven is the yeast or fermenting dough kept for making bread rise. In the Festival of Unleavened Bread all leaven made from grain belonging to the harvest of the previous year was thrown away. This marked a new beginning. Perhaps originally it was a sign that the evils of the past year should not affect people in the new year.

But after their escape from Egypt, the Israelites did not keep the festival only as a festival of the new barley harvest. They kept it in remembrance of God's goodness in setting them free from Egypt (Exod. 12.17). They kept it not only as a mark of the beginning of a new year, but also as marking the beginning of a new life of freedom from slavery in Egypt, a new life of service for God. Paul used it as a picture of the new life of holiness which the Christian should find in Christ (1 Cor. 5.8).

NOTES

11.1—12.36: This passage contains: (a) instructions for the first Passover in Egypt, and (b) instructions for later regular celebrations of the Passover and Festival of Unleavened Bread in Canaan (note Exod. 12.25). It is not always clear to us whether a particular instruction refers only to the first Passover in Egypt or to the later Passovers in Canaan, or to both.

The writer of Exodus clearly believed that the Unleavened Bread was connected with the Passover from the time of the Exodus. Many Old Testament scholars believe that the people of Israel did not begin to celebrate a barley-harvest festival until after they settled in Canaan. They suggest that the Israelites copied this festival from some Canaanite religious festival, although we have no knowledge of any festival of Unleavened Bread among the Canaanites. Those who hold this view do not agree about the time when the festival of Unleavened Bread was joined to the Passover, some say it was before the time of David, others say it was after the Exile. Since the whole theory is so uncertain, in our interpretation and comments here we have commented only on what the writer of Exodus says.

11.5. The maid-servant who is behind the mill: In Israelite homes it was the custom for men's wives to grind corn to make flour. But in Egypt grinding was considered the lowest form of work: it was usually done by poor women or prisoners.

12.2. This month: That is, the month Abib (Exod. 13.4). After the Exile the Jews called it by its Babylonian name, Nisan (Neh. 2.1; Esther 3.7). The Jewish civil year began in the autumn (Exod. 23.16). But the religious year began in the spring. Compare this with the way that in Christian countries the civil year begins in January, but the Church year begins about the end of November, on Advent Sunday.

12.9. Do not eat any of it raw or boiled: Among some tribes raw flesh is eaten because this is believed to be a way of gaining an animal's strength. Such a custom was forbidden to the Israelites. We do not know why the lamb was not to be boiled.

12.12. On all the gods of Egypt: Many of the Egyptian gods were pictured as having the form of animals. The writer of Exodus does not make clear whether the judgement on them was: (a) that they could not save the first-born sons of those who worshipped them, or (b) that they could not save the first-born animals whose form they had.

12.14. A memorial: When this word is used of the Passover it seems to mean something that will remind the people of Israel of what God has done for them, just as the stones set up by the river Jordan were to be a 'memorial' to remind each generation of the people of Israel (compare Exod. 12.14, 24–27 with Joshua 4.4–7).

12.15. Cut off from Israel: That is, excommunicated or prevented from taking any further part in the community and worship of Israel. We may compare this with a custom still followed by some Jewish and Muslim families. If any member of these families becomes a Christian, the rest of the family regards him as dead, and may even hold funeral rites for him.

12.23. The destroyer: Compare 2 Samuel 24.16. The destroyer or destroying plague is here pictured as an instrument of God's judgement. It is not a power of evil working against God.

12.26. Your children: That is, your sons. Women and girls had little place in the religion of Israel.

STUDY SUGGESTIONS AND QUESTIONS

REVIEW OF CONTENT

1. When were the Passover lambs to be: (a) chosen? (b) sacrificed? (c) eaten?
2. Why was the festival called the Passover?
3. For what reasons were the Israelites to celebrate the Passover?
4. (a) In what ways is the Passover similar to the Lord's Supper?
   (b) In what ways is the Passover different from the Lord's Supper?

5. The Passover was a 'memorial', a day of remembering. In what ways is such remembering more than simply thinking about what God has done in the past?

BIBLE STUDY AND REFLECTION

6. 'Christ, our paschal lamb, has been sacrificed for us . . .' (1 Cor. 5.8). In what ways do you think that knowing about the Passover festival can help us to understand more of the meaning of Christ's death?
7. In what ways do you think that the Passover helps us to understand the meaning of the Lord's Supper?
8. 'The Passover was a family celebration' (p. 63). Compare this with Christian religious festivals.
   (a) What, if anything, do you think there is for us to learn from it about religion in our homes?
   (b) What advice would you give to parents who say that they do not know how to teach their children about God?

12.29—13.22
The first-born Sons

OUTLINE AND CONTEXT

12.29–36: The death of the first-born. Pharaoh then told Moses that the Israelites must leave Egypt.
12.37–42: The Israelites began their journey out of Egypt. They went from Rameses to Succoth.
12.43–51: Further instructions about the Passover.
13.1–16: The consecration of the first-born and the Festival of Unleavened Bread, to remind the people of Israel how God had delivered them from Egypt.
13.17–22: The Israelites continued their journey, from Succoth to Etham.

Exodus 12.29–36 tells the story of the death of the first-born in Egypt. This is the climax of the long story about the plagues. It leads to Pharaoh's saying that the Israelites could leave Egypt. The story of their journey from Egypt to Mount Sinai is told in Exodus 12.37—18.27.

INTERPRETATION AND COMMENT

1. THE DEATH OF THE FIRST-BORN

The book of Exodus begins with the story of the suffering of the Israelites, and how they cried out to God for help. Now we hear another cry (Exod. 12.30): the mourning of the Egyptians over the death of their first-born sons. The fact that the leader of their country had already brought a similar sorrow to many Israelite families would in no way lessen the grief of Egyptians. To have the first-born son of a family die is a terrible tragedy, whether he is a full-grown man or a baby. The story makes us sad as we read it.

The writer of Exodus told this story because he believed:

(a) that it happened;

(b) that it showed God's power;

(c) that it was God's way of forcing Pharaoh to let the Israelites go free;

(d) that this tragic suffering could have been avoided if Pharaoh had been willing to obey God's command, and to let Israel go;

(e) that such a punishment was fitting, because Pharaoh would not let the people of Israel go (see Exod. 4.22–23).

But when we read the story, we may find that we have many questions in our minds. For example:

1. Did *all* the first-born of men and cattle die, or was the story exaggerated?

2. (a) Did God cause the death of the first-born?

(b) If He did, how can we believe what other writers of the books of the Bible say about God being loving and merciful?

3. (a) If the story is true, does God still act in a similar way?

(b) If He does, can we go on loving and worshipping Him?

When we think about these questions, we may find that we cannot give a clear answer to them. But it may help us if we remember these points:

(a) We often do not have enough knowledge to answer all the questions we can ask. When we study science, we may ask 'What was the date when men first lived on the earth?' We cannot answer this question. We do not have enough knowledge. We must be humble enough to admit that even in science, and in our study of life on the earth, there are many things we do not know—though we may discover some of the answers in the future.

(b) Jesus taught His followers that all people are by nature evil. God is a judge who must judge men truly. The fact that God punishes people does not mean that He ceases to love them. It is often a parent who loves his children most who is careful to correct them and discipline them when they do what is wrong.

(c) We can only see part of any person's life. We only know something about a person's life on earth and in time. God sees the whole of a person's life, both that part which is on our side of death, and the part which is beyond death. So we are not well able to judge the ways in which God deals with people during their lives on earth.

(d) We might try to avoid some of the problems that this story brings to our minds by saying: 'God did not cause the death of the first-born in

Egypt. This was only what the writer of Exodus thought. But God would not do nor allow anything so terrible.' But if we say this, we do not solve all our problems. We only move the problem a little. For we still live in a world full of suffering. We live in a world where people are continually at war, fighting and killing each other, where people are imprisoned and tortured by their fellow citizens, or are left to suffer poverty and starvation. Thousands of people die because the leaders of different groups are determined to keep their power or to gain power from others. Thousands die because richer neighbours refuse to help them.

How can such terrible things happen if the world has been made by a God who loves us? We do not know. We see that when people are proud and powerful, as Pharaoh was, they keep on causing distress and death to other people. We may perhaps believe that such suffering must be in some way necessary or God would not allow it.

When we read Luke 19.41–44 we find that Jesus wept for the people of Jerusalem. He knew that they were going to suffer. He did not want them to suffer. He wanted them to turn to God and to live in God's ways of peace and justice and love. But He saw that they were refusing to live in God's way. He knew that in the end this would lead to suffering and to sorrow. We learn from Jesus that God is not happy when people suffer from war and other disasters. He offers people a way of life, but if people refuse to listen to Him, and follow their own selfish ways, then sorrow and suffering is bound to come.

2. THE CONSECRATION OF THE FIRST-BORN SONS (13.1–2, 11–16)

Some of the people of Canaan used to sacrifice their first-born sons. They killed them as an offering to their gods. The Israelites learned that God did not want them to offer their children to Him in such a way (Gen. 22.1–14). But they did believe that their first-born sons should be specially set apart for God. Instead of sacrificing them, they gave five shekels of silver to the priest (Num. 18.15–16). This payment was to show: (a) that the child's life belonged to God, and (b) that God provides a way of life for His people instead of a way of death. The payment is called a redemption price. When the writers of the New Testament said that Christ died to redeem us from sin, they meant that through Christ who died for us we can belong to God, and we can share in the eternal life of God.

When the Israelites consecrated their first-born sons to God, they also remembered how their own first-born sons had been kept safe when the Egyptians died (Exod. 13.14–15). They remembered that God called them as a people to be like a first-born son among the nations (Exod. 4.22–23). Notice that in many different ways the writers of the Bible say to people, 'God has been good to you, so give yourself to Him and live for Him'.

3. IT SHALL BE TO YOU A SIGN ... AS A MARK ON YOUR HAND (13.9, 16)

The eating of unleavened bread for seven days, and the consecration of the first-born sons, are described as being like signs, like a mark on the hand or a jewel on the forehead. Among some tribes young men have cuts made on their faces when they are grown up and have become full members of the tribe. Among other people a woman may have a mark on her face, or may wear a particular jewel, to show her importance. The writer of Exodus must have known of such customs. But he saw that it is not important for people to be reminded of their own position or strength. It is much more important for them to remember God's goodness and power. The religious festivals and customs of Israel were to be such reminders.

When the people of Israel settled in the land of Canaan they lived among people who had very different ideas. In Canaanite religious festivals, people had to do special acts and speak special words. They believed that such acts and words would help the gods to bring fertility to the land, to the people, and to their flocks and herds. Their festivals and their sacrifices were to provide the gods with the things that the gods needed, so that in return the gods would help the people. But the people of Israel came to understand that when we worship God we are not giving Him something He needs so that we may persuade Him to help us (see Psalm 50.9–15). Their religious festivals were to help them to remember God and His goodness. They were not trying to remind God, because God does not forget (Isa. 49.14–16).

NOTES

12.37. Six hundred thousand men: Compare Numbers 2.18, 32. If there were 600,000 men over the age of twenty, then the total number of Israelites must have been about two million people. It is not likely that so many people could have travelled together out of Egypt and through Sinai. How can we explain this large number? We can suggest a number of explanations:

(a) The writer of Exodus exaggerated the number,

(b) The writer of Exodus made a mistake,

(c) The writer of Exodus wrote a smaller number, and this was later altered or copied wrongly by a scribe,

(d) The words written in the verse have been wrongly understood. Some scholars suggest that the Hebrew word *alluph* (armed man) was written in many places in Exodus and Numbers and later on mixed up with the word *eleph* (a thousand). If this suggestion is right, it would mean that the total number of armed men given in Numbers 1–2 would be about 18,000, and the total number of Israelites about 72,000.

12.38. A mixed multitude: As well as the Israelites, there were probably:

(a) some Egyptians who were married to Israelites (Lev. 24.10), and (b) other people who had migrated to Egypt from Palestine and had become slaves (Num. 11.4).

12.40. Four hundred and thirty years: Genesis 15.16 gives a round figure of 400 years. See Special Note C, pp. 84–88.

12.41. The hosts of the Lord: The word 'hosts' is in Hebrew *tsebaoth.* It refers to an ordered array; for example, of stars in the sky (Gen. 2.1) or of men in an army (Gen. 21.22). In the Old Testament books from 1 Samuel onwards the most frequent title of God is 'the Lord of hosts' (*Yahweh Tsebaoth*), but in the books of the Pentateuch (Genesis—Deuteronomy) this title is not found. This suggests that the books of the Pentateuch may have been written at an earlier date than the other prophetic and historical books of the Old Testament.

12.46. You shall not break a bone: Compare Num. 9.12; Pss. 34.20; John 19.46. We do not know why no bone of the Passover lamb must be broken.

12.49. One law . . . : See p. 11. When there are different laws for people of different races in a country, there is nearly always injustice.

13.2. Consecrate: That is: make holy, sanctify, set apart for the use of God. When people consecrated animals, they set them apart for God by sacrificing them. But what did it mean to consecrate or set apart a *person* for God? In Lev. 19.2 and 20.7 we see that men set apart for God must be holy because God is holy. The idea of God's holiness included the idea that He is set apart from all that is evil (Isa. 6.3–6; Hab. 1.13). So the Israelites learned that those who are consecrated to God must be: (1) set free from what is evil, and (2) ready for God to use them to do His work in the world.

13.9. The law of the Lord: In Exodus the word law (Hebrew *torah*) refers to commandments and instructions which God gave to the Israelites (Exod. 12.49; 13.9; 16.4, 28; 18.16, 20; 24.12).

13.18. The Red Sea: See note on 14.2, pp. 76, 77.

13.18. Equipped for battle: The Hebrew word translated 'equipped for battle' may mean 'organized in five groups' (compare Num. 2.2–31). The NEB follows the Greek translation (the Septuagint), and says 'in the fifth generation', but this seems unlikely to be correct, since (a) there is no word for 'generation' in the Hebrew text of this verse, and (b) 12.40–41 shows that the writer of Exodus believed the Israelites were in Egypt for much more than five generations.

13.21. A pillar of cloud . . . a pillar of fire . . . : See pp. 169, 170, section 3.

STUDY SUGGESTIONS AND QUESTIONS

REVIEW OF CONTENT

1. Why did Pharaoh tell Moses to take the people of Israel out of Egypt?

2. For what reasons do you think the writer of Exodus wrote the story of the death of the first-born in Egypt? What lessons did he want to teach?
3. What were the three most important ways in which the Israelites remembered how God had delivered them from Egypt (Exod. 12.43—13.16)?
4. What was the most direct way from Egypt to Canaan? Why did the people of Israel not go by that way?

BIBLE STUDY AND REFLECTION

5. What answer would you give to someone who said: 'I do not believe that God caused the death of the first-born sons of the Egyptians'?
6. What answer would you give to someone who said: 'I cannot believe in God because so many people suffer and die in the world'?
7. What lessons can we learn about suffering from each of the following passages?
   (a) John 10.11–15; (b) Luke 19.41–44; (c) Romans 1.18–32; (d) Romans 8.18–39.
8. The Israelites were told to consecrate their first-born sons to God. Timothy was told that a Christian should be 'consecrated and useful to the master' (2 Tim. 2.21). Use a Concordance and a Bible Dictionary to find out more about the meaning of being consecrated to God (look up these words: consecrate, holiness, sanctify). What difference do you think it should make to the life of people today if they are consecrated to God?
9. 'You shall redeem . . .' (Exod. 13.13). Use a Concordance and Bible Dictionary to study the meaning of the words 'redeem' and 'redemption'. Notice how often redemption is connected with the following ideas: (1) the payment of a price, (2) being set free by someone else, (3) being set free from a hostile power, (4) being set free to live a new kind of life. How do these ideas help you to understand what the writers of the New Testament mean, when they say that Christians have been redeemed by Christ?
10. 'God did not lead them by the way of the land of the Philistines' (Exod. 13.17). Do you know of any other people whom God has led by a way that they did not expect to go? If so, what do you think they have learned from their experience?

14.1–31

'The Lord brought us out of Egypt'

OUTLINE AND CONTEXT

14.1–4: God told Moses to lead the Israelites to the shore of the Sea of Reeds.
14.5–9: Pharaoh led his army against the Israelites.
14.10–18: Moses told the Israelites not to be afraid.
14.19–31: God divided the waters of the sea: the Israelites crossed in safety, but the Egyptians were drowned.

Exodus 14.1–31 continues the story of how the Israelites left the land of Egypt. The story began in Exodus 12.37–42 and 13.17–22. It leads on to the record in Exodus 15.1–21 of how the Israelites rejoiced because God had saved them so wonderfully.

INTERPRETATION AND COMMENT

The writer of Exodus told the story of the escape of the Israelites from Egypt, not only because it was a thrilling event, but also because it contains great truths about God and His purposes for people.

1. GOD DELIVERS HIS PEOPLE

The Israelites were in great danger. They were escaping slaves; they were not well armed. The Egyptians were ready to attack them with a force of well-trained and well-equipped soldiers. The Israelites could not defend themselves or rescue themselves. They thought they would be killed (Exod. 14.1–12). Then God rescued them (Exod. 14.13–31). What they could not do, God did for them.

The story shows that God delivers His people by His own acts and His own power. He does not expect people to be good enough or strong enough to save themselves. This is a truth which the writers of the New Testament clearly understood. For example, Paul wrote to the Christians in the town of Ephesus, 'God has saved you because He loves you (by grace) . . . and this salvation is a gift that God has given you: it is not the result of what you were nor of anything you did, so no one can boast about it' (Eph. 2.8–9). A woman who recently found new life in Christ said, 'I always used all kinds of bad language. Now I find I cannot use it any more. There is a new power in my life, a power that is not my own. God has changed me.'

2. GOD IS IN CONTROL

Like the story of the Plagues, the story of the crossing of the sea shows that

'God delivers His people' (p. 74).

At the shrine of the Blessed Virgin Mary at Lourdes in France, pilgrims gather to be delivered from sickness and pain. In a famine area in Africa, relief workers distribute water and food that will deliver some of the people from starvation. What likenesses and unlikenesses do you see between each of these 'deliverances' and God's deliverance of the Israelites from Egypt?

God is in control of the world He has made. He can use its natural forces to do what He wants done. Within the past century travellers have seen the waters of shallow lakes in Egypt parted or driven back by the wind. On one occasion the waters of Lake Menzaleh were driven back seven miles. As we read the story we need not be surprised that an east wind drove the water back (Exod. 14.21). But the writer of Exodus clearly meant us to learn a lesson from the fact that this happened at the moment when the Israelites were in danger, that it happened in answer to the prayer of Moses, and that it happened as God had promised (Exod. 14.15–16).

The story also emphasizes that God uses people who are ready to serve Him. He used Moses. He first of all told Moses what He was going to do (Exod. 14.16–18). Afterwards the Israelites would not say, 'We were lucky: the waters divided just when we needed to cross.' Because God had told Moses beforehand, the Israelites said, 'God helped us: He divided the waters when we needed to cross.'

This faith that God is in control, and that He wishes to use us to help others, was shared by two Christians travelling in a remote area of north-west China to tell people about Jesus. One day they had walked for most of the day across desert and mountains, and had seen no one. They stopped to pray. One of them prayed, 'Show us where to find the man you intend to bless through us.' Then they sang a hymn. Two Buddhist monks (lamas) high up on the mountain side heard the singing. They came from an isolated monastery where the monks had heard there was a God who loves. When they heard people singing they said, 'These are the messengers we are waiting for. It is only people who know God, who will sing.' The two Christians were invited to the monastery, and spent a week telling five hundred monks about the God who loves, and who has shown His love to us through Jesus Christ.

3. GOD PUNISHES THOSE WHO OPPRESS OTHERS

God had promised to set the Israelites free 'with great acts of judgement' (Exod. 6.6). An Israelite judge had to help those who were wronged or in distress (see p. 39 and Job 29.14–16; Pss. 10.17–18; 103.6). The other part of a judge's work was to punish those who had done wrong and oppressed others (Job 29.17; Pss. 1.5; 76, 7–8). The Book of Exodus shows that those who seem to be powerful, and to be able to oppress others, may in the end be punished. Evil does not in the end bring benefit to those who do it. God does care about human suffering, for He is the Creator of the world and all its people.

NOTES

14.2. Between Migdol and the sea: Migdol means 'Fortress'. There were a number of Egyptian settlements and fortresses that protected Egypt's border with Sinai. '*The Sea*' is in Exod. 15.4 called the Sea of Reeds or Reed Sea (the Hebrew is *Yam Suph* which does *not* mean Red Sea). Ancient Egyptian records refer to the 'Papyrus Lake'. It was probably a large but not very deep lake somewhere in the area of the present Lake Timsah and the Bitter Lakes.

14.6–7. The chariots of Egypt: Chariots became an important part of the Egyptian army in the time of the Hyksos kings (see pp. 84, 85). In the time of King Solomon the Egyptians still made the best chariots (1 Kings 10.29).

14.9. Horsemen: The Hebrew word means 'riders'; that is, the men who rode in the chariots. Horses were not ridden into battle until a later period (2 Sam. 1.6; 1 Kings 20.20).

14.19. The angel of God: See note on Exod. 3.2. Notice that in Exod. 14.24 it is the Lord Himself who is in the pillar of cloud and fire.

14.20. The night passed: The RSV footnote says that the Hebrew should be translated 'and it lit up the night'. Such a translation would not make sense. A better suggestion is that the Hebrew words mean: 'it restrained the night', that is, the cloud made it too dark for the Egyptians to make an attack by night on the Israelites (compare Joshua 24.7).

14.24. The morning watch: Between 2 a.m. and 6 a.m.

14.27. To its wonted flow: That is, to its usual level.

14.28. All the host of Pharaoh: There is no mention in this verse or in Deuteronomy 11.4 of Pharaoh himself. Later on, Jews believed that Pharaoh was one of those who was drowned, perhaps because they understood literally the poetic language of Psalm 136.15. The later Jewish traditions were followed by Muhammad. So the *Qur'an* says: 'Pharaoh sought to scare them out of the land, but we drowned him together with all that were with him.'

14.29. The people of Israel walked . . . : This is a summary of what happened: it is better to translate it, 'the people of Israel had walked . . .' (See NEB and JB.)

STUDY SUGGESTIONS AND QUESTIONS

REVIEW OF CONTENT

1. Why did the Egyptians not want the Israelites to leave Egypt?
2. How did they try to stop them?
3. What did the Israelites say to Moses when they saw that the Egyptian army was coming to attack them?
4. (a) What answer did Moses give to the Israelites?
   (b) What lesson do you think we can learn from this answer?

BIBLE STUDY AND REFLECTION

5. 'You have only to be still' (Exod. 14.14). Compare the message which

the prophet Isaiah gave to the king and to the people of Judah, when they were threatened by hostile armies. See especially Isaiah 7.7–9; 30.15.

(a) In what ways was the situation of Judah like that of the Israelites who were trying to escape from Egypt?

(b) What would you say to someone who said: 'My life is controlled by evil powers. There is nothing I can do to set myself free'?

(c) What would you say to someone who said; 'I do not need to do any work. God will provide all that I need'?

6. The waters of the Sea of Reeds were divided at the time when the Israelites needed to cross. How would you answer someone who said, 'They were lucky. It was a coincidence. I do not believe it had anything to do with God'? (pp. 74–78 section 2, and Isaiah 48.3–8 and Amos 3.7 may help you to answer).
7. Moses said to the people, 'Fear not' (Exod. 14.13).

   (a) What reason did he give the Israelites for not being afraid?

   (b) Read Isaiah 41.8–14; 43.1–7; 44.1–2, 6–8. What reasons did the prophet give Israelites at a later time for not being afraid?

   (c) What do you think most people are afraid of today?

   (d) Can you find in the passages you have read from Exodus and Isaiah, or in Romans 8.28–39, any reasons why they need not be afraid?

15.1–21

Songs of Victory

OUTLINE AND CONTEXT

15.1–19: The Israelites sang a hymn of victory:
(a) The Lord has delivered us from Pharaoh (15.1–12).
(b) The Lord will lead us into Canaan (15.13–18).
15.20–21: Miriam and the women of Israel danced and sang the song of victory.

Exodus 15.1–21 continues the story of Exodus 14, by telling how the Israelites praised God because He had delivered them from the Egyptian army.

INTERPRETATION AND COMMENT

1. PRAISING GOD

This passage tells us how the Israelites praised God. The story helps us to think about why we should praise God and how we should praise God. Notice particularly how these questions are answered:

(a) *Why did the Israelites praise God?* They praised God for what He had done for them (Exod. 15.1–12). He had rescued them from the Egyptian army which was going to kill them or make them slaves again. They also praised God for what He was going to do for them in the future (Exod. 15.13–18). He had promised to lead them to the land of Canaan, and they believed He would do this (Exod. 15.13–17).

But the people did not only praise God because of His actions. They praised Him because of His character: they knew that God acts in certain ways because of what He is. So they praised Him for being greater than any gods worshipped by other peoples (Exod. 15.11). They praised Him because He loved them and was faithful in keeping His promises (Exod. 15.13). They praised Him for being a King who rules over the universe and over all time (Exod. 15.18). When the Israelites thought about who God is, and what He has done, and what He has promised to do, they naturally wanted to praise Him. When Christians think about God in these ways they have the same experience.

(b) *When did the Israelites praise God?* The Israelites praised God when they had experienced His help in their own lives (Exod. 15.2). They had come to know Him, not only as the God of Abraham ('my father's God'), but also as their own God ('this is my God and I will praise Him'). It is particularly at times when people find that God is present and helps them in the difficulties they face, that they are moved to praise Him.

(c) *How did the Israelites praise God?* They praised Him with singing, music, and dancing. When we rejoice in the greatness and goodness of God, words alone are not enough. We need music, song, and dance to express our joy and our fellowship in praise. Throughout Old Testament times the people of Israel used songs and music to praise God (see, e.g., Psalm 150).

When we study the history of the Christian Church we find that almost every period of spiritual growth has been a time of singing. For example, in England in the eighteenth century, hundreds of thousands of people learned of God's love through the witness and preaching of men like John Wesley, George Whitefield, and John Newton. They experienced God's power to make them better people, and out of this experience a great number of hymns were composed which are still sung today—such hymns as 'How sweet the name of Jesus sounds', and 'O for a thousand tongues to sing my dear Redeemer's praise'.

The same happened in the Southern Sudan during the recent seventeen years of war. Many of the Christian congregations lost their homes and their Church buildings, but in this time of trouble they put their trust in Jesus Christ. As a result of this experience, many of the Sudanese Christians wrote new hymns expressing their faith in God, and praising Him.

Dancing has usually had a smaller place in Christian worship than singing. In many parts of the world this was because dancing was so closely connected with worship of other gods, or with drunkenness or sexual immorality. This is not a new problem; it was one which the Israelites also faced (see Exod. 32–6; 1 Kings 18.26). But in many parts of the world today Christian groups are seeking to find out how they can best use dancing to express their Christian experience and joy.

(d) *Whom did the Israelites praise?* In the Egyptian writings which remain from the thirteenth century BC we find songs of victory. These songs praise the Pharaoh, or the general who led the Egyptian army to victory over its enemies. But the song we find in Exod. 15.1–19 does not praise Moses or any Israelite leader. The Israelites praised God, because they knew that He alone had saved them when they could do nothing to save themselves (Exod. 14.10–30).

2. CONFIDENCE FOR THE FUTURE (15.13–18)

God had delivered the Israelites from Egypt, as He had promised to do (Exod. 6.6). So the Israelites were confident that He would also keep the other part of His promise, and would bring them into the land of Canaan (Exod. 6.8). Christians also have experienced part of the good things God has promised to give them through Christ, so they also look forward, to the time when God will do all that He has promised (see also Eph. 1.13–14; 2 Cor.1.19–22). This confidence is expressed in the lines of an English hymn:

> We will praise Him for all that is past;
> We will trust Him for all that's to come.

3. THE ISRAELITES' ATTITUDE TO THEIR ENEMIES

If we are learning from Christ to love our enemies (see Luke 6.27–28), we may have many questions in our minds when we read Old Testament passages like Exod. 15.3–12. For example, we may ask, (a) 'Were the Israelites right to rejoice when so many Egyptians had died?' or (b) 'Is God really "a man of war"?' (c) 'Should we follow the example of the Israelites in such rejoicing, or has Jesus shown people a different way?'

We do not find it easy to answer such questions. But there are a number of ideas that may help us if we keep them in mind.

1. First let us think about the Israelites and their attitude to the Egyptians:

(a) The Israelites did not say, 'We are glad that the Egyptians died, and we hope more of them will die.' They were not like many terrorists today, who kill people who are not involved in their quarrel and then seem proud that they have done so. The Israelites did not kill the Egyptians, and they rejoiced chiefly because they themselves had been saved from the Egyptians who wished to kill or enslave them (Exod. 15.9).

(b) The Israelites certainly hated the Egyptians, but this hatred was mainly a result of what the Egyptians had done to them (see Exod. chapters 1, 2, 5, 14). But the Israelites did not respond only with hatred. As we have seen (p. 11), the Israelites learned from their experience in Egypt that they should have a special care for people of other tribes and races with whom they came into contact.

(c) The writer of Exodus and other Old Testament writers give examples of how we can help our personal enemies, instead of rejoicing when they suffer—see Exod. 23.4–5; Job 31.29–30; Prov. 24.17; 25.21.

2. Questions about God: 'Is He a "man of war"' (Exod. 15.3)?

(a) The story told in the Book of Exodus makes it clear that the Egyptians were wrong to oppress the Israelites as they did (Exod. 1—2), and also wrong to seek to enslave them again or to kill them (Exod. 15.9). When people keep on doing what is wrong, even after God has warned them to change their ways, they may expect that in some way God will act to punish them (see also Luke 13.1–5).

(b) The Book of Exodus is only one part of the Bible. It is an early part. Over hundreds of years God was teaching people in Israel and in the Christian Church to understand His ways more clearly (see Heb. 1.1). In the New Testament it is made clear: (1) that God does not want people to perish, but to repent and be saved (1 Pet. 3.9), and (2) that God loves all people and has so taken upon Himself the evil men do, that He can forgive and restore all who come to Him (John 3.16, Rom. 3.21–26).

3. Questions about ourselves: 'Should we follow the example of the Israelites?'

(a) If we condemn the Israelites for hating the Egyptians, we must also judge ourselves. We must remember the times when we have been glad to see someone suffer, or have said, 'He deserved it.'

(b) When we read in the Old Testament what people did or said, we must not always say, 'They did that, so we should follow their example.' Many actions are described in the Old Testament which we are not meant to copy (compare Paul's teaching in 1 Cor. 10.1–13).

(c) The writers of the New Testament continually refer to a war in which we ought to take part. This is not a war against people. It is the continuing battle against evil. We are not to use weapons of war, but truth and love and prayer (2 Cor. 10.3–5; Eph. 6.10–17; 1 Tim. 6.11–12).

NOTES

15.1–18: This song is a poem. The ways of writing poetry change from time to time. If we read a line from an English poem and it says, 'And gladly wolde he lerne and gladly teche', we know from the spelling that this is not modern English. It was written several hundred years ago. If we read in Hebrew the poetry of Exodus 15.1–18, we find that it is not like the Hebrew poetry written in the time of David or later. It is more like the poetry of Canaan in the period 1700–1400 BC. It is similar in some ways to the Song of Deborah (Judges 5), but older in its style.

15.1. The horse and his rider: that is, the horses and the charioteers (see note on 14.9).

15.2. The Lord is my strength: The word 'Lord' here translates the Hebrew *Yah*; which is a shorter form of Yahweh. It is found most commonly in the word 'Hallelu*yah*', which means, 'Praise Yahweh'. *Yah* is also used in Isaiah 12.2. The prophet Isaiah used the story of the Exodus to encourage his hearers: (Is. 11.11–16). He said that God would once again deliver His people. Then they would sing songs of deliverance. In Isaiah 12 there is a list of the hymns or psalms they would sing. One of the songs in this list is the Song of Moses, which he refers to by quoting words from Exodus 15.2.

15.2. Salvation: In the Old Testament this word usually refers to deliverance from enemies, from danger, or from death. In the New Testament 'salvation' usually refers to deliverance from sin, from powers of evil and from spiritual death.

15.5. The floods: Hebrew *tehomoth*, a poetical word for the sea and its waves (Is. 63.13; Ps. 77.17). The same word was used in the Canaanite language to refer to the deep sea.

15.8. The blast of thy nostrils: A poetical way of referring to the wind, compare 2 Sam. 22.14–16. See also Exodus 14.21–22 which describes how the wind caused the water to be divided.

15.11. Who is like thee? This question assumes that there is no one like Yahweh. See also Exodus 9.14.

15.13. Steadfast love: The Hebrew word is *hesed*. It means faithful love, the sort of love to which a person is bound by a solemn promise (for example, the loyal love of a husband and wife who in a marriage service have promised to love each other and to be faithful to each other all their lives).

15.15. Have melted away: The Hebrew word probably means, 'they were disturbed, or overcome by fear'.

15.17. Thy own mountain: Scholars have interpreted these words in two different ways:

1. as referring to Mount Zion in Jerusalem, where Solomon had the temple built,
2. as referring to the mountainous land of Canaan.

The second view seems more likely, because:

(a) In Exodus all other passages which mention God as 'bringing Israel in' refer to the land of Canaan, not to Mount Zion (see 6.8; 13.5, 11; 23.20; and compare Deut. 6.10). The whole people of Israel could not be brought in to a single mountain.

(b) The Hebrew word translated in the RSV as 'thy own' means 'your inheritance, the land you have inherited'. God is pictured as the owner of an estate into which He brings His people so that they may work for Him there. It was not Mount Zion, but the whole mountainous land of Canaan, that God promised to give Israel as an inheritance (Deut. 4.21; 15.4; 19.10).

15.18. The Lord will reign: God is here pictured as a king. It was at the time of the Exodus that the idea of God's kingly rule over His people became an important part of Israel's faith.

15.20. Miriam, the prophetess: Old Testament writers say little about the spiritual and prophetic ministry of women, but compare Judges 4.4; 2 Kings 22.14; 2 Chron. 34.22; Neh. 6.14; Isa. 8.3. In 1 Cor. 11.2–16 Paul mentions women who prophesied and took part in public prayers in the Church at Corinth. This would not have happened in a Jewish Synagogue, where only men were allowed to take part.

15.20. A timbrel: A tambourine or drum. The Israelites used many different instruments to accompany their singing (see Psalm 150.3–5).

15.21. Miriam sang to them, 'Sing to the Lord . . .' This does not mean that Miriam sang only this one verse. She sang the song contained in 15.1–18. Compare the way we say: 'We sang "The Lord's my shepherd" ', meaning that we sang the whole of the psalm.

STUDY SUGGESTIONS AND QUESTIONS

REVIEW OF CONTENT

1. For what reasons did the Israelites praise God?
2. What does the Song of Victory say (a) about what God had done in the past, and (b) what God would do in the future, for His people?

BIBLE STUDY AND REFLECTION

3. *Praising God.* Study the following passages; and in each passage, find out (i) who was praising God, and (ii) why they were praising God; and consider (iii) whether you have any similar reason for praising God.
   (a) Psalm 40.1–3 (b) Psalm 103.1–5 (c) Luke 2.8–20
   (d) Luke 24.44–53 (e) Revelation 19.1–8.
4. Our attitude to our enemies: What do you think are the most important lessons to be learned from the following passages? Exodus 23.4–5; Job 31, 29–30; Proverbs 24.17; 25.21; Luke 6.27–31

5. The Israelites used songs, musical instruments, and dancing in their praise and worship of God. In what ways are songs, musical instruments, and dances used by:
   (a) Christians in your country;
   (b) people in your country who belong to other religious groups?
   Do you think that any changes are needed to make your worship more meaningful? Do you think you personally have any contribution to make? If so, what is it?
6. What do the following passages teach about the warfare to which Christians are called? (a) 2 Corinthians 10.3–5 (b) Ephesians 6.10–17 (c) 1 Timothy 6.11–12 (d) 2 Timothy 2.3–4

Special Note C: Exodus and Egypt

1. THE EXODUS AND THE HISTORY OF EGYPT

(a) EGYPTIAN CIVILIZATION

The Egyptians were one of the first peoples to make great progress in building, in writing, and in art. Egypt is still famous for its great pyramids, which are the memorial tombs of kings and other important people. Most of the pyramids were built in the period 2600–2200 BC. In that period Egyptian artists and writers produced some of the finest work ever done in Egypt.

When Moses was born, the pyramids were already a thousand years old. Egypt had been a land of cities and of culture for a longer period than England has been today. Because Moses lived more than three thousand years ago, we may be tempted to think that he lived in a backward and primitive culture. But in fact he lived when Egyptian civilization was already old.

(b) THE HYKSOS KINGS

From about 1710 to 1570 BC foreign kings ruled in Egypt. The Egyptians called them the Hyksos kings. The Hyksos people had moved into Egypt from Palestine and western Asia. Racially the Hyksos people were of the same type as the Israelites.

The Hyksos people were able to conquer Egypt and rule it because they had more powerful weapons than the Egyptians. They had chariots drawn by war-horses. Such chariots had not been known in Egypt before, but they continued to be the most important part of Egypt's army for many centuries (compare Exodus 14).

The Egyptians did not like the Hyksos foreigners who ruled over them. Perhaps it was partly this hatred of the Hyksos, passed down from generation to generation, which led them to hate and fear the Israelites (Exod. 1.8–14).

About 1570 BC the Egyptians drove the Hyksos out of Egypt. This victory led to a period in which Egypt was again a strong nation (1570–1100 BC), and its culture and civilization flourished. For much of this period Palestine was part of the Egyptian empire.

The capital of Egypt from 1570 to about 1300 BC was the beautiful and famous city of Thebes, about 800 km (500 miles) from the mouth of the river Nile. But in the time of Moses Egypt had a new capital city, in the Delta region, not far from the area in which most of the Israelites lived.

(c) RAMESSES II

Towards the end of the fourteenth century BC there was an army coup. An army officer became ruler of Egypt. His grandson, Sethos (or Seti), was Pharaoh about 1316–1304 BC. Sethos decided to make Avaris the capital city of Egypt. Avaris was a city in the Delta region, which had been the capital city in the time of the Hyksos kings. By the time of Sethos it needed to be rebuilt.

The son of Sethos was Ramesses II. He ruled Egypt for more than seventy years, about 1304–1229 BC, and did most of the planning of the new capital city. The Egyptians changed its name from Avaris to Pi-Ramesse (the House of Ramesses). The Israelites called it Raamses (Exod. 1.11).

Ramesses was a proud and powerful king. He liked to show his greatness by having huge statues of himself made by his Egyptian craftsmen. Several of these statues were 20 metres or more in height.

It is likely that Sethos was the Pharaoh who began to make the Israelites work on building projects in the Delta area, and that Ramesses II was Pharaoh at the time when the Israelites left Egypt.

(d) MERENPTAH

The next Pharaoh after Ramesses II was Merenptah. He was not a strong leader. During his reign a number of towns and tribes in Palestine revolted against the rule of Egypt, and Merenptah had to send an army into Palestine to try to restore Egyptian power. In a boastful inscription, written about 1220 BC, he listed many places and peoples which his army had attacked. The people of Israel are included in the list: 'Israel is laid waste,' he wrote, 'its seed is destroyed.'

But despite Merenptah's boasts, Egyptian power in Palestine was coming to an end. By 1100 BC the great days of the Egyptian empire were

'It is likely that Sethos (Seti I) was the Pharaoh who began to make the Israelites work on building projects in the Nile Delta, and that Ramesses II was Pharaoh at the time when the Israelites left Egypt' (p. 85). A wall-painting of brick-makers in the tomb of Rekh-mi-Re at Thebes shows the sort of labour the Israelites were probably doing in Egypt. A granite statue of Ramesses II is now in the museum at Turin in Italy.

over. Egypt had lost control of Palestine, and, except for a brief period, did not regain control of Palestine for more than 800 years.

2. WHEN DID MOSES LEAD THE ISRAELITES OUT OF EGYPT?

We do not know the date at which the people of Israel left Egypt. But we can find out the period at which this event is most likely to have taken place.

There are two main kinds of information that we shall find helpful: (1) information that we find in the Bible, especially in the Book of Exodus; (2) information discovered by archaeologists.

Archaeologists study the things left behind by people who lived long ago. They look at the remains of buildings, pottery, roads, tools, pictures, inscriptions on rock and stone, and other writings. Those who have worked in Egypt and Palestine have made many discoveries which help us to decide at what time the tribes of Israel probably left Egypt.

(a) EVIDENCE FROM EGYPT

The building of 'Raamses' is mentioned in Exodus 1.11. Ruins of the city were dug up about AD 1930. Many of the statues, columns, and fragments of buildings were marked with the name of Ramesses. An Egyptian schoolboy's letter to his teacher has been found, in which the boy described the city of Pi-Ramesse as 'a splendid city without rival'. In the early years of his reign Ramesses II was chiefly busy organizing the building of the city. So it is likely that Israelite workmen were among the many people at work there during the period about 1304–1280 BC.

Merenptah's inscription was engraved about 1220 BC. It shows that the Israelites were already in the land of Canaan by 1220 BC. So the evidence from Egypt, taken together with information from the Book of Exodus, suggests that the Israelites left Egypt some time after 1290 BC and at some time before 1220 BC.

(b) EVIDENCE FROM EDOM AND MOAB

On their way to Canaan, the Israelites passed by the country occupied by the kings of Edom and Moab (Num. chapters 21—22). Archaeologists who have studied the remains of Edomite and Moabite settlements say that these kingdoms were not established until after 1300 BC. If the Israelites had left Egypt before 1300 BC, they would not have found settled kingdoms in that area. So the evidence from Edom and Moab, together with our information from the Book of Numbers, suggests that the Israelite tribes left Egypt at some time after 1300 BC.

(c) EVIDENCE FROM CANAAN (PALESTINE)

Archaeologists have dug up the remains of many towns in Palestine. From a careful study of the sort of pottery they find in the ruins, and from tools and building styles and inscriptions, they can often find out approximately the date when a town was built or was destroyed.

They have discovered that in the period about 1250–1220 BC many towns in Canaan were attacked and destroyed. Among these towns were Bethel, Debir, Lachish, and Hazor. The Book of Joshua mentions that the Israelites captured all these towns. For example, Joshua 10.38 refers to an attack on Debir. When archaeologists dug up the remains of Debir, they found that the remains of the Canaanite town were covered in a layer of ashes. This suggests that the town was captured and destroyed by fire. Above the burnt layer they found the remains of an Israelite settlement. So it seems clear from the evidence from Canaan, taken together with information from the Book of Joshua, that the Israelites invaded Canaan at some time in the period 1250–1220 BC, and probably near the beginning of it.

The biblical accounts say that the Israelites spent about 40 years in the Sinai Peninsula before they invaded Canaan (Num. 10.11–12; Deut. 2.14; Ps. 95.10). If they are correct, and if the invasion of Canaan began at some time about 1250–1240 BC, then it is most likely that the Israelites left Egypt at some time in the period 1290–1280 BC, or not long afterwards.

(d) CONCLUSION

Evidence from Egypt, from Edom and Moab, and from Canaan, taken together with information given in the books Exodus—Joshua, suggests that the tribes of Israel left Egypt in the early part of the thirteenth century BC, perhaps at some time in the period 1290–1280 BC. We do not know the exact date, but this is not an important question: we can understand the message of the Book of Exodus without knowing the exact date of the Israelites' escape from Egypt.

PART 2 15.22—18.27

GOD LED THE ISRAELITES TO MOUNT SINAI

15.22—17.7

'Is the Lord with us?'

OUTLINE AND CONTEXT

15.22–26: *The journey from the Sea of Reeds to Marah:*
The Israelites travelled to Marah. There they complained because the water was bitter (15.22–24).
Moses prayed, and God showed him how to make the water drinkable (15.25).
God promised that if the Israelites would obey Him, He would keep them free from diseases which the Egyptians suffered (15.22–26).
15.27—16.36: *The journey from Elim to the Wilderness of Sin:*
The Israelites reached the Wilderness of Sin. They complained that they were dying of hunger (15.27—16.3).
God promised to give them meat and other food (16.4–12).
A flock of birds provided meat (16.13).
For other food the Israelites collected manna each morning, except on the Sabbath (16.14–31).
A jar of manna was kept in the Ark of the Covenant (16.32–36).
17.1–7: *The journey from the Wilderness of Sin to Rephidim:*
The Israelites reached Rephidim. They complained because there was no water (17.1–3).
Moses prayed, and God showed him a rock from which water would flow when he struck it with his rod (17.4–7).

Exodus 1.1—15.21 has told the story of how God set the Israelites free from Egypt. Exodus 15.22—18.27 tells the story of how God led the Israelites from Egypt to Mount Sinai, and how He showed them that He was with them. The story of the journey to Mount Sinai prepares the reader for chapters 19—40 which tell how God made His covenant at Sinai with the people He had rescued from Egypt.

INTERPRETATION AND COMMENT

1. THE ISRAELITES COMPLAINED

They had been singing songs of victory, praising God for setting them free from Egypt. But not long afterwards they were complaining that Moses had done wrong in bringing them out into the wilderness (15.24; 16.2–3; 17.1–3). The story shows how quickly the people of God can pass from praising Him to complaining.

Farmers who use horses for ploughing like to have a horse that will work steadily all day. Such a horse is much more useful than a horse which starts off quickly and soon becomes tired. In the parable of the Sower Jesus compared people who receive God's word with enthusiasm but soon give up when trouble comes, and those who patiently hold fast to God's word (Luke 8.13, 15).

The Israelites complained first about Moses. They blamed him for bringing them into difficulties (16.2–3). But it is clear that they were really complaining about God (16.8; 17.7). When we ourselves complain about our leaders, or about our situation, it may sometimes be because we are angry with God for bringing us into such a situation.

A young Christian teacher felt that God had called her to teach in a certain place. After a few years she went to the pastor of her church and complained bitterly about how difficult her life had been and how badly the older teachers had treated her. The pastor listened, and then asked her, 'Why are you angry with God?' This question helped her to see that the greatest trouble was not in the other teachers but in herself, and that she must learn afresh to trust God to uphold her in the way in which He wanted her to go.

2. GOD PROVIDES WHAT HIS PEOPLE NEED

God led the Israelites along a way that was not easy. Compare the words of Jesus to those who are ready to follow Him: 'If any man wants to follow me, he must say "no" to self, and take up his cross and follow me' (Mark 8.34).

But the stories in Exodus 15.22—17.7 show that along the way that He leads them, God will give His people what they really need. At Marah and at Rephidim what the Israelites needed was already there: a tree at Marah to make the water drinkable, and a spring of water in the rocky ground at Rephidim. When Moses prayed, God showed him how to make use of them. In many of the problems which people face, they may find that God has already provided a way to help them.

The story about quails and manna (Exod. 16) teaches us that the world which God has made can produce the food that His people need. But if we wish to enjoy fully the blessings which God has prepared for us, we must be ready to do what He tells us to do (Exod. 15.26; 16.23–30). This is not surprising, for if a person wishes to benefit from the help of a doctor, he must be ready to do what the doctor tells him.

3. GOD AND HEALTH

In Exodus 15.26 God speaks of Himself as 'the Lord, your healer', and says that His people's health will depend on whether they obey Him. The teaching of this passage, and of the Bible as a whole, is that: (a) God is concerned that people should be healthy, (b) because God loves us He is at work both to save us from becoming ill and to heal us when we are ill, (c) when we live according to God's will and are seeking His glory we are more likely to be healthy, and (d) refusal to trust in God and to obey His commands can lead to ill health.

So when we are ill, we should not say, 'It is God's will. There is nothing we can do about it.' We should ask ourselves, 'Is there any way in which I have been failing to live as God wants me to live? Is there something that God wants me to learn from this illness?' Then we should trust that God will be our healer. But when other people are ill, we must be careful not to make the mistake that Job's friends made. They told him that all sickness was a result of a person's own sin. So they said to Job, 'Repent of your sins and you will be healed' (Job 11.13–15; 22.21–27). In Job's case, his sickness and suffering were as a test and proof of his real faith in God. Job's suffering was not a result of his sins. In the end Job also came to know the Lord as his healer (Job 42).

If we ask, 'How does God heal people?' we cannot give a simple answer. Sometimes He heals people mainly through the work of doctors, nurses, and others who teach healthy ways of living. At other times He heals people mainly through prayer and the laying on of hands, or anointing with oil. The story of how the bitter water at Marah was made drinkable shows that the way of medicine and the way of prayer are not two completely separate ways. The tree was like a medicine put into the water, but Moses only learned about it when he prayed. Prayer and medical research are both needed as we seek for health. Faith and medicine can be like two hands that work together.

4. 'IS GOD WITH US OR NOT?'

God had promised Moses and the people of Israel: 'I will be with you' (Exod. 3.12; 6.7). The Israelites had not yet learned that the presence of trouble and difficulty does not mean the absence of God. It was when the writer of Psalm 23 was in 'the valley of deep darkness' that he knew most clearly that God was with him (Ps. 23.4). A young Swedish woman who was found to be suffering from tuberculosis in both lungs wrote to a friend, 'I discovered then how real God's strength is in such circumstances . . . and I thanked Christ because I felt him nearer and more real.' The difficulties and sufferings we face should not lead us to think that God is not with us. It may be only when we are passing through times of suffering that other people may become aware of the presence of God with us (compare Daniel 3.23–25).

NOTES

15.22—17.7. Shur, Marah, Elim, Sin, Rephidim and Horeb: These were all places or areas on the western side of the Sinai Peninsula (see map, p. xii). We are not certain of the exact position of all the places on the route by which the Israelites travelled, but travellers who have visited Sinai report that the story in Exodus fits in well with what they have observed. Note that Sin (the Wilderness of Sin) is the name of a place. It has nothing to do with the word 'sin' meaning evil or wrong doing.

15.25. He cried to the Lord: That is, he prayed to God for help.

15.25. He proved them: God tested them. In Exodus 14—17 the writer shows that when God's people face dangers and difficulties it is a test which shows whether they are really willing to trust in God and obey Him. See also Matthew 4.1–11; 1 Peter 1.5–6; Job 23.10.

15.26. Diligently hearken to the voice: That is, listen carefully to what he says, and then do it.

16.4–31. Manna: In the Sinai Peninsula there are many tamarisk trees. Insects which feed on these trees produce drops of a sweet substance rather like crystallized honey. In the early summer it can often be found on the ground in the morning. It is a nourishing food. Bedouin Arabs call it *mann*.

In this passage manna is, in English translations, called 'bread' (16.8, 15, 22, 29, 32). But the Hebrew word (*lehem*) can mean more generally 'food'. So in John 6.41–59 when Jesus spoke of Himself as the 'Bread of heaven', and as being superior to manna, he meant that He was the true food which brings eternal life. He did not mean us to ask, 'Why does He say He is bread, and not potatoes, or millet, or meat?'. Similarly, in the Lord's prayer, when we say, 'Give us today our daily *bread*', we mean, 'Give us today the *food* we need.'

16.13. Quails: These birds live in the Mediterranean area. They migrate to Africa in the winter. In the spring they fly north again, crossing parts of Egypt and Sinai. They fly in large flocks, only a few feet above the ground. When they stop for rest they can easily be caught. Their flesh is good to eat.

16.16. An Omer: A measure of capacity equal to about four pints or two litres.

16.22–30. The Sabbath: This is the first use in the Old Testament books of the technical term 'sabbath', meaning the day of rest. (In Genesis 2.2–3 it is not called 'the sabbath' but 'the seventh day'.) The idea that the seventh day should be a special day seems to have been common among Semitic peoples. The Babylonians thought that the seventh, fourteenth, twenty-first, and twenty-eighth days of the month were dangerous days. These were days on which they specially feared the anger of their gods. For the Israelites, however, the sabbath was not a day of fear, but of peace and rest. They regarded it as a gift which God gave to Israel (Exod. 16.29; Isa. 58.13; Mark 2.27). Jews still keep the sabbath (Saturday) as a day for rest and worship; but most Christians keep Sunday as their holy day, because on that day Jesus came to them after He had risen from the dead (John 20. 1–4, 1 Cor. 16.2). See also p. 109.

16.32–36. Before the testimony (v. 34): This means that the pot of manna was put in the sacred box (the Ark of the Covenant) beside the stone tablets on which the Ten Commandments were written. See also the passage on 'the two tablets of the testimony' on pp. 149–150.

The writer of Exodus mentions here the whole period of forty years during which the Israelites ate manna in the wilderness. He is not saying that the manna was put in the Ark of the Covenant in the Wilderness of Sin, that is, before the Ark was made at Mount Sinai. Rather, he is describing here something that was done later on, because it has to do with manna, which is the subject of his story. Students of the Gospels will know that the Gospel writers also sometimes arranged what they wanted to write according to the subject or theme, and not always according to the time at which it happened.

STUDY SUGGESTIONS AND QUESTIONS

REVIEW OF CONTENT

1. *Difficulties*
   (a) What difficulties did the Israelites face on their journey from the Sea of Reeds to Rephidim?
   (b) How did they feel and what did they say when they faced these difficulties?
   (c) What did Moses do when he was faced with these difficulties?
2. In what ways did God provide what the Israelites needed?
3. What is said in Exodus 15.21—17.7 about:
   (a) God's laws? (b) the Sabbath?

BIBLE STUDY AND REFLECTION

4. *Complaining:* Notice the complaints of the Israelites in Exodus 14.11–12; 15.24; 16.2–3; 17.1–3; Numbers 11.4–6; 20.2–13; 21.4–9. See also Deuteronomy 1.27; 6.16; Psalms 78.1–55; 95.7–9; 1 Corinthians 10.10; Hebrews 3.1–19.
   (a) What lessons can we learn from the complaints of the Israelites?
   (b) What do we ourselves most often complain about, and why? Do you think that in any of these cases we make complaints, instead of ourselves doing something to improve the situation?

5. *Anger:* 'Why are you angry with God?' (p. 90). If we have suffered and we are angry with God, do you think it is best for us: (a) to tell God about our anger, (b) to keep our anger to ourselves, (c) to express our anger by violent action against someone or something else, or (d) to see if there is some sin we ought to confess? Give reasons for your answer.
6. *Leadership:* 'The Israelites complained first about Moses' (p. 90).
   (a) What complaints do people make about their leaders, (i) in the Church, and (ii) in the state?
   (b) Which of these complaints do you think are reasonable?
   (c) What do you think the leaders should do about these complaints?
   (d) Do you think it is possible to be a leader and to escape from all complaints?
   (e) How do you think we should react when people complain about us?
7. *Healing:*
   (a) 'Faith and medicine can be like two hands which work together' (p. 91). What would you say: (i) To someone who said: 'When Christians are ill, they should only pray and trust in God, they do not need medicines'? (ii) To someone who said, 'When people are ill, they only need medicines. They do not need to pray'?
   (b) Which do you think are the most important causes of ill-health in your community? (Consider the following: Eating too little; Eating too much; Refusing to be immunized against diseases; Dirt and lack of hygiene; Inherited diseases; Lack of prayer and faith in God; Refusing to forgive wrongs; Overwork; Worry; Poverty.)
   (c) What do you think are the most important things that people should do to improve the health of your community?
8. *Our needs:* 'God provides what His people need' (p. 90).
   (a) What do you most need?
   (b) What do you most want?
   (c) What is the difference between wanting something and needing it? (Can you express this difference in some other language you know?)
   (d) Read Matthew 6.25–34. What did Jesus say that His followers should seek for most? Why did He say that they need not be worried about other things (e.g. money, food, clothing)?

17.8—18.27
'The Lord is with us'

OUTLINE AND CONTEXT

17.8–16. *The Israelites defeated the Amalekites*
The Amalekites attacked the Israelites at Rephidim. The Israelites defeated them while Moses prayed (17.8–13).
The story of the attack of the Amalekites was written down (17.14–15).
18.1–27. *Jethro visited Moses*
Jethro arrived to visit Moses. He rejoiced that God had delivered the Israelites from the Egyptians (18.1–12).
Jethro advised Moses to appoint other men to help him in his work as a leader and a judge (18.13–27).

Exodus 15.22—17.7 has shown how the Israelites asked, 'Is the Lord with us or not?' (17.7). Exodus 17.8—18.27 contains two more stories which emphasize that God was with them.

INTERPRETATION AND COMMENT

1. GOD'S PRESENCE BRINGS VICTORY

The Amalekites attacked the Israelites and killed some of them (see Deut. 25.17–18). On the next day, Joshua led Israel's fighting men into battle, while Moses went up to the top of a hill to lift up his hands in prayer (compare Psalm 134.2 and 1 Tim. 2.8). The Israelites defeated the Amalekites.

After the victory perhaps some of the Israelites said, 'We won because Joshua and his men were good at fighting.' Perhaps others said, 'We won because Moses was good at praying.' But Moses built an altar and named it 'The Lord my banner' (*Yahweh-nissi*). He was saying to the Israelites, 'We did not win the victory only because Joshua fought and I prayed. We won because God was with us and He helped us.'

Christians are involved in a fight against evil (Eph. 6.12). In this warfare the weapons are not material but spiritual (2 Cor. 10.4). One of the main weapons is prayer (Eph. 6.18). When we pray, we become channels through which God's power is brought to people in need. So long as we remember that it is only a sort of picture, we may liken a person who prays to an electric wire. A generator produces electricity. A wire conducts the electricity to a light which shines or to a motor which works. The wire itself is not powerful or clever. It cannot produce light or power; yet it can be the channel through which power passes from the generator. When we pray we do not have to be strong or clever ourselves, but we can be channels through which the power and love of God are made known in the world.

2. 'THE LORD WILL HAVE WAR WITH AMALEK'

The Israelites believed that God wanted them to go on hating the Amalekites and fighting them 'from generation to generation' (17.16). In the life and teaching of Jesus we can see a different way, a way of loving and forgiving those who hate us and hurt us (Luke 6.27–38; 23.33–34).

There are many times when we find that it is easier to think and act as the Israelites did before Christ came into the world, than it is to think and act as Christians.

In some parts of Northern Ireland people march through the streets each year in remembrance of battles that were fought three hundred years ago. For some people perhaps it is only an occasion when they enjoy being able to march behind a band as it plays. But such marches also encourage people to remember past hatred, and to go on hating other groups in the community 'from generation to generation'.

In Burundi, after many thousands of people of one tribe had been killed by members of another tribe, one man who survived said, 'This will never be forgotten. We will tell our children and they will tell their children.' This is a natural reaction. But there were also some Christians in Burundi who died praying for their enemies, as Christ did, 'Father, forgive them.'

The story of the Amalekites and the Israelites may make us aware: (a) that if we use violence and attack other people, we are likely to provoke them to use violence against us, and (b) that we have a great need to learn and to practice forgiveness and love.

3. 'CHOOSE ABLE MEN' (18.21)

As a leader and judge Moses had too much to do. Nearly every leader is tempted, like Moses, to try to do too much himself. Jethro could see that some of the work of Moses could only be done by Moses himself (18.19–20), but that other parts of the work could be shared with other men (18.21–22). He advised Moses to choose men who could help him in his work as judge (compare Judges 11; Luke 6.12–16; Acts 6.1–7). Moses did what his father-in-law advised. A wise leader listens to what other people say, and follows their advice when it seems to be good.

4. JETHRO

In Exodus 18.12 we read that Jethro 'offered a burnt offering and sacrifices to God.' A number of scholars, when writing about the origin of Israel's faith in Yahweh, have suggested that Jethro taught Moses how to worship and sacrifice to Yahweh. There is, however, nothing in Exodus 18 which could form a sufficient foundation for such a view:

(a) Jethro is never called a priest of Yahweh.

(b) Exodus 18.12 says that Jethro provided a sacrifice for God (Elohim), not for the LORD (Yahweh).

(c) We cannot even be certain who killed the sacrificial animal, Jethro, or Moses, or Aaron. (The Hebrew text only says that Jethro *took* a burnt offering; compare Lev. 9.1–16 in which the Israelites took sacrifices and Aaron offered them.)

(d) Exodus 18.1–11 shows that it was Moses who told Jethro about Yahweh, and not Jethro who told Moses.

There is no clear evidence in the Bible or anywhere else to show that Moses learned about God from Jethro. Since the religious beliefs of the Midianites and Kenites, so far as we know of them, were quite different from those of the Israelites, there is no sufficient reason for believing that the Israelites learned from the Midianites or Kenites how to worship Yahweh as the one true God.

NOTES

17.8. Amalek: The Amalekites were a nomadic tribe. They lived in the desert areas of Palestine, south-west of the land in which the Israelites eventually settled. It does not seem likely that a very large number of them would have been at Rephidim in southern Sinai. How then can we explain this story of their attack on the Israelites? There are a number of possible explanations. For example:

(a) Perhaps on this occasion a large number of Amalekites had travelled far from their homes;

(b) Perhaps the writer made a mistake; the Amalekites may have attacked Israel later on, when they were nearer to Palestine;

(c) The attack happened later, but the writer of Exodus chose to put the story at this point in the book because he saw that it gave an answer to the question asked by the Israelites, 'Is the LORD with us or not?' (17.7).

We cannot be sure which of these explanations is nearest to being correct.

17.9. With the rod of God in my hand: In Egypt many sorts of rod were used for religious purposes. The high priests of many Egyptian gods had special rods, and were often called 'the priests of the rod'. So the mention of the rod here probably shows that it was as a priest that Moses went up the hill, to pray for God's help for the people.

17.14. Write this in a book . . . and recite it: In the time of Moses people usually wrote on tablets of clay or stone, or on pieces of leather. Any kind of written record was called a 'book' (Hebrew: *sepher*). Writing materials were costly, so when a record had been made in writing of some important event, people were usually taught about it orally, by word of mouth, without making more copies in writing (compare Deut. 31.9–13; 2 Sam. 1.18).

17.16. A hand upon the banner of the Lord: The Hebrew text of this verse is difficult to understand. Here are some suggested translations:

(a) 'saying, "Power is with the banner of the LORD".'
(b) 'because he said, "lay hold of the banner of Yahweh".' (JB)
(c) 'and said, "My oath upon it . . .".' (NEB)

There are similar passages in Genesis 22.14 and 1 Samuel 7.12 which describe how a place is named to remind people of an event in which God showed His power to save and help His people. So Exodus 17.16 probably gives an explanation of the giving of the name Yahweh-nissi. The NEB translation is probably wrong. There are many passages in the Old Testament where we cannot be certain of the correct translation, but in whatever way we translate the difficult words, the main meaning and teaching of the whole passage remains the same.

18.2. After he sent her away: This does not mean that Moses had divorced his wife. Probably after Moses returned to Egypt he had sent his wife and children back to Jethro so that Pharaoh could not harm them. See note on 4.20 (p. 30).

18.7. Moses did obeisance: That is, Moses bowed low before Jethro, as a sign of respect.

18.16. The statutes of God and His decisions: Moses explained how the laws which God had given were to be applied in each case. The word translated 'decisions' is in Hebrew *toroth* (laws). This word in the Old Testament usually refers to written laws giving particular directions about what must be done.

18.18. You and the people with you will wear yourselves out: Moses would be tired by too much work and the people by too much waiting.

18.21. Choose men . . . who hate a bribe: That is, men who will not accept a bribe. Bribery was common in the courts of many countries. Old Testament writers condemn both those who take bribes and those who offer them (see Ps. 26.10 and Job 15.34).

STUDY SUGGESTIONS AND QUESTIONS

REVIEW OF CONTENT

1. The Israelites had asked a question (17.7). The stories in Exodus 17.8—18.12 give an answer. What was the question? In what ways do the stories in Exodus 17.8—18.12 answer it?
2. What were the two things that Moses did in order to help the Israelites to remember their victory over the Amalekites?
3. *Jethro's visit:*
   (a) What did Moses tell Jethro when he came to see him?
   (b) What was Jethro's response to what Moses told him?
   (c) What problem did Jethro see that Moses needed to deal with?

(d) What advice did Jethro give Moses?

BIBLE STUDY AND REFLECTION

4. Read Genesis 22.14; Exodus 17.15–16; 1 Samuel 7.12.
   (a) Why did Abraham, Moses, and Samuel give special names to a place, an altar, and a stone pillar?
   (b) What did they want people to remember?
   (c) What did they expect would be the result in people's lives, of remembering these things?
   (d) Is there any way in which the names that we give to people or places can help people to think of God and of His goodness?
5. Read Numbers 14.41–45. Compare it with Exodus 17.8–13.
   (a) What are the main differences between these stories?
   (b) What do you think we can learn from them?
6. 'If we use violence and attack other people, we are likely to provoke them to use violence against us' (p. 96).
   (a) Give some everyday examples of this, if you can.
   (b) Why do you think so many people use violence to try to get their own way?
7. 'Moses told his father-in-law all that the LORD had done' (Exod. 18.8).
   (a) What has God done for you? for your Church? for your people?
   (b) How can you best tell other people about this?
   (c) The writer of Exodus wrote his book in order to tell people 'all that the LORD had done'. (i) Is there any way in which you could help people by writing a letter or a book about what God has done for you? (ii) Is there any programme in your Church for training people to read? If there is, can you help in any way? If there is not, do you think there is anything that you and other people can do to start such a training course?
8. Choose able men (Exod. 18.21).
   (a) What kind of abilities do you think men and women need to have in order to be good leaders, (i) in a Church or congregation? (ii) in a nation?
   (b) Do you think there are any ways in which the system of choosing leaders could be improved, (i) in your Church, and (ii) in your country? If so, how?
9. Choose men . . . who hate a bribe (Exod. 18.21).
   Read 1 Samuel 8.3; 12.3; Psalm 26.10; Isaiah 33.15; Amos 5.12.
   (a) What is bribery?
   (b) What sort of results does bribery have: (i) for those who give bribes? (ii) for those who receive them? (iii) for poor people in the community?
   (c) How common is bribery in your country? Do you think anything should be done to prevent it? If so, what?

Part 3 19.1—40.38

GOD MADE HIS COVENANT WITH THE ISRAELITES

19.1–25

The Covenant—Introduction

OUTLINE AND CONTEXT

19.1–2: The Israelites arrived at Mount Sinai.
19.3–9: An introduction to the Covenant: at Mount Sinai God promised to make the Israelites His special people, and the Israelites promised to obey God.
19.10–25: A solemn preparation for the giving of the Covenant law.

Exodus 1—18 has described the deliverance of the Israelites from Egypt. The purpose of the deliverance is now shown to be that the Israelites might live in a special relationship to God. This special relationship is fixed by a solemn Covenant. Exodus 19 introduces the central idea of the Covenant, and leads on to Exodus 20—40 which describe the Covenant, its laws, and its meaning in detail.

INTERPRETATION AND COMMENT

1. THE WORD, 'COVENANT'

The word 'Covenant' is one of the most important of all the words used in the Bible. It is also one of the most difficult words for us to understand, because we do not use it much in our everyday lives. When a husband and wife promise to love and to honour and help each other, we usually refer to this as the making of *vows* or *promises*: we do not call it a Covenant. To understand the word 'Covenant' in the Old Testament we must think of the love and joy and confidence that people can feel at a happy wedding. The Covenant which God gave to Israel meant first of all that He had chosen them to be His, and had promised to bless them.

When countries make an agreement to support and help each other, we usually call this a *pact* or a *treaty*: we do not call it a covenant. But in the Old Testament such an agreement was called a 'Covenant'. So when we think of the Covenant, we must think of the security and peace that

'When we think of the Covenant, we must think of the security and peace that countries can enjoy when they are joined together by a treaty which they are happy to keep' (pp. 100, 102).

When Presidents Sadat and Gadafy made a treaty joining Egypt and Libya together as one state, the two leaders clasped hands to symbolize their countries' unity. What is the chief difference between the covenant God made with Israel, and the covenants or treaties made between one country or nation and another?

countries can enjoy when they are joined together by a treaty which they are happy to keep.

Marriage between a man and woman, and treaties between countries, may be agreements between equal partners. But the Covenant between God and Israel was never thought of as an agreement between equal partners. It was a promise and a call by God, whose greatness and goodness are beyond our understanding, to a people who were called to love and obey and worship Him. (See also Special Note D, pp. 114–118.)

2. GOD CHOOSES PEOPLE AND RESCUES THEM FROM TROUBLE SO THAT THEY MAY SPECIALLY BELONG TO HIM AND SERVE HIM (19.3–9)

The words of Exodus 19.5 show that God was speaking to the Israelites as a king who expected His subjects to obey Him. He expected them to obey Him gladly because they already knew Him to be good and kind and powerful (19.4). In a good family, young children will usually be glad to do what their parents tell them, because they know that their parents love them and want what is best for them. So also the Israelites were glad to hear what God said, and were ready to obey Him (19.8).

In Exodus 19.3–9 the writer was introducing the story of the Covenant. He showed the most important points of the whole story which he was going to tell more fully in chapters 20—40. These important points are:

(a) After God delivered the Israelites from Egypt, He promised that they should be His special people. This meant that they must obey Him.

(b) The people promised to obey God.

This pattern of first being rescued and called to belong to God, and then of being called to serve Him together with other people in a new way of life, is repeated in the New Testament. New Testament writers say: (1) that God has set Christians free from sin and death, through the death and resurrection of Jesus Christ; and (2) that Christians should gladly obey God, doing what is good and holy and loving, through the power of the Holy Spirit. (See for example Rom. 12.1–2; Eph. 2.1–10; 1 John 3.1–3.)

3. GOD IS GREAT AND HOLY AND POWERFUL (19.10–25)

After the Israelites had prepared themselves for two days, God appeared on Mount Sinai, with fire and smoke and thunder, to give Moses the law of the Covenant. God is so much greater and so much more powerful than human beings that it is difficult to describe Him. At Sinai, thunder and lightning and fire and smoke helped the Israelites to feel the greatness and holiness of God. 'God's greatness is beyond our reach . . . so men should bow in reverence and awe' (Job 37.23–24).

When the law was given to Israel, the people received it as something which had the authority of God in all His holiness. In many countries today people face a crisis because they no longer recognize any authority which should control human action. They think that all standards and all laws are produced by human beings for their own benefit or convenience: and if human beings produce all laws, so they can equally well change them or disregard them.

The story in Exodus 19.10–25 also emphasizes that although human beings are called by God to belong to Him, they are not of themselves good enough or holy enough to come near to God. The people of Israel were instructed to keep at a distance from the mountain.

NOTES

19.3. Out of the mountain: That is, 'from the mountain' (JB), from higher up the mountain. The Hebrew word translated 'out of' in the RSV does *not* mean from inside the mountain.

19.3. The house of Jacob: This means 'the people of Israel', because they were descended from Jacob. In the Old Testament the word 'house' is used with several meanings. Here it means people. In Exodus 20.2 '*house* of bondage' means the *land* in which the Israelites had been slaves; in 20.17 it means *family and property*. See also Mark 3.25, where the 'house' that may be in rebellion against itself is a *family*.

19.5. Keep my covenant: The Covenant was not an agreement between Israel and God, which the Israelites might have called '*our* Covenant'. Their part was to receive the Covenant and to keep it by obeying God's commands.

19.5. My own possession: This word (in Hebrew, *segullah*) shows that Israel was to belong to God, like the special treasure of a king which he can use as he chooses (1 Chron. 29.3), or like a servant who is always loyal and obedient to his master (Deut. 7.6; 14.1–2; 26.16–18). If God 'chooses' us, this does not mean that we are specially good, nor that we shall have an easy life; it means that we must spend our lives serving God and serving our fellow men.

19.5. For all the earth is mine: Compare Genesis 12.1–3. When God chose Abraham, it was so that He might bless all the nations of the world through Abraham and his descendants. This story of the making of the Covenant at Sinai also reminded the Israelites that all the world belongs to God and that God is able to help people whatever land they live in. (See also Amos 9.5–7; Isa. 42.1–4; Jonah 3.10—4.11.)

19.6. A kingdom of priests: The king of this kingdom is God. The Israelites were to be His priests. In Israel the priests were concerned both with sacrificial worship and with teaching God's ways to the people. So for Israel to be a kingdom of priests perhaps meant: (1) that all the Israelites should worship God, and (2) that they should know that they were called to teach other peoples the truth about God, and to draw them to Him. But very few of the Israelites saw themselves as called to be missionaries to the world.

19.6. A holy nation: The Israelites were called upon to be *holy*: to be set apart from what is evil, so that they might share in God's goodness (Lev. 11.44–45). The whole *nation*, in its laws and government and actions, must be holy.

19.6. These are the words: Words are often the clearest way in which we can make our thoughts and wishes known to other people. The writers of the Old Testament believed that God made His will known to Moses and the Israelites in words, so that they could clearly understand. Throughout the Old Testament God is pictured as both the 'God who acts' and the 'God who speaks'.

19.6. The children of Israel: Elsewhere in the RSV this phrase is correctly translated as 'the sons of Israel' or 'the people of Israel'. Earlier English translators who used the expression 'children of Israel' have caused a certain amount of confusion.

19.11. The Lord will come down: The writer of Exodus did not think that Sinai was the place where God lived, but a place where He chose to reveal Himself.

19.15. Do not go near a woman: The Israelites knew that sexual intercourse was part of God's good plan for the lives of men and women (Gen. 1.26–31; 2.24–25). They did not, however, think that it was a proper part of religious ritual or worship. But in Canaan and other neighbouring countries there were many peoples and tribes who believed that sexual intercourse was a necessary part of their religious ceremonies. They thought that sexual intercourse between a king and priestess, or between men and special prostitutes, could influence their gods and persuade them to make the land fertile. Some Israelites were tempted to share in such worship. They needed to be reminded that this is not what God wants.

19.16–18. Thunders and lightnings, and a thick cloud . . . : Some scholars have suggested that this story of God's appearance to Moses on Mount Sinai was based on the eruption of a volcano. But there are no volcanic mountains in the Sinai Peninsula. It is better to confess that God's ways of revealing Himself to people are a mystery beyond our understanding. Perhaps we need to hear afresh God's words to Moses, 'The place on which you are standing is holy ground' (Exod. 3.5).

19.23. Thou thyself didst charge us: This means, 'you warned us and commanded us.'

STUDY SUGGESTIONS AND QUESTIONS

REVIEW OF CONTENT

1. At Mount Sinai God called the people of Israel to be in a special relationship to Himself. In what three ways are the people described in Exodus 19.5–6?

2. In the story of God's appearance to Moses on Mount Sinai, which parts of the story indicate:
   (a) God's greatness? (b) God's holiness? (c) God's glory?
3. Explain the meaning of the word 'Covenant' in the Old Testament. What sort of thoughts and feelings do you think the word 'Covenant' would stir up in the minds of the Israelites?

BIBLE STUDY AND REFLECTION

4. The Israelites were called to obey God because He had already been good to them (Exod. 19.4). Think about the sermons you hear, or the sermons you preach. Do these sermons teach that people obey God: (a) out of love, because He is good, or (b) out of fear because He may punish them? Do you think there is any change of emphasis needed in the preaching? If so, of what sort do you think it should be?
5. 'All the Earth is mine' (Exod. 19.5).
   (a) What would you say to someone who said 'God is only concerned to help those who are Christians'?
   (b) What would you say to someone who said: 'Other people have their own religious beliefs, we should not try to make them accept ours'?
   (c) A Christian minister said recently, 'I have been converted twice, first of all to Christ, and then to the world which God has made. When I first trusted Christ I did not realize that art and music and drama, and man's ability to make things, are important parts of the life God means us to live.' What is your opinion about this?
6. Read 1 Peter 2.9 and compare it with Exodus 19.5–6.
   (a) In what ways did Peter say that Christians were like the Israelites?
   (b) What did Peter say Christians had been delivered from? What do you think he meant by this?
   (c) Why do you think some writers call Christians, 'the new Israel'?
   (d) In the Old Testament there are many promises about what God will do for Israel. What people do you think should be expecting those promises to be fulfilled for them: Jews? or Christians? or people who live in the land of Israel? (Read 2 Cor. 1.20 and Matt. 21.33–43.)
7. 'I am coming to you' (Exod. 19.9).
   (a) In what important ways do writers in the New Testament develop this idea that God comes to us?
   (b) Do the other religions in your country teach that God comes to people, seeking to call them to Himself, or that He is far away, so that people must struggle hard to reach Him? What would you say to people if you were asked to preach a sermon on the text, 'I am coming to you'?
8. 'Moses consecrated the people and they washed their garments' (Exod. 19.14).

What lessons can we learn about holiness from each of the following passages?
(a) Ps. 15.1–5; (b) 51.6–12; (c) Joel 2.13; (d) Mark 7.1–23; (e) Rom. 2.25–29; (f) Gal. 5.16–24

20.1–17
The Covenant: its Foundations

OUTLINE AND CONTEXT

20.1–2: *Introduction to the Covenant:* God called the Israelites to obey Him because He had set them free from Egypt.
20.3–17: *The foundations of the Covenant:* Ten basic commandments.
(a) Duty to God: to be loyal to Him and obey Him (20.3–11).
1. Have no other gods (20.3).
2. Do not worship any images (20.4–6).
3. Do not use God's name wrongly (20.7).
4. Do not work on the sabbath day (20.8–11).

(b) Duty to other people: to be loving and honest (20.12–17).

5. Honour your father and mother (20.12).
6. Do not murder anyone (20.13).
7. Do not commit adultery (20.14).
8. Do not steal (20.15).
9. Do not give false evidence against anyone (20.16).
10. Do not covet what belongs to someone else (20.17).

Exodus 19 describes the majestic appearance of God on Mount Sinai. The glory and greatness of God give emphasis to the commandments of God described in 20.1–17. These commandments are the foundation upon which are built the laws and demands unfolded in Exodus 20.18—40.38.

INTERPRETATION AND COMMENT

1. THE FOUNDATIONS OF THE COVENANT'S LAWS

As Israel's Great King, God gave His people the laws of the Covenant. We can picture the faith and worship of the Israelites as like a large building. A large building must have good foundations resting on firm enough ground. The firm ground of God's Covenant with Israel was His love for them. He had shown His love in setting them free from Egypt (20.2). The foundations are the Ten Commandments.

2. THE BASIC DEMANDS: LOYALTY AND LOVE FOR GOD AND FOR OTHER PEOPLE

In a country ruled by a king, the king expects his subjects to be loyal to him, and not to work against him on behalf of another country. He also expects his subjects to be united, and not to fight against each other. In a similar way, the basic demands of God's Covenant were:

1. That the Israelites should be loyal and obedient to Him, and not worship any other god (Exod. 20.3–11);
2. That they should treat each other kindly and honestly, respecting the life, family, possessions, and reputation of other people (Exod. 20.12–17).

The peoples of Egypt, Canaan, Babylonia, and other lands around the Fertile Crescent worshipped many different gods. Scholars have found the names of many hundreds of them. There were gods of war, of fertility, of hunting, of trading, of the sea, of the land, and of many other things. The demand (command) 'You shall have no other gods besides me, and you shall worship me without images' was something new in the history of religion. From this beginning there have grown three great religious groups, Jews, Christians, and Muslims. They are all agreed that there is only one God, and that men should worship Him alone. It is this that makes them missionary religions: for if there is only one true God who is the source of all being and all true joy, then those who worship many gods or spirits or stars or anything else, must be wrong. Those who are beginning to know the truth, and to experience the love of God, will naturally desire to spread this knowledge and experience to other people.

The Covenant law of Israel was also unusual in putting proper treatment of other people as one of the two most important aspects of a religious life. In most of the other lands around the Fertile Crescent people thought that what the gods wanted was primarily the right kind of prayers and sacrifices. But in Israel people began to learn that God is much more concerned that people should treat each other well. So the second section of the Ten Commandments (Exod. 20.12–17) is all about how we behave to other people: this is more important than religious rituals and sacrifices. Compare Hosea 4.1–2; 6.6; Isaiah 1.12–17; Jeremiah 7.21–23; Mark 12.32–33.

3. GOD'S COMMANDMENTS BROUGHT THE ISRAELITES JOY

The writers of the Old Testament knew that obeying God's commands helps people to live a good life. It helps them to trust in God who gives freedom (Exod. 20.2–3), to enjoy work and rest (20.8–11), and not to harm each other (20.7, 12–17). So these writers often express the joy that God's commands brought them: 'more to be desired are they than gold . . . sweeter also than honey . . .' (Psalm 19.10). Read Deut. 4.7–8; Psalm 19.7–10; Psalm 119.1–16; 97–105. These passages refer to the whole covenant law of Israel, of which the Ten Commandments are the foundation.

At Sinai the Israelites accepted God's law gladly (Exod. 19.7–8) because He had already accepted them as His people and had set them free from Egypt. They knew that the commandments were good, and that they would bring blessing to those who kept them.

Hundreds of years later, many Jews began to think of God's laws in a different way. They thought that they must first keep all God's laws perfectly, and then afterwards God would accept them as good people. When we read the New Testament we find that in the first century AD very many Jews had this wrong idea about God and His laws.

Saul of Tarsus tried hard to keep all the Jewish laws. He failed. He was disappointed and crushed, because he had thought that it was only by keeping the Law perfectly that he could persuade God to accept him. The Law had shown him that he was a failure (Rom. 3.19–20; 7.7–12; Gal. 3.10). It was only when Paul came to know Jesus that he found out that God accepts people because He loves them, and not because they are perfectly good. Jesus said, 'I did not come to call people who have kept the Law: I came to call people who are sinners' (Mark 2.17).

4. THE TEN COMMANDMENTS AND THE CHRISTIAN

Jesus said that He came not to abolish the Law, but to fulfil it (Matt. 5.17). He made people think about the inner meaning of the Commandments (Matt. 5.21–28). So His followers today must still ask what God wants to teach them through the Ten Commandments. In this Guide we have only space to indicate some of the questions that we may ask as we study the Commandments. For example:

1. *No other God.* For some people this may mean facing the question 'Can I still speak of Mount Everest as the Mother Goddess?', or 'Can I worship Vishnu and Siva and other gods?' For others it is a question of what we put first. Do we put God first, or our wealth, or our power, or our family, or political leaders, or a political ideology? Jesus said that it is only as we put God first that everything else will find its proper place in the pattern of life that God has prepared for us (Matt. 6.24–34).

2. *No images.* God is God. No one and nothing can be compared with Him. If we make an image of God, we make something we can control. The writers of the Bible challenge us to let God control our lives.

Also, if we make images to help us in our worship, we put something between ourselves and God. Jesus said that God the Father loves us so much that He hears and answers our prayers. Even Jesus Himself does not have to pass on our prayers to the Father (John 16.26–27).

In the history of the Church this commandment has been differently understood. For the first four or five hundred years of the Church's history, people who were not Christians were amazed to find that there were no statues or images in Christian churches. In the following thousand years the practice grew, first of making images of the saints and martyrs, of Mary, and of Jesus. Then people began to offer the same sort of worship to the images as they did to what the images represented. At the time of the Reformation in the sixteenth century, most of the Reformers said, 'The Commandment of God says, do not make images and worship them. Let us follow God's command, not the tradition of the Church.'

3. *Do not use God's name wrongly.* People who know that Christians worship God will often judge God by what Christians do. If we pray, 'Hallowed be your name,' our lives must be holy. If we pray to God who is love, we cannot properly desire to harm or hurt other people, however badly they treat us. If we worship God who is holy and true, we are called to be holy in what we do and say. To do evil, or to use bad language, or to promise what we do not mean to fulfil, are all ways in which we can break the commandment.

4. *Do not work on the Sabbath day.* As we have seen (p. 93), most Christians keep Sunday as a holy day, in honour of Christ's resurrection. When we consider how Jesus used the Sabbath, we can find guidance for ourselves. It was His custom to meet with others to pray, to worship God, to hear and preach His word (Luke 4.16). Jesus also used the Sabbath as a day to heal and help people in need (Luke 6.1–11; 13.10–17; 14.1–6). Christians are not bound by all the Jewish rules about the Sabbath (Col. 2.16).

5. *Honour your father and mother.* If we have parents, this commandment challenges us to care for them when they are old, to obey them in all that is good while we are young, to respect them during the years when we are becoming adults, and to love them always. If we are parents, it challenges us to be people whom our children can love, honour, and obey. A parent who is always harsh or unkind does not help a child to keep this commandment, nor does a parent who allows a child always to do as it likes (Eph. 6.4).

6. *Do not murder anyone.* Jesus said that this also means 'Do not hate anyone' (Matt. 5.21–22). He set before us a way of seeking good for those who harm us (Luke 6.28). His apostles taught the same lesson (Rom. 12.14–21; 1 John 2.9–11; 3.11–17). When a person is wrongly treated and is able to love those who treated him wrongly, he is sharing in God's love.

We need also to take seriously the simple command: 'Do not murder anyone.' In many parts of the world terrorists are ready to murder other people. Some Government leaders are ready to kill those whom they consider to be a threat to their policies. Not many years ago one such leader launched a campaign with the slogan: 'It is better that nine innocent people should die than that one enemy of the people should escape.' But in most countries more people are killed in motor accidents than by bombs or bullets. We need to do much more to make our roads safer.

7. *Do not commit adultery*. This commandment, like the others, refers to both men and women. Yet in some cultures we find that men and women are treated differently. In some, a man may have more than one woman and no one takes much notice; but when a woman becomes pregnant by a man who is not her husband she is made to suffer.

Jesus made it quite clear that the same standards of love, of loyalty, and of purity, apply to both men and women (Mark 10.11–12). But, because people were more ready to blame a woman than a man, he showed special concern for women involved in adultery—so that He might set them free to live a new and better life (John 8.1–11).

8. *Do not steal*. We may possess only a little, but we do not want other people to steal it. It is easy for us to see that a thief does wrong when he takes what is ours. But what do we think about the person who could work but is idle: who prefers to live on welfare or some form of government aid? Is he not also stealing from those who work to produce wealth? And what should we say when we see that in the world as a whole about 80% of the world's wealth is in the hands of about 20% of the world's population? Paul put together the ideas of hard work and helping the poor. He said to the Christians at Ephesus, 'The thief must give up stealing. Instead he must work hard and honestly . . . so that he may have something to share with the needy' (Eph. 4.28).

9. *Do not give false evidence*. We can harm other people by our words, by telling lies about them, by refusing to speak kindly, by refusing to admit when we have done wrong and so letting other people be blamed. The positive side of this commandment is that we should 'speak what is good and helpful, and so bring blessing to those who hear what we say' (Eph. 4.29).

10. *Do not covet*. When we see that someone else has something that we would like to have, we can do one of two things. We can either envy them, and try to deprive them of what they possess in order that we may have it; or we may be encouraged to work harder, and to save our money, so that we may be able to get something similar for ourselves. It is the first of these attitudes and aims, envy, that the commandment forbids.

This commandment showed the Israelites that God is concerned not only about what we do, but also about our motives and our desires.

5. A SUMMARY OF THE COMMANDMENTS

Jesus said that the most important commandments of all are: (1) that we should love God, and (2) that we should love other people (Mark 12.29–31). Paul said that if we love other people we should do all that God's law demands (Rom. 13.8–10), for if we love a person we shall respect his life, his marriage, his possessions, and his reputation. The commandments are not like prison walls to prevent us from doing what we want to do, they are like a road that leads us safely in a direction we need to go.

NOTES

20.2. The house of bondage: See note on 19.3, 'the house of Jacob' (p. 103).

20.3. No other gods before me: The RSV footnote is better: 'no other gods besides me'. Compare JB: 'no gods except me'. The commandment does not mean 'you can have other gods so long as you put them after me'. See also note on 15.11 (p. 82) and Joshua 24.14–15.

20.4. Anything in heaven above . . . in the earth . . . in the water under the earth . . . : That is, for the purposes of worship the Israelites were to make no images of birds, land animals, or of any creatures that live in the sea. The 'water under the earth' means the sea. In English we commonly speak of the land as being 'above sea-level'. In Hebrew it was more usual to put it the other way round, and speak of the sea as being 'below land-level'.

20.5. A jealous God: We usually use the word 'jealous' to mean 'envious' or 'resentful'. But here 'jealous' means 'caring deeply for what is right and opposing what is wrong'. God loves His people and longs for them to do what is right. He is grieved if they are unfaithful to Him, as a good husband is always sad if his wife is unfaithful to him.

20.6. To thousands: This should be translated 'to the thousandth generation' (see NEB footnote and Deut. 7.9). Notice that this phrase is used in contrast to 'the third and fourth generation' in 20.5. It shows that unfaithfulness to God affects the whole of one's family (three or four generations may be alive together—see Job 42.16), but that God's blessing for those who obey Him extends much further. Wrong translations of this verse have made it difficult for people to see its emphasis on the tremendous love and goodness of God.

This verse also shows that the writer of Exodus thought of God as the Lord of time and history, whose plans may take thousands of years to complete.

20.7. . . . in vain: The Israelites were allowed to use God's name in swearing solemn oaths (Deut. 6.13). But they were not to use God's name to swear oaths which they intended to break (Lev. 19.12), nor in a curse which was intended to bring harm to an innocent person.

20.7. . . . will not hold him guiltless: That is, 'will not leave unpunished' (NEB).

20.12. Honour your father and mother: Notice that this implies that the normal Jewish family was made up of one father and one mother and their children (Gen. 2.24; Prov. 31.10–31). Some Jewish men were polygamous, having more than one wife at a time: but the Old Testament stories show that this was a cause of jealousy and trouble—as it often is today.

Honour was to be paid to both father and mother. Both are equally important in the life of the family.

20.13. You shall not kill: No one must kill a personal enemy or an innocent person. For murder the death penalty was laid down (Gen. 9.5–6) but it must only be imposed after a proper trial. Accidental killing was distinguished from murder (Num. 35.15–34).

20.17. . . . your neighbour's house. . . . : That is, his family and possessions. The list of the main parts of a family and possessions begins with the most important: 'your neighbour's wife'. In Deuteronomy 5.21 the word 'house' refers to a building, so it is put in the list after the man's wife.

STUDY SUGGESTIONS AND QUESTIONS

REVIEW OF CONTENT

1. What reasons are given in Exodus 20.1–17, why the people of Israel should obey God?
2. All the ten commandments showed what God wanted the people to do.
   Which of the commandments refer chiefly to:
   (a) loyalty to God
   (b) proper treatment of other people?
3. How was the Sabbath to be kept holy? Why was it to be kept holy?

BIBLE STUDY AND REFLECTION

4. 'Love is the fulfilling of the law' (Rom. 13.10). Read again each of the Ten Commandments, and then consider these questions about each of them:
   (a) Is it true that if we love God and love other people we shall keep this commandment?
   (b) In what ways do you think this commandment is most often broken?
   (c) Does the teaching of Jesus give any deeper meaning to this commandment? If so; what?
   (d) List any circumstances in life today which you think make it particularly necessary to emphasize this commandment, or particularly difficult to know how to apply the commandment and obey it?
5. The Ten Commandments show the importance of two things; first, loyalty to the LORD as the only God, and secondly proper treatment of other people.
   (a) Study the following passages in Amos: 1.6, 9; 2.4, 6–8; 3.14; 4.1–3; 5.4–5, 7, 14–15, 24, 25–27; 8.4–6, 13–14.
   Which of these passages refer to disloyalty to the LORD? Which of

them refer to wrong treatment of other people? Which of these demands of the Covenant do you think Amos emphasized most?

(b) Study the following passages of Hosea: 4.1–2, 13–14, 17; 8.4–6; 10.5–6, 13.

In these passages Hosea speaks of actions which break the Ten Commandments. Which of the Ten Commandments were broken? Does Hosea give greater emphasis to the breaking of the commands to be loyal to the LORD or to the breaking of the commands to treat other people rightly? (Note that in Hosea the words 'adultery' and 'harlotry' usually refer to the worship of images or other gods.)

6. Study carefully Matthew 5.17–48.

(a) In this passage what did Jesus teach about:

(i) the Commandments?

(ii) the way Jewish teachers had interpreted them?

(iii) the meaning of the Commandments for His followers?

(b) To whom was Jesus speaking in Matthew 5.17–48?

(c) Jesus said that He came to seek and to save the lost. Do you think He believed that people were able to keep the Ten Commandments perfectly? If not, why do you think he gave the Commandments so important a place in His teaching?

7. Read (a) Exodus 20.1–11. Compare it with passages (b) and (c) below:

(b) Money is the greatest god. You must consider it more important than family or health. You shall worship the things that money can buy. You may make any false statement that will protect your money. You must work whenever you can at any kind of job, particularly on Sunday if you will be paid extra money for working on that day.

(c) There is no god; the Party is supreme. You shall not worship anything except the State and the Chairman of the Party. You shall put up the picture of the Chairman in your home and your place of work; you shall not speak against him. If you make a promise to an enemy of the people, you need not keep it. Your time belongs to the State, and you shall work at all times as you are directed.

Do you know any people who have views similar to those set out in passage (b) or in passage (c)? Who are they? Would you prefer to live in a country where people follow the ideas set out in Exod. 2.1–11, or those in passage (b) or those in passage (c)? Give reasons for your answer.

8. Read (a) Exodus 20.12–17. Compare it with passages (b) and (c) below:

(b) When your parents are old, spend no money on them. You must make progress at any cost. Do all you can to take over the business and wealth of other people. Give full expression to your sexual powers in whatever way you think will bring you pleasure. To get on in politics or business, be ready to say that your rivals are bad people. Try by all means to become richer, and be jealous of everyone who has more than you.

(c) If your parents do not support the Party, you must denounce them. Enemies of the people must be killed. You shall report to the authorities on everything you see other people doing. You shall covet everything that belongs to capitalists and nothing that belongs to the leaders of the Party.

Which ideas in passage (b) and passage (c) are accepted by any people you know? Do you think they are good ideas? Give reasons for your answers. Do you think that following the ideas in (b) and in (c) will benefit people and make them happy? What would you say to someone who said, 'We do not need the Ten Commandments'?

Special Note D: The Covenant and Hittite Treaties

In the world today some countries are much more powerful than others. They often impose agreements on weaker countries, so that a weaker country promises to support the policies of the stronger one. Sometimes such a pact or treaty includes promises of what the powerful country will do to help the weaker one; for example, to defend it against invasion.

In the period 1600–1200 BC, one of the most powerful states near to Palestine was the kingdom of the Hittites. The Hittites lived in Asia Minor. Their kings conquered many smaller countries. They forced the rulers of those countries to serve the Hittite kings as vassals. When they did this they made a treaty or 'Covenant' with them. In the Covenant or vassal-treaty the Great King of the Hittites laid down rules about what the vassal chief must do. A study of these covenants can help us to understand the covenant described in the book of Exodus.

Scholars have discovered and studied more than twenty of these Hittite covenants or vassal-treaties. The treaties have a common form. Nearly all of them have the same five parts in the same order, i.e.:

1. *An Introduction:* (a) giving the name of the Hittite King, and (b) showing what the Hittite King had done for the vassal.

2. *Commands:* showing what the vassal must do, including (a) basic demands for loyalty to the Hittite King and his empire, and (b) detailed instructions.

3. *Orders about the treaty:* that (a) a written copy must be placed in the temple of the vassal's god, and (b) that at certain times the treaty must be read out publicly to the vassal's people.

'When the Hittite kings conquered smaller countries they made a treaty or "covenant" with them . . . a study of these treaties can help us to understand the covenant described in the Book of Exodus', which reflects 'the way that similar covenants were made in the time of Moses' (pp. 114–118).

The Hittite treaties were written on small clay tablets—the picture shows some fragments of these discovered by archaeologists in Asia Minor, with a scale to show their size.

4. *Witnesses:* a long list of gods who were to be witnesses of the treaty.

5. *Curses and Blessings:* (a) curses on the vassal if he should break the covenant, and (b) blessings on him if he should keep it.

Here are some parts of the treaty between the Hittite King Mursilis and a vassal chief called Duppi Tessub. (The numbers are *not* part of the text of the treaty—they are added to help us to see the parts listed above.)

1. (a) These are the words of the Sun Mursilis, the Great King the King of the Hittite land . . . (b) When your father died . . . I put you in the place of your father.
2. (a) So honour the oath of loyalty to the King . . . and just as I shall be loyal to you, so I shall be loyal to your son. But you, Duppi Tessub, remain loyal to the King of the Hittite land. . . . Do not turn your eyes to anyone else. With my friend you shall be a friend . . . (b) If you hear that someone is to rise in revolt . . . go immediately to the aid of the King of the Hittite land . . . If a fugitive comes to your country, seize him.

There is then part of the treaty missing. Other Hittite treaties at this point have part 3: orders about the treaty and where the copies must be kept.

4. The Storm god of heaven, the Sun goddess Arinna . . . Anu, Antu, Apantu, Allil, Nintil, the mountains, the rivers . . . let these be witnesses to this treaty.
5. (a) . . . should Duppi Tessub not honour these words of the treaty . . . may these gods destroy him together with his wife, his son, his grandson, his house, his land, and everything that he owns. (b) But if Duppi Tessub honours these words of the treaty . . . may these gods of the oath protect him . . .

The Covenant offered by God to the people of Israel at Sinai was in many ways similar to the Hittite treaties. Notice these parts, as they are described in Exodus, Leviticus, and Deuteronomy:

1. *Introduction:* (a) Giving God's name; and (b) stating what He had done for Israel (Exod. 20.1–2).

2. *Commands:* (a) Basic demands (Exod. 20.3–17); and (b) detailed instructions (Exod. 21—23 and 25—31).

3. *Orders about the Covenant:* (a) To put the written record of the Covenant in a sacred place (Exod. 25.16; 34.1, 28—29); and (b) to read it publicly (Deut. 31.10–13).

4. *Witnesses:* Twelve pillars (Exod. 24.4; compare Joshua 24.27).

5. *Blessings and Curses:* (Lev. 26; Deut. 28; and see Exod. 19.5–6; 20.5–7).

A careful study of this treaty form helps us (1) to understand the

Covenant made at Sinai, and (2) to evaluate some of the ideas that scholars have put forward about the Covenant.

1. UNDERSTANDING THE COVENANT

It is clear that it was as a Great King that God gave the Covenant to Israel. This confirms our view that the Covenant was not an agreement between equal partners, but a bond between God and the Israelites which He offered and they accepted.

In the Hittite treaties the Great King set out the good things he had done for the vassal chief; for example, 'When your father died I established you as chief in his place'. The Hittite king gave this as a reason why the vassal chief should be loyal and obedient. This makes more plain to us the importance of Exodus 20.1–2. It is because God has been so good and loving to His people that He calls on them to be loyal and obedient.

The promises made by the Great King to be loyal to his vassals, and to protect them from invasion, help us to see that the Covenant promise: 'you shall be my own possession' (Exod. 19.5), was meant to give the Israelites a great sense of security. The many passages in the books of the prophets and in the Psalms about God's goodness and mercy reflect this sense of security—that God will loyally care for His people because He has chosen to bring them into a covenant-relationship to Himself.

2. COMPARING THE DIFFERENT IDEAS OF SCHOLARS ABOUT THE COVENANT

Some scholars suggest that the idea of the Covenant only became important in Israel's religion in the sixth century BC, at the time of the fall of Judah and the Exile in Babylonia. Other scholars believe that it was the central idea in Israel's religion from the time of Moses. Study of treaty forms in the period about 800–500 BC shows that they were in important ways different from the international treaty forms of the Hittites in the period 1600–1200 BC. The Covenant described in the books of Exodus and Deuteronomy is similar in form to the earlier Hittite treaties. It is therefore probable that those scholars are right who have argued that the covenant idea was central in Israel's religion from the time of Moses.

Some scholars have suggested that in Israel there were at first a number of stories told about Israel's escape from Egypt, and then other stories about a covenant made at Sinai. They suggest that the stories about the Sinai covenant were not linked in any way to the stories about the escape from Egypt until a later period, when editors joined them together. But other scholars have argued that the story of the escape from Egypt and the making of the Covenant was one story from the start.

Study of the Hittite treaties helps us to see that this second view is much more likely to be correct. It was a necessary part of a Hittite vassal-treaty for the introduction to show what good things the Great King had done for the vassal chief. So we can see that Exodus 20.1–2 was a necessary part of the basic document of the Covenant. The story about Israel's escape from Egypt gives the reason why Israel should accept the Covenant. It is not likely that stories about the Sinai Covenant could ever have been separate from stories about how God set the Israelites free from Egypt.

The Hittite treaties contain two different forms of command. Some are direct commands: for example, 'Remain loyal to the king.' Others begin with the word 'if'; for example, 'If a fugitive comes to your country, seize him.' Similarly in Exodus some of the commands are direct; for example, the Ten Commandments (Exod. 20.3–17). Other commands begin with 'if'; for example, 'If a man steals an ox . . . and kills it . . . he shall pay five oxen for an ox.'

Before the Hittite treaties were well known, many scholars argued that the different forms of command in Exodus showed that the laws belonged to documents or traditions that were originally separate. It is now clear, however, that this is not so. Before the time of Moses there were covenant documents which contained a variety of forms of command. If we want to divide up the laws in Exodus we shall have to find other arguments to support our case.

The Hittite empire came to an end about 1200 BC. The period 1200–1000 BC was one of constant wars and changes in the lands around the Fertile Crescent. These changes also affected the forms of the covenants made at that time. For example, in later Assyrian treaties there is no historical introduction, there are no blessings for keeping the treaty, and the order of the parts of the treaty is variable. The story in the Book of Exodus reflects the way that treaties were made in the time of Moses and earlier. It does not reflect so well the way that treaties were made in later centuries. This is a fact that we shall have to take into account when we consider the views of scholars who suggest that the stories in the book of Exodus were not written down until the period 800–500 BC.

20.18—22.17

The Covenant: Its Laws (1)

OUTLINE AND CONTEXT

20.18–21: The people of israel were afraid to hear God speak.
20.22–26: Commands about making an altar for sacrifices.
21.1—22.17: Detailed laws:
About slaves (21.2–11).
Listing crimes for which death was the penalty (21.12–17).
About bodily injury (21.18–27).

About injury caused by cattle (21.28–36).
About damage to property (22.1–15).
About sexual intercourse with an unbetrothed virgin (22.16–17).

Exodus 20.1–17 gave the basic demands which God made in the Covenant He offered to Israel at Sinai. 20.18—23.19 contains some of the detailed instructions which made up the Law of the Covenant. These laws are arranged in groups, according to their subject and the penalties that were laid down for those who broke them.

INTERPRETATION AND COMMENT

Many of these laws may seem strange to us as we read the Book of Exodus today. We must remember that they were laws for a people who lived long ago. They may not suit the different circumstances of our lives, but perhaps there will be something for us to learn from them.

1. ANCIENT ISRAELITE LAWS

Most of the laws of ancient Israel had been handed down from generation to generation (see Ruth 4.7). We may call them customary laws.

Many of Israel's customary laws were similar to the laws of people who lived in Babylonia, Assyria, and Syria. This is not surprising, since Abraham's ancestors had lived in Ur and in Haran.

One of the best known lists of laws from these lands is a code of laws drawn up by the Babylonian king Hammurabi about 1700 BC. Much of the law that he caused to be written down was older customary law. There are many laws in Exodus 20—23 which are similar to Hammurabi's laws. So the background of the laws in Exodus is very ancient. Most of them are probably laws which had been made before the time of Moses.

2. WHY WERE SOME CUSTOMARY LAWS INCLUDED IN THE COVENANT?

As we have seen (p. 114), detailed instructions were a normal part of a treaty or covenant. The Books of Exodus, Leviticus, and Deuteronomy do not contain all the customary law of Israel. For example, there are no laws about marriage and divorce. We cannot be certain why some laws were included in the Covenant and some were not. It may be that the laws contained in the Covenant are chiefly:

(a) laws about sacrifice and worship, for these were subjects which needed to be made clear as the Israelites learned to worship only one God and not the many gods worshipped by the peoples of Egypt and Palestine, and

(b) laws which were needed to make changes in the earlier customary laws, to make them express more clearly care and concern for people.

3. PEOPLE MATTER MORE THAN THINGS

The Covenant laws of Israel set a supreme value on human life. The Babylonian laws set a supreme value on property. So the Babylonian laws were less severe in cases of murder and more severe in cases of theft.

In Babylonia many offences to do with property were punished by death: for example, a wife who stole from her husband would be put to death. In Israel no kind of theft or damage to property was punishable by death.

In Babylonia a murdered person's family could accept a payment in compensation from the murderer. In Israel, for deliberate murder the only penalty was the death penalty. This sterner penalty indicates the greater value which the Israelites put upon human life.

In Babylonia a man who caused the death of another man's daughter could be punished by having his own daughter put to death. But in an Israelite court a judge could not order one person to be put to death for a crime known to be committed by someone else (Deut. 24.16).

In Babylonian law there was little to protect women. In Israelite Covenant law there were several laws to protect the right of women. In Babylonia many of the laws gave a special position to the wealthy nobles. In Israelite law there was, by contrast, special concern shown for the poor and the immigrants.

People matter more than things. And all people matter, whether they are men or women, slaves or free, young or old, rich or poor. These are some of the lessons of Israel's Covenant law.

4. CAN WE APPLY THESE LAWS TODAY?

We do not live in ancient Israel. The laws of Exodus 20—23 refer to situations which may not be common in our lives today. In many parts of the world today, people are more troubled by cars which knock them or their children down, than by cattle which stick their horns into them. Trade union rules may be more important to us than regulations about slavery.

So we cannot apply all the Old Testament laws directly to our lives today. But they may help us to consider the importance of law in the life of our country, and to think more clearly about the sort of laws we have. A study of Israelite law will make us ask: Do we give a supreme value to human life? Or do we regard wealth or party ideology as more important than the lives of other people? Or we may ask: Does everyone in our country have an equal position under the law—or do we have laws which favour some groups of people more than others?

The laws of the Covenant concerned social and family life, and worship. They suggest that God has a plan for every part of our lives. They make us ask, 'Is there any part of our life which we are trying to live without God?'

'We cannot apply all the Old Testament laws directly to our lives today, but they . . . may help us to think more clearly about the sort of laws we have' (p. 120).

In Fiji special regulations protect pedestrians from danger. Policewomen in Hong Kong check on parking meters as part of a scheme to control motor traffic in the city. What connection, if any, can you see between the ideas on which these controls and regulations are based, and the laws recorded in Exodus 21.12–14; 21.22, 23; and 21.28, 29? Which of the Ten Commandments, if any, reflect these same ideas?

NOTES

20.18–20. The thunderings and the lightnings: The purpose of the revelation of God's law amid thunder and lightning and smoke was not to make the Israelites afraid of God, but to make them reverence His law and so turn away from evil.

20.23. Gods of silver: This verse gives emphasis to the second commandment (20.4–5): in their worship the Israelites must not even use valuable gold and silver images such as the Egyptians and Canaanites used.

20.24–25. In every place . . . I will come to you: The Israelites needed to know that God would go on revealing Himself in new places. He was not limited to Sinai. In each place where God made Himself known there was to be only one altar.

Burnt offerings were made primarily as gifts to God, and for forgiveness of sins (Lev. 1.3–4). The peace offerings helped the people to show their thankfulness to God, to rejoice before Him, and to share in fellowship as they ate the sacrificial meal together.

Here in Exodus, sacrifice is set out as a proper part of worship for those who in the Covenant were called to be loyal to the LORD (Exod. 20.1–11) and to treat one another justly (Exod. 20.12–17). The prophet Hosea preached to people who were disloyal to the LORD: they worshipped Canaanite gods, and treated other people wrongly (Hos. 4.1–2). To such people Hosea said, 'God desires steadfast love and not sacrifice, the knowledge of God more than burnt offerings' (Hos. 6.6). By 'steadfast love' Hosea meant loyal obedience to the basic demands of the Covenant (compare Amos 5.21–24; Isaiah 1.10–17; Psalm 51.15–19). It is made clear by the prophets that loyalty to God and obedience to His laws are essential if sacrifice is to have any meaning and value.

21.1. Ordinances: The detailed laws and instructions of the Covenant.

21.2–6. Laws about Hebrew slaves: Legal language is often difficult to understand. This is partly because written laws remain fixed, while a spoken language changes. In English law a 'parcel' of land means a small area of land, but in spoken English 'parcel' means a package. In Exodus 21.2–6 there are similar problems. For example, does 'a Hebrew slave' mean an Israelite slave, or a slave belonging to nomadic people? Such people were often made slaves in Egypt and other lands, and they had to serve as slaves as long as they lived. So if the latter is the right meaning, Israelite law was kinder: such a slave must be set free after six years of service. Yet if he wished to remain as a slave, he could do so. The slave was to be treated as a person, not as a piece of property.

We do not know whether 'to bring to God' meant 'to bring to the doorway of the man's house', where the household gods were kept by those who believed in such gods, or 'to bring to court', where an oath might be made in God's name.

21.12–17. Offences for which the penalty was death: These offences were deliberate murder (21.12, 14), striking or cursing one's father or mother (21.15, 17), and kidnapping (21.16).

The laws about them were meant to prevent the practice of blood-vengeance, by which one murder could lead to a whole series of killings, each in revenge for the last. They also gave a murderer no right to escape punishment by taking sanctuary at an altar. But if a man killed someone by accident, he was not to be put to death (20.13, and see Num. 35.9–34; Josh. 20.1–9). In some parts of the world, if a child runs into the road and is killed by a car, the local people kill the driver of the car, even if it is clear that the accident was not the driver's fault. They have something to learn from this law.

21.18–27. Laws about bodily injury:

1. A man who injured another man must pay him: (a) compensation for the time he could not work, and (b) the cost of medical treatment (21.18–19).

2. A man who beat his slave to death must be punished as a murderer. But if it was clear that he did not intend to kill the slave, then he was considered to have suffered a sufficient penalty in the loss of the slave (21.20–21).

3. If men were fighting together, and they happened to hurt a pregnant woman and cause her child to be born prematurely, then: (a) if the woman and child both recovered, a fine must be paid by the man responsible, as laid down by the court, in response to her husband's request. But (b) if permanent harm or death resulted, then a different penalty must be paid (21.22–25).

In similar laws in Babylonia, the punishment depended on the social class of the person who was hurt. Also the penalty might be inflicted on the wife or daughter of the man responsible.

4. A slave must be set free if his master destroyed his eye or his tooth. In Hammurabi's laws and in the Hittite laws no penalty was paid by a man who harmed his own slave. The Covenant law of Israel is the only one of those ancient law codes which gave protection to slaves (see also 21.7–11, 20–21).

21.24. An eye for an eye: Note that this was a legal penalty which would only be imposed by a judge, after investigating a case. Some Jewish teachers of the law understood it to mean that in daily life whatever someone does to us we may do to them in retaliation. Jesus taught his followers a different way (see Matt. 5.38–42; Luke 6.27–31).

21.28–36. Laws about injury caused by cattle or to them:

1. An ox which killed a person must itself be killed (21.28–32).

2. If the owner knew that the ox was likely to kill and failed to control it, he too must be put to death or fined (21.29–32). If a man's son or daughter was killed by someone else's ox, the owner of the ox must pay the penalty.

In Babylonia the owner's son or daughter would have been put to death!

3. For injuries caused to another man's cattle, proper compensation must be paid (21.33–36).

21.32. Thirty shekels: The price for a slave in the time of Moses was about 30 shekels. The price had risen since the time of Joseph, who was sold for 20 shekels. After about 1000 BC the price of slaves rose to 40 or 50 shekels. So this law reflects conditions in the time of Moses.

22.1–15. Laws about theft and damage to property: When someone had been found to have stolen something, he must do two things: (a) return what was stolen or an equivalent sum of money; and also (b) pay an extra amount as compensation for the trouble he had caused (compare Lev. 6.1–5).

In Hammurabi's laws in Babylonia the penalties laid down for stealing included chopping off the thief's hand, or putting him to death. Israel's Covenant law was based on the understanding that people (even thieves) are more important than property. The only case in which a thief might be killed was if he was breaking into a house at night and the owner killed him in self-defence (22.2–3).

22.16–17. A virgin who is not betrothed: Betrothal, or engagement, was very important in Israelite life. It was the first stage of the marriage. In the case of a betrothed girl the law was the same as for a married woman. But if a man had sexual intercourse with a girl who was not engaged, he must pay the girl's father the customary bride-price. He must also marry the girl, unless her father refused to allow the marriage.

STUDY SUGGESTIONS AND QUESTIONS

REVIEW OF CONTENT

1. What are the main lessons you think we should learn from our study of the laws in Exodus 20—22?
2. What are the main differences that have been mentioned between Israel's Covenant law and Hammurabi's Babylonian laws?

BIBLE STUDY AND REFLECTION

3. *The death penalty:* The Law of the Covenant did not allow the death penalty to be imposed for theft or damage to property.
   (a) If the death penalty is used in your country, for what kind of crimes is it imposed?
   (b) What does this show about what is most valued in your country?
   (c) If there is no death penalty, do you think that this makes murder seem an unimportant crime? Does the lack of a death penalty bring danger of death to other people from the activity of criminals, terrorists, or their supporters?

4. *Murder:* (a) What do you think are the main reasons for which people commit murder? (b) What do you think could be done to reduce the number of murders?
5. The laws of Israel set a supreme value on human life (p. 120). What are the most common causes of accidental death, (a) amongst children, and (b) amongst adults, in your country? What efforts are being made to reduce such accidents? What else do you think should be done?
6. *Israelite and Babylonian laws:* Many of the Covenant laws of Israel were similar to Babylonian ones, but others were different. Some of the differences suggest that the Israelites were learning more clearly that God cares for all people. Discuss the following statement: 'God's people may use what is good in the customs and cultures of their own lands, but they must always be ready to make changes in traditional ways.'

22.18—23.33
The Covenant: Its Laws (2)

OUTLINE AND CONTEXT

22.18—23.19: Detailed laws about:
Loyalty to the one true God (22.18–20),
Care for the weak (22.21–27),
Offerings made to God (22.28–31),
Truth and justice (23.1–9),
Sabbath rest for the land and for all who work (23.10–13),
Festivals and offerings (23.14–19).
23.20–33: God promised to guide, protect, and bless His people as they obeyed Him.

Exodus 22.18—23.19 continues and completes the section of detailed covenant laws which began at Exodus 20.22.

INTERPRETATION AND COMMENT

1. CARE FOR THE WEAK AND THE NEEDY

When we read the laws recorded in Exodus 22.21–27 and 23.1–9, we see that the Israelites were to be specially careful in their treatment of weak and needy people: immigrants, widows, orphans, and the poor. They were to do this because they had learned through their own experience that God is kind: 'I am compassionate' (22.27). Also, they had suffered in Egypt.

They knew what it was like to be oppressed, to be a stranger in a strange land (23.9). Similar concern for people in need is shown throughout the Old Testament.

A group of young soldiers were being rather harshly treated by those who were training them to be officers. Several of them said, 'We are being made to suffer. When we are in positions of authority we shall be able to make others suffer!' A few of them said, 'When we are officers we must treat people in a better way than this.' Most people suffer at one time or another. If we let God teach us His compassion, then suffering will not make us bitter: it will help us to understand and help other people.

2. LOYALTY AND WORSHIP

The Israelites were warned not to take part in, nor to copy, the religious practices of the Canaanites (22.18–20; 23.18–33). Exodus 22.18–19 and 23.19 refer to magical practices by which the Canaanites hoped to get fertility for crops and herds.

As we have seen, the Canaanites believed in many gods, some of which represented the powerful forces of nature—for example, Hadad was a god of the storm. The Canaanites did not believe in a single God who is the creator of everything that exists, but in gods who emerged out of an original chaos, and who needed the powers of magic in order to control what would happen.

Old Testament prophets and writers condemned such beliefs and practices, because they believed in one God who is the source of all that exists: by His power He is able to control everything.

When we study stories about the Canaanite gods, we find that the people believed they were often fighting against each other, and that they needed food and sexual intercourse, and could suffer sickness and death. The Israelites' faith, as we find it expressed in the Book of Exodus, was totally different. Moses and the prophets saw that there was no possibility of combining these different religions. So they warned the Israelites to take no part in Canaanite worship. (See also p. 164). But many of the people did not listen to such warnings. The Book of Judges and the Book of Kings (1 Kings and 2 Kings) have much to say about the way in which the Israelites accepted pagan religious beliefs and practices.

Christians who live in countries where other religions are strong often have difficult decisions to make. One African Christian recently said, 'We used to pour out offerings of beer to the spirits of our dead ancestors. Can we do the same thing at the burial places of Christian martyrs?' When we try to answer such questions we have to consider, 'What kind of beliefs about God and about the world and about human beings lead people to such a practice? Do these beliefs fit in with our Christian faith in one God who has called us to be His through Jesus Christ, and has promised that His Holy Spirit will fill us and direct us? If not, can we accept the practices? And if we do them, will it help other people to trust in God through Jesus Christ?' Compare what St Paul had to say about eating meat that had been offered to idols (1 Cor. 8.1–13; 10.14–33).

3. THE SABBATH AND SPECIAL FESTIVALS

In 23.12–17 the law of the Sabbath is repeated. There is special emphasis that the Sabbath is to be a holiday for all employed workers. This reminds us that if we employ other people to work for us, God expects us to be concerned for them as people, and to see that so far as we can we provide good conditions of work, reasonable hours and pay, and a proper opportunity for people to join in the worship of God.

There are also instructions about the three special festivals when the Israelite men were to gather 'before the LORD' (23.17). At these festivals they were to come to God as their King and pay Him homage, and to renew their loyalty and obedience. Some Christian people say that all our time belongs to God, and so we do not need to have special times for worship and prayer. But if we do not have special times for worship, we are likely to use all our time as if it belongs to ourselves.

Some of the Hittite vassal-treaties (see special Note C, pp. 114–118) laid down that vassals must appear at certain times before the Great King. This was so that they could express and renew their loyalty to the King, receive his instructions, and then return to their own lands to continue as his loyal subjects. When we have a special festival, or a daily time for prayer, it should be so that we can return to our daily work and other activities to spend our time for God. There is a danger that we may sometimes fail, if we think: 'I have set aside a special time for God. Now I can use the rest of my time in any way I choose.'

4. GUIDANCE

God promised to bring the Israelites 'to the place that I have prepared' (23.20). This place was a land which they had not seen. It would not be easy for them to enter it, because it was occupied by strong tribes who lived in well fortified towns. But as it was a place prepared for them by God, the people of Israel could go forward with confidence.

We all face an uncertain future. But if we belong to Jesus Christ we can go forward into the future with confidence, because we know that God has prepared a way for us. Paul says that we are God's workmanship: 'created in Christ Jesus to do those good things that God has prepared for us to do' (Eph. 2.10). And we can also face death with confidence, for Jesus promised his followers: 'I am going ahead to prepare a place for you' (John 14.1–3).

NOTES

22.19. lies with a beast: (Compare Lev. 18.23–25.) One Canaanite poem tells a story of how the god Baal had sexual intercourse with a cow in order to save himself magically from death. Hittite laws allowed sexual intercourse with some animals. The Israelites were learning to understand sexual intercourse as a gift from God to bind together a woman and her husband in a loving unity (Gen. 2.18–25). Wrong uses of sexual powers can spoil what God intends to be a blessing.

22.25. as a creditor: Creditors used to take possession of the land of those who owed them money and could not repay it. Such debtors and their families were often sold as slaves (see Lev. 25.36; Deut. 23.20; Ps. 15.5; Jer. 15.10). Notice that this verse (22.25) does not condemn lending money to people in order to help them. Very often a poor person who has a bad harvest or is out of work can best be helped by someone who will lend him money. What the law forbids is the exploitation of poor people by those who are rich, and who might take advantage of a person's poverty or trouble, not to help him but in order to gain something from him. (See also Ps. 37.26; Matt. 5.42.)

22.26. take in pledge: That is, take as proof that the man owed a debt.

22.27. I am compassionate: That is, merciful, kind, and helpful. The idea that God is merciful is one which strongly influenced Muhammad. Nearly every chapter of the Qur'an begins: 'In the name of God, the merciful, the compassionate'. Sura 57.27 refers to Christians as those in whose hearts God has placed 'mercy and compassion'. In orthodox Islam the doctrine of God's difference from what He has made (*mukhalafa*) means that although He calls Himself 'The Merciful' we cannot know that He is in any way like a merciful person. In Christian teaching Jesus's compassion, His love and care and healing power, are seen as a true revelation of the loving mercy of God.

22.29. The first-born of your sons: See the section 'The consecration of the first-born sons' on p. 70.

23.1. You shall not join hands: Joining hands meant coming to an agreement.

23.2–6. In a suit: That is, in a legal case in court.

23.4–5: Compare Leviticus 19.17–18 and Matthew 5.44–48.

23.6–9: These laws were for judges. In Israel, as in other countries, bribery was a constant temptation. See also Isaiah 1.21 and Amos 5.12.

23.11. lie fallow: That is, remain uncultivated. Such a practice is also good for the land, and many farmers use a period of fallow in the rotation of their crops.

23.14–17: These three festivals marked the main stages of the Israelite farmer's year: (1) the beginning of the barley harvest, (2) the end of the corn harvest, and (3) the end of the harvest of vines and olives.

23.19. The first of the first-fruits: The first part of the barley harvest to become ripe. Deuteronomy 26:1–11 records a special form of offering and prayer to be used when the Israelites first settled in Canaan. Because they were thanking God for giving them the land, the prayer began by mentioning how Jacob had left the land of Canaan to go to Egypt (Deut. 26.5).

23.19. You shall not boil a kid in its mother's milk: This refers to a Canaanite fertility rite.

23.21. For my name is in him: The name of a person, in the Old Testament, often reveals his nature. One Jewish commentator says that this phrase means, 'I reveal myself to you through him. I and he are the same.' Many Christians see in this angel a foreshadowing of God's way of making Himself known to people through Jesus, to whom He has given 'the name that is above every name' (Phil. 2.9). See also notes on 3.2, The angel of the Lord (p. 22).

STUDY SUGGESTIONS AND QUESTIONS

REVIEW OF CONTENT

1. In what ways do the Covenant laws make special provision for strangers, widows, orphans, enemies, the poor, and employees?
2. What reasons are given why there should be such special concern for people in need?
3. What results would follow, according to this passage, (a) if the Israelites obeyed God? and (b) if they worshipped other gods?

BIBLE STUDY AND REFLECTION

4. *People in need*

   (a) 'Concern for people in need is shown throughout the Old Testament' (p. 126). In the following passages, what people are mentioned as needing special help, and in what ways is it said that they could be helped? Job 29.11–17; 31.13–23; Ps. 146.9; Isa. 1.17; 2 Sam. 12.1–15; 1 Kings 2.1.

   (b) What did Jesus teach about our responsibilities to people in need? (See Matt. 25.34–40; Luke 10.30–37; John 13.3–17; and compare 1 John 3.16–17; James 2.14–16.)

   (c) In the place where you live, what people do you think are most in need of help?

   (d) If someone is poor and hungry because he refuses to work, in what way do you think he needs to be helped?

   (e) If someone is poor and hungry because (i) there is no job for him to do, or (ii) he does not know how to work efficiently, in what way do you think he needs to be helped?

5. *Other religious beliefs and practices*
   (a) Why were the Israelites warned not to take part in Canaanite religious practices?
   (b) Do you think any similar warnings are needed today? If so, what do you think are the wrong beliefs and practices that people are tempted to follow, and why do you think they are wrong?
6. *Sabbath and Sunday*
   (a) Do you think people need to rest from work for one day each week? Give reasons for your answer.
   (b) Do you know any people who work every day and never have a regular rest or holiday? What result does this have for them?
   (c) What would you say to a Christian shop-keeper who said, 'I sell more goods on Sunday than on any other day. I must keep my shop open on Sundays or I would not earn enough to live on'?
   (d) What do you think are (i) the main values, and (ii) the main dangers, of having special times for prayer and worship?

24.1–18

Israel accepts the Covenant

OUTLINE AND CONTEXT

24.1–2: God told Moses to prepare the leaders of Israel to worship Him on the mountain side.
24.3–8: The making of the Covenant: the Israelites promised to obey God.
24.9–11: God revealed Himself to the leaders of Israel as they worshipped Him.
24.12–18: Moses was called to be with God on the mountain top.

Exodus 20.1—23.33 set out the basic demands of the Covenant and its detailed laws, and mentioned the blessings that God would give His people if they obeyed Him. Exodus 24.1–18 describes how the Israelites accepted the Covenant, and by telling how Moses was called up the mountain, leads on to the account in Exodus 25—27 of how he was instructed about the Tabernacle.

INTERPRETATION AND COMMENT

1. GOD'S PEOPLE ACCEPT HIS COVENANT

Moses told the Israelites 'all the *words* of the LORD and all the *ordinances*' (24.3). This means that he told them the '*words*' (20.1) which were the basic demands made by their heavenly King (20.2–17), and also the '*ordinances*' (21.1) which were the detailed laws of the Covenant (21.2—23.19). Then, when they had heard them, the people prepared to take the great oath of the Covenant: 'All that the LORD has spoken, we will do.' Genesis 26.31 and Joshua 9.15 show that the making of a solemn oath was the normal climax of a covenant ceremony.

But before the oath was taken an altar was built, pillars were set up, and a sacrifice was made. Half of the blood of the sacrifice was sprinkled on the altar and half on the people. This sacrifice and sprinkling of blood show:

(a) That the people came to God as sinners who needed to be forgiven;

(b) That they realized how important the Covenant was, and that if they broke it they would deserve to die as the sacrificial animal had died; and

(c) That God and His people were brought together in unity by the Covenant.

By accepting the Covenant, the people of Israel accepted the LORD as their King. They would obey Him gladly because He had done so much for them. At the heart of Israel's religion is the prayer, 'Thy will be done.'

2. PERSONAL RESPONSIBILITY

At Sinai the people of Israel as a whole committed themselves to God to walk in His ways. Many of God's promises were made not to individuals, but to all the people together. Because of this, some scholars put forward this idea: it was not until the time of the prophets Jeremiah and Ezekiel that the Israelites had a clear idea of people as separate individuals, each with his personal responsibility. But when we study the Ten Commandments and the other Covenant laws, we find that many of them are addressed to each individual person. For example, the command in Exodus 20.13 (RSV 'You shall not kill') is 'Thou shalt not kill'. It is a command to each person. And if a person did commit murder, it was that person alone who was held responsible and punished. Unless each individual person commits himself to God to walk in His way, it is not possible for God's will to be done in the world. We cannot hide from God in a crowd of other people.

But the Sinai Covenant was also accepted by the Israelite people as a whole. God's will cannot be done in the world unless people who live and work together in groups are willing to do His will. Nations and states, employers' groups and Trade Unions, families and communities of friends, all have a responsibility to God. We cannot escape from God by saying 'God is only interested in what we do in our private life as individuals.'

3. THE TERMS OF THE COVENANT WERE WRITTEN DOWN (24.4, 7)

For more than five hundred years, in Mesopotamia, Palestine, and Egypt, the ancestors of the Israelites had lived among people who wrote down the things which were important to them. In Babylonia the king Hammurabi had had his laws written down. He included a curse on anyone who should alter what he had written. The Hittite treaties were also written documents. If anyone should 'change the wording of the tablet', all the gods of the oath were called upon to punish him.

So, when the Israelites accepted the Covenant, its terms were written down. They accepted the Covenant law as a law that must not be changed. This is perhaps the beginning of the growth of the idea of Scripture amongst Jews and Christians; the idea that there is a written word of God to guide His people in their lives, a word that should not be changed or added to by men.

4. GOD REVEALS HIS GLORY (24.9–11)

In this chapter the writer tells us about the great event of the making of the Covenant (24.3–8). No other event in Israel's life, except the escape from Egypt, was more important. But the writer of Exodus shows us that something else happened which was even more wonderful and full of mystery and splendour. After the people had accepted the Covenant (24.3–8), the leaders of Israel responded to God's call (24.1) and went up the mountainside. There God revealed Himself to them (24.9–11).

We do not know what they saw. The verses do not tell us what God's appearance was like. They only describe some kind of dazzling blue floor that seemed to be beneath Him. We may compared this with Ezekiel's vision (Ezek.1.4–28). Ezekiel described in detail the appearance of a chariot throne above which God revealed His glory (1.4–26). But when Ezekiel spoke of God's glory he could only say that it was 'a likeness as it were of a human form' surrounded by fiery brightness (1.26–28).

Perhaps the experience the Israelites had was in some ways similar to our experience when we look at the sun. We may say, 'I saw the sun'. Yet scientists tell us that we do not see the sun itself but only some of the light that is continually streaming from it. The writer of John's gospel knew and believed the Old Testament, yet he could say, 'No man has ever seen God' (John 1.18). Perhaps he too understood that in Old Testament times men saw the appearance of God's glory, but without being able fully to see God as He is in Himself.

We may notice also that God took the initiative in revealing Himself. It was He who called the Israelites up the mountainside. In the account in Exodus the invitation was given before the Israelites accepted the Covenant. This vision of God's glory was not something they earned by accepting the Covenant; it was God's gift to those whom He had called to be his people. Christians who are called to live under a new Covenant believe that its climax will come when God is seen in all His glory and dwells among His people as their light and joy (Rev. 21.1–5; 22.1–5).

As we learn how God still reveals Himself to people today, we often notice that He comes to people in ways they do not expect, and in ways which emphasize His initiative and His love in coming to us. Not long ago a woman lay seriously ill in hospital. One night, many miles away, her sister and some other Christians prayed that God would help her and make her aware of His presence and love. A night or two later the woman was lying in bed, almost asleep. Thinking the nurse had tapped her on the shoulder, she opened her eyes and looked. There was no nurse there. Then she looked towards the end of her bed. She saw Jesus standing there, smiling at her. She says His face was so full of love, it was wonderful. Then, raising His hand, He blessed her. She wrote to her sister with great joy: 'All the years of pain are as nothing to me now. I have seen Jesus! I know He is alive! . . . And He blessed me.' We cannot tell when or how God may choose to reveal Himself to anyone, but when He does they are made conscious of His love, His glory, and His holiness.

NOTES

24.1. Nadab and Abihu: They were sons of Aaron (Exod. 6.23). They were chosen to be priests when Aaron their father was made the chief priest of Israel (Exod. 28.1). For the story of their death, see Leviticus 10.1–2.

24.4. Twelve pillars: These were to represent the twelve tribes of Israel (compare Josh. 4.1–7). Some scholars have argued that not all the Israelite tribes were originally in Egypt, and that fewer than twelve tribes were at Sinai. There is no factual evidence to support such a view. All the Old Testament documents support the view that all twelve tribes were at Sinai.

In Genesis 31.51–52 we read how Laban and Jacob set up a pillar to be a witness to a covenant they made. Moses may have set up the twelve pillars as witnesses. We have seen that in several ways the Covenant was similar to the Hittite vassal treaties (see pp. 114–118). Here is one way in which it was quite different. In the Hittite treaties we find long lists of gods who were called to be witnesses. In the Covenant described in Exodus there is no list of gods: the Israelities believed that there is only one God.

24.8. Moses took the blood and threw it upon the people: We cannot be certain of the meaning of this action. Some scholars suggest that it symbolized the sharing of a common *life* by God and His people. But it is more likely to symbolize *death*, and Israel's recognition that breaking the Covenant oath would make them worthy of death (compare the Hebrew oath form 'May the LORD do so to me and more also, if . . .' which originally meant, 'May God make me as dead as the animal which has been sacrificed, if . . .').

For the use of the word 'blood' as meaning death, life laid down in death, or responsibility for death, see Genesis 4.10–11; 42.22; Numbers 35.33; Joshua 2.19; 2 Samuel 1.16; Acts 5.28; Romans 5.9–10; Hebrews 12.4; 9.16–18.

24.11. . . . and ate and drank: That is, they lived and did not die: compare Exodus 33.20; Joshua 6.22–23; 13.21–23. Some scholars have suggested that 'they ate and drank' is a description of a covenant-making ceremony, the eating of a sacred meal. But this is not likely to be so. In Exodus 24.1, 9–11 the whole emphasis is on the *leaders* of Israel seeing God: in the covenant ceremony all the people were involved.

24.12. . . . the tables of stone: See section on 31.18 (pp. 149, 150).

24.14. Whoever has a cause: That is, 'If anyone has a dispute' (NEB).

STUDY SUGGESTIONS AND QUESTIONS

REVIEW OF CONTENT

1. What did Moses do at the Covenant-making ceremony?
2. What did the people do?
3. What did the elders of Israel do after the people had accepted the Covenant?

BIBLE STUDY AND REFLECTION

4. 'All that the LORD has spoken, we will do' (24.7).

   (i) What does each of the following passages tell us about how well the Israelites in later generations kept the Covenant?

   (a) 2 Kings 8.54–61 (b) 2 Kings 11.1–11 (c) Hos. 4.1–2 (d) Isa. 1.2–4, 21–23 (e) Jer. 7.8–10?

   (ii) In the following passages, what hope did the prophets Hosea, Jeremiah, and Ezekiel give to people who had failed to keep the Covenant?

   (a) Hos. 2.18–23 (b) Jer. 31.31–34 (c) Ezek. 36.22–27.

   (iii) Have you made any promises to God? If so, how well have you kept them?
5. What do you think Jesus meant when He described His blood as 'the blood of the Covenant' (Mark 14.22–24)? How is this idea developed in 1 Peter 1.3—2.10?
6. Read 2 Corinthians 3.4—4.6. Paul says that he was called to be a minister 'of a new covenant.' In what ways does the passage show that the new covenant is: (a) similar to the Covenant made at Sinai; and (b) different from it?
7. *Jesus and Moses:*

   (a) In a concordance look up the references to 'mountains' and 'hills' in the Gospels. In which of these passages do you think the writers meant their readers to think of Jesus as a new and better Moses?

   (b) In what ways do you think Jesus was like Moses and in what ways was He different from him?

   (c) What does the writer of the Epistle to the Hebrews say about Jesus and Moses in Hebrews 1.1–3; 3.1–6?

25.1—27.21
How to make the Tabernacle

OUTLINE AND CONTEXT

25.1–9: The gifts which the Israelites must bring.
25.10–40: The ark, the table, and the lamp.
26.1–37: The Tabernacle; its curtains, framework, and veil.
27.1–21: The altar and the court of the Tabernacle.

Exodus 25.12–18 told how Moses was called to the top of Mount Sinai where the glory of the LORD appeared. Exodus 25—27 continues the story by describing the instructions given to Moses on the mountain.

INTERPRETATION AND COMMENT

1. THE TABERNACLE

The Tabernacle was a sacred tent. It was a symbol of God's presence and His holiness. It was made with a wooden frame, covered with curtains. It could be taken to pieces, so that it could be carried by the Israelites on their journey.

The Tabernacle itself consisted of two rooms: the inner one was the most holy place, and could only be approached through the outer one. The sacred tent was surrounded by a courtyard formed by curtains hung on wooden poles.

Many books have been written by people who have tried to explain every detail of the Tabernacle and its meaning. In this Study Guide we shall not attempt to study the Tabernacle in detail, for these reasons:

(a) The writer of Exodus does not give us any clear explanation of the meaning of each part of the Tabernacle. There is therefore no certain way of deciding between the different ideas that may be suggested. For example, the curtains of the Tabernacle were decorated in blue, purple, and scarlet (26.1). Did the colours have a meaning, or were they simply the best colours that were available? We do not know. If they had a meaning, did blue suggest God's heavenly nature (Exod. 24.10) or His kingly power (Esther 8.15)? Did scarlet stand for wealth (2 Sam. 1.24), or for the blood of sacrifice through which sinful men can come to God? We do not know, and it is not sensible to spend much time on such questions. If we want to know, for example, about God's kingly power, there are many passages in the Bible which speak of it clearly. We do not need to find details in the Tabernacle to explain it to us.

(b) If we devote too much attention to the details of the Tabernacle and its ritual, we are likely to find that we have forgotten one of the main principles of Biblical religion. Both in the Old Testament and in the teaching of Jesus we find it clearly stated, that what matters most in religion is loyal love for God and humble trust in Him, combined with practical love for our fellow men. The prophets and Jesus pointed out that if we concentrate on details of sacrifice and ritual, we may fail in the most important matters of faith and practice. When people asked Micah what kind of sacrifices God required, the prophet answered: 'What does the LORD require of you but to do justice and to show loyal love, and to walk humbly with your God' (Mic. 6.8). To people who were very interested in details of the law of tithing, Jesus said that the central demand of God's law is for 'justice and mercy and faith' (Matt. 23.23). To people who were concerned about ritual washing. He said that purity of heart does not come from outward ceremonies (Mark 7). As Paul wrote to the Christians in Rome, 'The Kingdom of God is not a matter of what we eat or drink, but of the righteousness, peace and joy that the Holy Spirit gives' (Rom. 14.17).

So in this Study Guide we shall attempt only to show the main meaning that the Tabernacle seems to have had for the people of Israel.

2. THE TABERNACLE WAS TO SHOW THAT GOD IS WITH HIS PEOPLE

Moses was told (25.8) to make a holy place so that God could dwell among His people. We are sometimes tempted to think that God is far away. The message of the Tabernacle for the Israelites was: 'God is near. God is personal. God cares for you. He will not leave you, and you cannot leave Him behind when you travel to another place.'

3. THE TABERNACLE WAS TO SHOW THAT GOD IS HOLY

The holy place, where God's presence was to be made known, was closed in with curtains. Its central part was dark and mysterious. The ordinary people and the priests were not allowed to enter it. The high priest went in only once a year, after making special sacrifices. So the Tabernacle also had this message for the people of Israel: 'God is holy, and you are not worthy to come into His presence.' In the words of a later prophet, 'Your sins have made a separation between you and your God' (Isa. 59.2).

But, in the courtyard which surrounded the holy tent, there was an altar for sacrifices and a bronze bowl for washing. They showed that God is ready to forgive those who have done wrong, and to restore them to fellowship with Himself: 'I am He who blots out your transgressions. I will not remember your sins' (Isa. 43.25).

4. THE TABERNACLE WAS TO SHOW THAT GOD'S WORD MUST GUIDE HIS PEOPLE IN THEIR LIVES

In the centre of the holy place was a sacred box, the ark. In the ark Moses

'Moses was told to make a holy place so that God could dwell among His people' (p. 136).

When a new Coptic cathedral was being built in Cairo, the clergy consulted with the architect about details of the construction. Do you think that God dwells with His people only when they have made a holy place for Him? If so, what sort of a place does it have to be? How far do you think that the way people worship God is affected by details of the building where they gather for prayer?

put two stone tablets with the Ten Commandments written on them (25.21). And God said to Moses, 'There I will meet with you . . . and I will speak with you of all that I will give you in commandment to the people of Israel' (25.22). So another message which the Tabernacle had for the people of Israel was: 'You must obey the written commandments of God. You must also keep listening to what God has to say to you. What He says to you in the present and in the future will be in harmony with the Commandments which He has already given you.'

God does not contradict Himself. So if anyone claims to have a message from God, we need to ask; 'Does it fit in with what God has already revealed to us in Jesus Christ and through the Holy Scriptures?' Of the people who wanted to consult mediums and spirits, the prophet Isaiah said, 'To the law and the testimony! If they do not speak according to this word, surely there is no light for them' (Isa. 8.20). When John found that people were teaching in the Churches things that were contrary to what Jesus had revealed and taught, he wrote his letters to set out again the message that had been made known 'in the beginning'. He warned Christians to be careful: 'the man who runs ahead and does not keep to the teaching of Christ is without God' (2 John 9).

NOTES

Chapters 25—27. The Tabernacle: The Tabernacle was a portable building, with its wooden framework covered with curtains. The Egyptians had used portable buildings of similar construction for more than a thousand years before Moses. One Egyptian picture, painted about 2200 BC, shows the framework of a large 'Tent of Purification'. Remains found in the tomb of the Pharaoh Tutankhamun show that the Egyptians were skilled in covering woodwork with a thin layer of gold—as the Israelite craftsmen did, according to Exodus 25.11; 26.29.

When the Pharaoh Ramesses II went to fight in Syria against the Hittites (about 1290 BC), he took with him a portable tent. The god-king camped in the middle of his army, which was spread out in a square formation round his tent. Perhaps Moses used his experience in Egypt not only in making the Tabernacle, but also in the plan for Israel's camp (Num. 2 and 10).

Ancient Canaanite stories show that many of the features of the Tabernacle were known in Canaan before the time of Moses. One Canaanite writer described the god El as dwelling in a building that is called both a tabernacle and a tent (he used the same two words as we find in the Book of Exodus). The description of El's tent mentions boards that were put up on special bases (compare Exod. 26.15–25).

One of the Canaanite gods, Baal, had a temple with a throne, a footstool, a lamp, and a table with utensils. All these things were similar to things which the Israelites made for the Tabernacle. But there was one major difference. In Baal's temple there was a statue of the god. The priests of Baal had to go in each day and dress the god, and take him food, and at night undress him and put him to bed. So Baal's temple contained also a chest-of-drawers for his clothes and a bed for him to sleep on. The fact that in the Tabernacle there was no statue of the LORD and no bed for Him to sleep on, shows how very different were the ideas of God held by the Israelites from those of the Canaanites.

Most of the scholars who have written about the Tabernacle in the past century have taken the view that:

(a) The story of the Tabernacle was written down by Jewish priests during the time of exile in Babylonia (about 590–550 BC).

(b) These priests used old traditions about a holy tent used by the Israelites in the time of Moses, but

(c) The tent was a very simple one, and the priests who wrote the story based it not only on the early tradition about a holy tent, but also on their knowledge of the Jerusalem Temple. Therefore the account in Exodus does not tell us about a Tabernacle which actually existed: it tells us only what the Jewish priests imagined to have existed.

In this Study Guide we are mainly concerned with the meaning of the Book of Exodus. The spiritual lessons that the writer of Exodus intended to teach remain the same, at whatever date and in whatever way he wrote the book. So we have not discussed these questions in detail.

However, there have always been some scholars who have argued that the account of the Tabernacle was written very much earlier than the time of the Exile in Babylonia. This view has been strengthened by recent discoveries and studies of the literature of ancient Egypt and Palestine. When we find that the methods of construction, the materials, the utensils, and the ideas connected with the Tabernacle are all to be found in Egypt and Palestine in or before the time of Moses, then we are more likely to believe that the story of the Tabernacle belongs to the early history of Israel, and not to the time of the Exile.

In this Study Guide we take the view that, whether every detail of the Exodus account is accurate or not, the Tabernacle was constructed at Sinai as a portable Shrine to symbolize God's presence among His people as their King and leader.

25.3–7: The materials for making the Tabernacle are all such as would have been available in Egypt and Sinai. Many scholars have commented on the large amounts of metal required. If there were about 72,000 Israelites (see note on 12.37), each one would have had to give about half an ounce of gold, one and a half ounces of silver, and one ounce of bronze. Egypt was rich in these metals (see also Exod. 12.33–36).

25.10–22. The ark: The ark was a wooden box. It was thought of as God's footstool (Pss. 99.5; 132.7–8; 1 Chron. 28.2). It was thus a specially suitable place for the 'testimony' (25.21), that is, the tablets that recorded the covenant law. When the Hittites and the Egyptians made a treaty about 1280 BC, two copies of the treaty were made: one was placed 'beneath the feet' of Teshub, a Hittite god, and the other in an Egyptian temple, 'beneath the feet' of the god Ra.

25.18–22. Cherubim: These were carved figures with wings. They formed: (a) part of a visible throne for the invisible God (Exod. 25.22; Ps. 99.1), and (b) a protection for the Covenant documents (see Gen. 3.24 for cherubim as protecting).

26.31. The veil: This formed a screen of fine linen to divide the most holy place from the holy place. In Solomon's temple there was a similar veil (2 Chron. 3.14). In Herod's temple in Jerusalem the veil was sixty feet long and thirty feet wide. It was as thick as the palm of a hand. It symbolized the fact that sinful men cannot stand in the presence of God. It was this thick veil that the writers of the Gospels say was torn from top to bottom when Jesus died (Matt. 27.51; Mark 15.38; Luke 23.45). This was to show that in his death Jesus bore the sins of the world, and opened a new way for men to be forgiven, to be cleansed, and to live in fellowship with God.

STUDY SUGGESTIONS AND QUESTIONS

REVIEW OF CONTENT

1. What were the main lessons about God that the Tabernacle expressed?
2. What was contained in the ark, and what was its importance?

BIBLE STUDY AND REFLECTION

3. 'The Tabernacle was to show that God was with His people' (p. 136).
   (a) Read the following passages: Isaiah 4.4–6; Jeremiah 3. 16–17; Ezekiel 37.24–28. Make a list of the ideas which are connected with the Covenant, the glory of God revealed at Sinai, and the Tabernacle. What blessings do they say God's people will enjoy when the whole city and all God's people become a Tabernacle in which God dwells?
   (b) Read John 1.14 and Revelation 21.1–4. In both of these passages the Greek word translated 'dwell' actually means 'tented' or 'tabernacled'. In what ways do you think the writers' ideas about God's presence are similar to, and different from, the ideas of: (i) the writer of Exodus? (ii) the prophets Jeremiah and Ezekiel?
   (c) In what ways do you think God makes His presence known among people today?
4. The Tabernacle and its sacrifices showed that there was a way for sin to be forgiven.

(i) How did the writer of each of the following passages say that sinful people could come to God?
(a) 1 Peter 1.18–21 (b) Heb. 10.11–25 (c) 1 John 1.5—2.2
(d) Eph. 2.1–10.
(ii) Do you think the story of the Tabernacle can help people today to understand the holiness of God? If so, in what ways can it help them?
(iii) What would you say to someone who said to you, 'I am not good enough to come to God'?

5. 'God's word must guide His people' (p. 136).
(i) In each of the following passages what did Jesus teach about the Old Testament scripture?
(a) Matt. 5.17 (b) Mark 12.24–27 (c) Luke 24.25—27.44–47
(d) John 5.39; 10.35.
(ii) (a) In what ways did Paul say that the Old Testament writings were useful? (Note 2 Tim. 3.14–42; 1 Cor. 10.11.)
(b) What would you say to someone who said: 'Since Jesus is the Word of God through whom He has spoken to us, we do not need the Bible'?
(c) How would you answer someone who said: 'The Bible is not the only Scripture we need, we must also accept the Book of Mormon'?

28.1—29.47

'Make Aaron the Priest'

OUTLINE AND CONTEXT

28.1–39: Robes for Aaron to wear as priest.
28.40–43: Robes for Aaron's sons.
29.1–37: How Aaron and his sons must be consecrated as priests.
29.38–47: The morning and evening offerings.

Exodus 25—27 described the Tabernacle. Exodus 28—29 gives instructions about the priests who must offer sacrifices in it. Exodus 39.1–30 and Leviticus 8—9 tell how these instructions were carried out.

INTERPRETATION

1. 'TO SERVE ME AS PRIESTS' (28.1, 4, 41; 29.1, 44)

Aaron and his son were to serve God as priests. Because God is glorious, His servants were to have clothes which would give them 'glory and beauty' (28.2). The main work of the priests was to bring the people's sacrifices to God (see Lev. 1—7), to pray for the people of Israel, and to seek God's blessing for them (Num. 6. 22–27).

We do not know in detail what meaning each of the sacrifices had. But it is clear that in offering sacrifices the Israelites were:

(a) seeking that God would forgive them for what was wrong in their lives; that He would accept the sacrifice instead of punishing them;

(b) worshipping God, and giving Him the best of what they possessed;

(c) thanking God for His goodness, and rejoicing in His nearness and love;

(d) seeking for God's blessing, for the peace and prosperity that He gives.

Forgiveness, worship, offering, thanksgiving, and blessing should all have a place in the life of those who seek to love and serve God. The ways in which we express them today may be different from the ways in which the Israelites worshipped, but our own experience may help us to understand the importance of the priests for the worship of Israel.

2. PRIESTS AND SACRIFICES IN THE NEW TESTAMENT

From the time of Moses the priests had a central part in the religion of the Israelites. When we read the Gospels we find many references to the High Priests, Annas and Caiaphas. But when we study the New Testament we find that among the followers of Jesus none were chosen out from the rest to be priests. Nor do we find in the teaching of Jesus and the Apostles anything about offering animals in sacrifice on an altar.

Jesus was brought up as a Jew, and so were most of His first followers. We might expect that Jesus would have appointed some of His disciples to be priests. Why did He not do so? The writer of the Epistle to the Hebrews gives us the fullest explanation. He was writing to Christians who had once been Jews, and who therefore understood about Aaron and the high priests of Israel. He explained to them that the high priests of Israel were sinful men, who had to offer sacrifices repeatedly, and that such sacrifices of animals could not fully bring forgiveness of sins (Heb. 5.1–3; 9.9; 10.1–4, 11). Unlike those priests, Jesus came as a perfect high priest, and made a perfect offering of Himself through His death on the cross. By this sacrifice of Himself, made once without any need of repetition, Christ has done all that is needed to put away sin and bring forgiveness (Heb. 7.26–28; 9.11–14, 25–26; 10.10–14). So, the writer concludes, where there is forgiveness, 'there is no longer any offering for sin' (10.18).

Instead of feeling that they were cut off from God, the first Christians learned to know and trust Him as a Father (Rom. 8.14–16; 1 John 3.1–2). Jesus had taught them that they all belonged to one heavenly Father, and this meant that they should live and act as brothers. None must claim a position of honour and respect like that claimed by Jewish religious teachers and leaders (Matt. 23.1–12). So the Church began its history without priests, and the sacrifices which it offered were the praise and thanksgiving and the lives of its members (Heb. 13.15–16; Rom. 12.1).

When we study the history of the Church we shall find that there have been many changes in what Christians have believed and taught about sacrifices. In the third century AD, Tertullian, a Christian leader in North Africa, wrote in answer to people who were puzzled by the fact that Christians had no temples, and offered no animals or incense in sacrifice: 'We do sacrifice, but in the way that God has commanded; that is by prayer alone; for God the creator of the Universe does not need any incense or blood.' And again; 'Prayer is the spiritual offering which has done away with the ancient sacrifices.' But from the third century AD onwards, we can trace the rise of the idea that in the Holy Communion (Eucharist, or Mass) the priest is offering a sacrifice to God for the remission of people's sins, and that this sacrifice is either a continuation or repetition of Christ's sacrifice on the Cross, and His offering of Himself to God. Later on this view was rejected by such reformers as Luther, Zwingli, and Cranmer.

3. THE PRIEST'S ROBES

For his holy task as one who was to bring Israel's sacrifices before God and to bring God's blessing to His people, the priest was dressed in very beautiful clothes (Exod. 28.4–43). This is another way in which the religion of the Israelites differed from that of the first Christians. For the first three or four hundred years of the Church's history Christian leaders wore no special robes, though when they came together to worship God they probably wore the best clothes they had. In Rome, in AD 423, the bishop Celestine complained that some clergy were introducing special robes. He wrote: 'By dressing in a pallium and wearing a girdle round their waist they think to fulfil the truth of Scripture, not in the spirit but in the letter. . . . We should be distinguished . . . by how we live, not by what we wear; by purity of thought, not by special clothes.' Between the ninth and twelfth centuries AD, many of the clergy thought that they should wear robes similar to those worn by Aaron, and a number of books were written on the subject. Some Christians today consider that it is good for the clergy to wear special clothes when they are leading services: others do not. In each case we need to ask, 'Is this a practice which helps people to worship God and to know the power of His Spirit in their lives?'

NOTES

28.1. Priests: In English the word 'priest' comes from the Greek word *presbyter*, which means 'elder'. It was shortened, first to 'prester', and then to 'priest'. We do not always use separate words to distinguish between (a)

'To serve God as priests' (p. 141).

At a seminary in the Philippines a lecturer leads a discussion with students training for the ministry. List some of the ways in which people are prepared for priesthood or other ordained ministry in the Church today. What sort of ministry do you think the students in the picture are likely to carry out?

a priest who offers sacrifice, and (b) a minister or elder or pastor who is the spiritual leader of a Christian congregation. This sometimes causes misunderstanding between Christians. Some may call their leaders 'priests', while others, who think of a priest as one who offers sacrifice on behalf of others, may feel very strongly that a Christian minister should not be called a priest.

28.6–14. The ephod: This was a kind of loin-cloth or skirt (1 Sam. 2.18; 2 Sam. 6.14). It was fastened by a girdle round the waist (28.8). It had two straps which went up over the priest's shoulders (28.7). The bottom edge of the breast-piece was fastened to these straps (28.26–28), so it is clear that the ephod did not cover the upper part of the body.

28.15–30. The breast piece: This was doubled over to form a square bag. On its front were fastened twelve precious stones, each engraved with the name of one of Israel's tribes.

Inside the bag were placed the Urim and Thummim. These were probably two sacred stones used for casting lots. When the leader of Israel sought for God's guidance (Num. 27.18–21; 1 Sam. 28.6), the priest probably put his hand in the bag and pulled out a stone. One stone would show the answer was 'Yes', and the other that it was 'No'. There is no reference to the actual use of Urim and Thummim after the time of David.

28.36–38: The golden plate on Aaron's forehead would show: (a) that Aaron was holy, and (b) that all Israel's gifts were meant to be holy. The prophet Zechariah looked forward to a time when every part of the life of God's people would be as holy as the gold plate on the High Priest's forehead (Zech. 14.20). In the Old Testament the word 'holy' has a fairly wide range of meaning. It means 'set apart for God', but it often means more than that. Holiness is part of God's nature; in saying 'Be holy, because I am holy' He is calling His people to reflect His nature. The holiness of God makes men feel both their littleness and their sinfulness: it calls forth both worship and humble confession of sin (Isa. 6.3–5). Thus a thing may become 'holy' by being set apart for a sacred use, but a person cannot be 'holy' unless he begins to share in the purity and goodness of God.

29.1–37: These commands were carried out after the Tabernacle had been made. You might find detailed notes in a commentary on Leviticus 8.

29.10–37. The offerings: The priest would look fine in his special clothes; but he was still a man. He was not perfect. Before he could serve as a priest, special sacrifices must be made. Even for a priest there was no way to come to God except by admitting he was a sinner and seeking to be forgiven.

Almost all religions have some ceremonies or methods of purification. These bear witness to the truth that 'all have sinned and fall short of the glory of God' (Rom. 3.23).

29.44. Priests: Since there was only one complete set of clothes (28.4–40), it is clear that Aaron was to be chief priest, and his sons were to be assistants. The title 'chief priest' or 'high priest' was not used until later in Israel's history—see Jeremiah 52.24; 2 Kings 22.4, 8; 2 Chronicles 19.11; 24.11; Haggai 1.1; Zechariah 3.1.

29.44: 'I will consecrate . . . Aaron': Special clothes and sacrifices were used to set apart Aaron and his sons for their holy work. But only God is truly holy. Only God can make people holy. Sacrifices by themselves cannot make people holy. So the climax of these instructions is a promise: God will come; by His presence He will make holy His people, their place of worship, and their priest (29.43–44).

STUDY SUGGESTIONS AND QUESTIONS

REVIEW OF CONTENT

1. What was the main work of the Israelite priests?
2. What were the main purposes of the Israelite sacrifices?
3. Write two or three sentences to show the meaning of the word 'holy'.

BIBLE STUDY AND REFLECTION

4. The Israelite priests offered sacrifices to God. God did not need the sacrifices (Ps. 50.10–13). Why do you think the Israelites needed them? Give examples to support your answer.
5. What can you learn from each of the following passages about the other work the priests did, besides offering sacrifices?
   (a) Num. 6.22–27 (b) Lev. 13—14 (c) Deut. 33.10 (d) Ezra 7.6 (e) Neh. 8.1–8
   Which of these priestly activities do you think Christians should also perform?
6. In the New Testament there are many leaders—apostles, elders, prophets, evangelists, deacons, and deaconesses. None of them are ever given the title of 'priest'. Why do you think this is? In what way do the following passages help us to find an answer?
   John 16.26–27 Heb. 9.24–28; 10.11–14 Matt. 23.1–12 Eph. 2.11–22.
7. The Israelite priests wore special clothes. In what ways do you think it may be (a) helpful and (b) unhelpful for Christian pastors to wear special clothes: (i) when they are leading services for a congregation, and (ii) at other times?

30.1—31.18

The Tabernacle: more Instructions

OUTLINE AND CONTEXT

30.1–10: The golden altar for incense.
30.11–16: The silver half-shekel for atonement.
30.17–21: The bronze bowl for washing.
30.22–38: Spices for the anointing oil and incense.
31.1–11: The craftsmen to make the Tabernacle.
31.12–17: The Sabbath must be kept.
31.18: The two stone tablets of the Covenant.

Exodus 28—29 described the priests who were to serve in the Tabernacle. Exodus 30 gives further instructions for making the Tabernacle, especially for the things the priests would need in order to carry out their work. Exodus 31 completes the instructions for making the Tabernacle by telling of the craftsmen who were to do the work.

INTERPRETATION AND COMMENT

1. THE INCENSE ALTAR

Spices and gums were mixed to make incense (30.34–36). The incense was burned on a special altar within the holy place. Because of its sweet smell, incense has been used by people of many religions, both as an offering to God, and as a means of producing a pleasant and suitable smell in the places where people meet for worship.

In Psalm 141.2 and Revelation 5.8 and 8.3–4 incense is mentioned as a symbol of prayer. As we read about the costly incense which Aaron had to burn each morning and each evening, we may think about the importance of prayer in our own lives. Do we pray each day? Is it helpful to pray each morning and each evening? We sometimes say, 'Time is money'—are we ready to set aside for God each day something that is costly? Or do we say, 'Yes, I would like to pray, but I really haven't got time'?

Once each year the chief priest of the Israelites had to perform a special rite of atonement. This was on the tenth day of the seventh month (Lev. 16.29). Notice in Leviticus 16.16 how many different words are used to show that there is something wrong with the people whom God calls to be His: for example, uncleanness, transgressions, sins. Even the purest of their offerings (30.35) were not worthy of God to whom they were offered. So the ritual of the Day of Atonement had two important lessons to teach the people of Israel: (1) 'You are not good enough for God' (compare Heb.

10.3); and (2) 'God loves you and forgives you, for it is He who has provided this way of sacrifice' (compare 1 John 1.5—2.2). We should never separate these two truths. A woman patient in a mental hospital refused to eat food or drink water: she had been told that she was a sinner and she felt she did not deserve to live. She found it difficult to believe that God loved her and wanted to forgive her. It is true that we are all sinners, but when we tell people this truth we must always tell them also about God's love for us, and about His ways of forgiving us and cleansing us from every sort of sin.

2. THE RANSOM MONEY (30.11–16)

As a symbol of atonement, the people were to give money offerings for the making of the Tabernacle. The money was collected when the census, or count, of the people was made (see note on 30.11, p. 150). Notice that each person gave the same amount (30.14–15). Every person's life is of equal value to God. He does not favour rich men more than poor (Job 34.19); nor should we (James 2.1–9). A man's wealth made no difference to the ransom that must be paid for his life.

In the Old Testament the word 'ransom' usually means a payment made so that a person need not die (Exod. 21.30; Job 33.24; Prov. 13.8). So when a writer mentions a ransom he usually has the following ideas in mind:

(a) Some wrong has been done.
(b) As a result, someone is in danger of death.
(c) Something costly is given so that the person may be set free. What is given may be gifts, money, or a life laid down in sacrifice.
(d) The person is then set free, and is able to live again as a free person.

When a ransom is offered to God these ideas also are found:

(a) People have offended God.
(b) He is rightly opposed to all that is evil.
(c) Yet He Himself provides the way of offering by which people may be restored and live in a right relationship to Him (notice Lev. 17.11, in which the blood of atonement is described as something which 'God has given for you upon the altar').

Many of the New Testament writers used these ideas of ransom as one way of explaining the meaning of Christ's death.

3. ANOINTING

In Israel priests were anointed (Exod. 30.30), and also kings (1 Sam. 15.1; 1 Kings 1.39). The anointing marked them out as men chosen by God for a special position or special work. Isaiah 61.1 refers to someone specially chosen by God and anointed by His Spirit: 'The Spirit of the Lord God is upon me, *because the Lord has anointed me* to bring good tidings to the afflicted; He has sent me to bind up the broken hearted, to proclaim liberty to the captives and the opening of the prison to those who are bound.' Jesus said that He was the one to whom this prophecy referred (see Luke 4.16–21). It was because His followers recognized Him as the Anointed One that they gave Him the title *Messiah*, or Christ. (*Messiah* is a Hebrew word for 'the anointed one', and *Christos* is the Greek for 'the anointed one'.)

In the Christian Church, the practice of anointing with oil has been used in ministry to sick people. (See James 5.14–16 'Is any among you sick? Let him call for the elders of the Church, and let them pray over him, anointing him with oil in the name of the Lord.' Compare also Mark 6.13.) But the practice is not used in all Churches. If it is to be more widely used, we need to renew our faith that Christ is still at work to heal people today.

4. GOD GIVES HIS SERVANTS CREATIVE ABILITIES, SO THAT THEY CAN WORK FOR HIM

God told Moses that He had given skill to the men who would make the Tabernacle (Exod. 28.3; 31.3–4). He is the great creator (Gen. 1). What He makes is good (Gen. 1.31). Skill in making beautiful things is a gift from God.

God is the God of the whole of our lives. He does not limit His interest only to our prayers and our preaching. Some Christians in a rural area in Mexico invented new and better ways of weaving cloth and making ropes. This helped them and other people to earn more money and to improve the way they lived. The Christians said, 'God has redeemed our minds, and God has redeemed our hands: that is why we can learn to do things better and to help other people.'

If we believe that God gives us our wisdom and abilities, we shall not boast about them. Paul, in his first letter to the Christians at Corinth, said, 'If you have received a gift from God, how can you boast about it as if it was something you had achieved yourself?' (see 1 Cor. 4.6–7, and compare James 3.13–18).

5. THE TWO TABLETS OF TESTIMONY (31.18)

A better translation is 'the two tablets of the covenant'. Psalm 99.7 shows that the word here translated in the RSV as 'testimonies' means 'laws that must be kept'. Exodus 24.12 and 34.28 show that what was written on the tablets was the 'words of God'; that is, the Ten Commandments (see Exod. 20.1–17). These set out: (a) God's claim to be Israel's Lord and King, and (b) the two basic demands of the Covenant: that the Israelites should be loyal to the LORD as the only God, and that they should be honest and loving to other people.

We may wonder why there were *two* tablets. The stone tablets were inscribed on the back as well as on the front (32.15), so the words would fit on quite a small tablet. It is at first difficult to understand why two were needed. Perhaps we can find the reason for making two tablets when we study the international treaties of the time. When such treaties were made, the kings or chiefs usually made two copies of the treaty or covenant (see note on 25.10–22, p. 139). This was (a) so that each king or chief could have a copy of the treaty to keep in his land, and (b) so that no one could easily change the words of the treaty. One Hittite treaty says, 'Whoever changes even one word of this tablet, may the thousand gods of this tablet root that man out of the land of the Hittites.'

So it seems likely that on each of the two tablets of the Covenant there was written all ten of the Commandments. The making of two tablets would show: (a) that both God and Israel should be faithful in keeping the promise made in the Covenant; and (b) that the laws of the Covenant were fixed and should not be changed.

NOTES

30.1–38: The subjects mentioned in this chapter seem to have been arranged by the writer in order, according to the materials that were to be used: 30.3 gold; 30.13 half shekel, which is silver; 30.17 bronze; 30.22 spices. This is the same order of materials as we find in 25.3–6: 'gold, silver, and bronze . . . spices for the anointing oil and for the fragrant incense . . .'

30.1. An altar to burn incense upon: Egyptians, Canaanites, and Babylonians all used incense in their worship. Special altars for burning incense have been found in many parts of Palestine. Most of them belong to the period 1000–300 BC.

30.6. Before the veil: The incense altar was to be placed in the holy place, near to the veil which shut off the most holy place (see diagram).

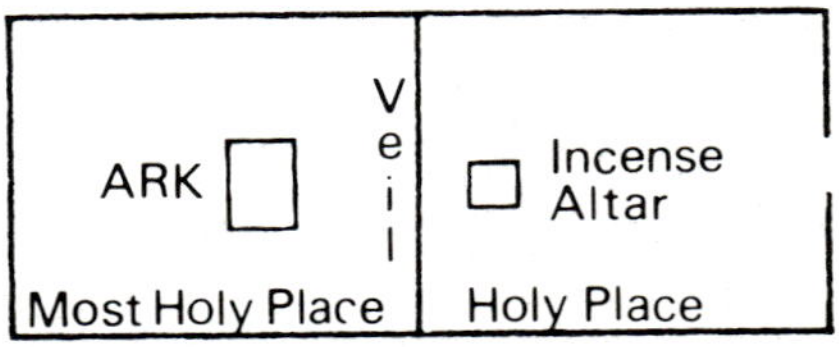

30.7. When he dresses the lamps: That is, when he cleans the lamps and trims their wicks.

30.10. Once a year: See Leviticus 16.1–34, for the Day of Atonement.

30.11. The census: The census was a recording by name and counting of all men over twenty years old. Men over twenty could be called on to serve as soldiers. In Mesopotamia the taking of a census was considered to be dangerous, so special ceremonies of purification were carried out.

We cannot be certain why people were afraid. Perhaps they had noticed that whenever there was a census, more people than usual fell ill. They did not at that time know that some diseases are infectious and can be widely spread when a large number of people have been meeting together. Or they may have been afraid: either (a) that their gods might be angry that men were finding out what only the gods should know, or (b) that the writing down of their names would give some god or man a magic power over them.

30.16. Money: The Hebrew word means 'silver'.

30.16. For the service of the tent: This means 'for the construction of the Tabernacle' (compare 25.1–9; 35.21; 36.3–5). It does not mean that they collected the money for sacrifices or services of worship in the Tabernacle.

30.17–21. A laver of bronze: The bronze laver was a round bowl to contain water for washing the hands and feet of the priests. In Solomon's temple there was not just one laver, but ten small ones and one enormous one (1 Kings 7.23–29).

30.22–33. The anointing oil: The spices would be soaked in water for several days and boiled. The scented liquid would then be mixed with the olive oil (30.24). The anointing was done by sprinkling a little oil on each person or article (Lev. 8.11). Spices were rare and costly, and some had to be brought from far tropical countries. So the trade in spices was very profitable (Gen. 37.25).

31.1. I have called by name . . .: This means, 'I have appointed the named person to do a special work' (compare Isa. 43.1; 45.4; 49.1).

31.18. Written with the finger of God: Compare 8.15, where the words 'with the finger of God' mean 'by God's power'. We need not suppose that the Israelites thought that God actually had a finger and wrote on stone tablets with it. According to 34.27–28, it was Moses who did the inscribing.

STUDY SUGGESTIONS AND QUESTIONS

REVIEW OF CONTENT

1. What lessons were taught by the Israelite rites of atonement, (a) about people, and (b) about God?
2. What do the Old Testament writers mean by the word 'ransom'?
3. What was the purpose and meaning of anointing?
4. What is the meaning of the words 'Messiah' and 'Christ'?
5. What were 'the two tablets of testimony'?

BIBLE STUDY AND REFLECTION

6. *Failure:*

   (a) 'Each year the chief priest had to perform a special rite of atonement', because even the purest of the people's offerings were not worthy of God (p. 147). People who try to serve God often feel that they have failed to do as well as they should, or have failed to be the sort of people they ought to be. What do you think we should do if we have such feelings?

(b) When other people look at the work of Christian Churches and missionaries, they often say, 'You have not done well enough.' How do you think we should react if people criticize us in this way?

7. *Ransom:* Look up the following New Testament references to 'ransom': Mark 10.45; 1 Timothy 2.6; 1 Peter 1.18–19. Which of the ideas mentioned in section 2 of the Interpretation (p. 148) best help you to understand what these New Testament writers meant, when they said that Christ gave Himself as a 'ransom' for us?
8. *Gifts:* Read again Exodus 31.1–5.

(a) Some people consider that practical skill and craftsmanship is something quite different from the spiritual gifts of love and faith. Others consider that both practical and spiritual 'talents' are gifts from God, which people may use to glorify Him and to help other people. Which opinion do you think most people hold? What is your own opinion?

(b) What encouragement is given to art and to craftsmanship in your country? In your Church? Are you yourself satisfied with things as they are? If not, what changes do you think need to be made? Do you think there is anything that you yourself should do? If so, what?

(c) 'If we believe that God gives us our wisdom and abilities, we shall not boast about them' (p. 149). What can we learn from the following passages: (1) about the pride of those who trust in their own wisdom, and (2) about the humility of those who know that their gifts are given to them by God? Isa. 10.12–19 Ezek. 28.1–10 Dan. 4.28–33 1 Cor. 4.6–7 James 3.13–18.

32.1–35

The Israelites break the Covenant

OUTLINE AND COMMENT

32.1–6: The Israelites made a golden bull and worshipped it.
32.7–14: Moses prayed for the Israelites.
32.15–35: The Israelites were punished.

Exodus 19—31 has told the story of the making of the Covenant, and the instructions for the building of the Tabernacle as a place where God, the giver of the Covenant, would manifest His presence. Exodus 32 shows how the people of Israel broke the Covenant, even before the Tabernacle was made. This leads on to the renewal of the Covenant (Exod. 33—34) and the construction of the Tabernacle (Exod. 35—40).

INTERPRETATION AND COMMENT

1. WHAT DID THE ISRAELITES DO, AND WHY?

Moses had been on the mountain top for a long time. The people of Israel were afraid that he might never come down. They seemed to have lost the man who led them out of Egypt. But this was not their only fear. Their journey through the wilderness was difficult. Ahead of them was the land of Canaan, an unknown land full of tribes who would be their enemies. As they faced these difficulties without Moses there to lead them, they also felt that God was far off. Some of the Israelites decided that they needed to have a god with them, a god who would go at their head on the journey that lay before them. So they made a golden image of a bull. They said, 'This is our god'. They offered sacrifices, and they drank and danced before the golden bull.

The Israelites had been living in Egypt, where the people believed that there were hundreds of gods. These gods were represented by thousands of images. Probably many of the Israelites thought it was sensible for them to have an image too.

And why a bull? In Egypt and in Canaan bulls were symbols of the gods of fertility, sexual power, and strength. As the Israelites went forward into Canaan they would need strength to defeat their enemies, and fertility for the land they conquered. So a god represented by a young bull would be suited to their needs.

In Canaan, as we have seen, sexual intercourse was an important part of some religious festivals. The Canaanites believed that it would persuade the gods to grant fertility to the people, to their flocks, and to their soil. The Israelites probably shared this sort of belief as they ate and drank and danced before the golden bull (32.6, 19).

2. WHY WERE THE ISRAELITES WRONG IN WHAT THEY DID?

The writer of Exodus clearly believed that the Israelites were wrong in making the golden bull and worshipping as they did. But we may ask, 'Why were they wrong? Should people not be free to worship God in whatever ways they consider to be helpful?' Here are some of the reasons which the writer of Exodus and other Old Testament writers give, to show why the Israelites were wrong:

(a) *They were disobeying God* (32.8): God had told them not to make images to use in worship (20.4–5, 23). But they thought they knew a better way. This reminds us of the story of Man as it is told in Genesis 3: Adam (Man) was given one clear command by God, but he thought he could do better by disobeying God the creator. When man uses a machine of any sort, he needs to follow the maker's instruction. If the maker's instruction says 'Use only petrol in this machine', the man will spoil the machine if he tries to make it run on kerosene. Similarly, we can spoil our lives if we choose not to follow our Maker's instructions.

(b) *They were breaking their promise:* The people of Israel had promised to keep the laws which God had given them (24.7). Those laws said, 'Do not make any image and worship it' (20.4–5). So the Israelites were breaking their promise.

We live in a world where many people make promises. Parents make promises to their children. When they marry, men and women make promises to each other. Employers and those whom they employ make promises about the wages they will pay and accept. Politicians promise what they will do if they are elected. In our prayers, we make promises to God. The making and keeping of promises is an important part of life.

(c) *They were worshipping something they had made:* They thought they were worshipping God (Exod. 32.4–5), but in fact they worshipped something which they themselves had made (compare Ps. 106.19–22 and Isa. 2.8). When people do this, they easily forget what God is really like (see Isa. 40.12–26; 44.6–20; 46.3–11). Idolatry tends to turn true religion upside down. In the place which should belong to God who makes us, we put an idol we have made. Instead of a God who desires to control us, we put an idol which we can control.

Someone wrote a book called 'Your God is too small'. If we make an image, we have a God who is too small. And this remains so, whether the image is made of something material, or whether it is made as a picture in our minds. If we make a picture in our minds of God as an old man, it may help us to think of God as being wise, but it will also make us think of God as being weak: we shall have a God who is too small. God is not small: He is the creator of the whole vast universe.

(d) *They were taking part in dances and sexual practices like those in Canaanite fertility rituals:* Such dances expressed a wrong idea about God, a wrong idea about the world, and a wrong idea about sexual intercourse. People who took part in them believed that God could be helped by their rituals, that power could thus be released in the world of nature. They believed that sexual intercourse was a channel through which that power could be released. The prophets of Israel taught that God does not need the help of any religious rituals. He alone has all the power that is needed to control the world He has made, and sexual intercourse is not a part of the worship He demands.

In many parts of the world today, dancing and drinking go together with practices which Christian people find they want to avoid. A Sioux Indian woman in America said: 'I used to be a wicked woman . . . but one time people came and prayed for me. And Jesus set me free from all the things, all the bad things I was going through, especially the Indian dances, all the witchcraft and everything I've done.' An English girl wrote, 'I am 15 years old. I am pregnant. I am not married. This only happened because I

'The people said: "Make us gods, who shall go before us"' (Exod. 32.1). 'In the place which should belong to God we put an idol' (p. 154).

Women and girls in Gambia wear dresses printed with the portraits of political leaders and pop stars, and some people say that these are the 'idols' of today. What other sorts of 'gods' do people mainly worship today instead of the Lord?

went to a party. After we had been drinking, my boy-friend made love to me.' This does not mean that all dancing is bad and that all drinking is bad. But it does suggest that, before we take part in dancing and drinking, we need to ask ourselves: 'Is this something which God would want me to do?'

(e) *They did this because they were afraid:* The people of Israel were afraid of what might happen to them in the future. Aaron was afraid to refuse to do what the people wanted. When we are afraid of suffering, of losing a job, or losing our reputation, it is very easy to tell lies or to do what is wrong. But if we know that God is in control of the world and of our lives, then we need not be afraid. As you read the books of the Old Testament, notice how often God's message to His people was, 'Do not be afraid.'

3. MOSES PRAYED FOR THE PEOPLE OF ISRAEL

Moses cared very much for the people whom he had been called to lead. So he prayed for them (32.11–13, 30–32). He knew they had done wrong (32.31), but he was not selfish. He was not prepared to receive God's blessing for himself while they could not receive it (32.10). If they had to suffer for what they had done, he wanted to suffer and die with them (32.32).

Moses also cared very much for God. In his first prayer he said, 'You told the Egyptians that you wanted us to leave Egypt. If they hear that we have been destroyed, they will think: "The God of the Israelites has no power".' (32.11–13.) Moses also said, 'You promised to give the land of Canaan to the descendants of Abraham—not to my descendants. People must see that you keep your promises' (compare Neh. 1.4–11).

These prayers of Moses can help us to think about our own prayers for other people. It is not easy for us to pray for people who are in trouble or in need. When we pray for them we may sometimes feel within ourselves the anxiety or sin or suffering which they bear. We may also find ourselves called to go and suffer with them and to work hard for their deliverance. This is the way of Jesus, to come and bear the suffering brought by the world's sin, so that He may set us free. This is the way the Japanese Christian, T. Kagawa, walked, when he went to live and work among the poorest people in Japan.

Moses prayed for the people of Israel not only because he cared for them but also because he cared about God. He wanted other people to be able to say, 'They trusted in God and He helped them.' In all our prayers for ourselves and for others we need to ask that the answer to our prayers may cause people to trust in God and to follow Him.

4. PUNISHMENT (32.25)

When we read this story of how the Levites killed about three thousand men, we are likely to ask many questions. For example, 'Did God really want them to kill all those people, or did Moses and the Levites fail to understand what God wanted them to do?' This is not an easy question to answer.

Some Christians say: 'God was guiding Moses. His Spirit inspired the writing of the Book of Exodus. Therefore we can be sure that God wanted the Levites to kill those who were guilty of idolatry.' Other Christians say: 'God is not pleased by the death of sinners. He would rather give them a chance to live, and to turn back to Him. Therefore we believe that when the Book of Exodus was written, the people of Israel had not yet learned enough of the truth of God's love and mercy.'

Perhaps there is some truth in both of these views. God did reveal Himself more fully to people in the life and death and resurrection of Jesus. From Jesus's example and His teaching, from His power to heal, to encourage, and to change men and women, we have learned more of what God is like. Jesus did show and teach a way of forgiveness, and of willingness to suffer as a result of the evil that people do. But he did not ever say that people must not be punished for doing what is wrong. When the Roman soldiers crucified Jesus, they also crucified two men who had taken part in rebellion, violence, and murder. These men asked Jesus to save them. Jesus did not say to them, 'I am sorry you must suffer like this: it is all the fault of a wrong system of government.' But to the man who admitted that he deserved to be put to death for the evil he had done, Jesus said, 'You will be with me, today, in Paradise.'

Even when we have learnt from Jesus His way of loving and forgiving, we still find ourselves in a world spoiled by human hatred and wrong-doing. In such a world there is a place for punishment, just as there is a need for pain. No one likes to suffer pain. Yet it is good for us that we can feel pain. A man with leprosy is likely to burn and cut and damage his hands and feet, because he has lost the sense of pain that would warn him not to approach too near the fire, nor to handle the blade of a knife. A surgeon who worked for many years among lepers said, 'If I could give them one gift it would be the gift of pain.' We do not like pain, but we need to be able to feel it. We do not like punishment, but it would not be good for us to live in a world in which those who do evil were never punished.

5. AN UNCOMFORTABLE GOD

Sometimes people say, 'There is no God.' Then they try to explain how it is that so many people believe in God. And they say something like this: 'People find life difficult. They often feel lonely, and unable to face the sorrows and problems of life. So they invent a God, and believe that He will be with them and help them. In this way they find comfort as they face the loneliness and the difficult problems of their lives.'

To people who say this, we can reply that the God who is revealed in the Scriptures of the Old Testament and the New Testament is not a comfortable God. He is a consuming fire, not a comfortable chair. He is a God who calls us to love our fellow men, to pray, to work, and to suffer for their good. He is a God who disciplines those who trust in Him, and who judges those who turn away from Him. If people had wished for a divine friend to comfort them, they would have invented a God very different from the One who reveals Himself to us through the written Word of the Scriptures, and through the living Word who is His Son.

NOTES

32.1–24: Notice how the writer of the Book of Exodus tells this story in a way which shows: (a) that idolatry is both foolish and dangerous, and (b) that Aaron acted weakly in doing what the people demanded. An action is not made right simply because many people demand that we should do it. Compare with this story the story of Balaam (Num. 22—24), which shows how foolish it is to try to use any kind of religion, magic, or prophecy to oppose God's will for His people.

32.1. To Aaron: The Hebrew word translated 'to' in the RSV should perhaps be translated 'against', as it is in Numbers 16.3, 19. The people came to Aaron with a demand: they wanted him to do as they said, whether he liked it or not.

32.4. A molten calf: The Hebrew word translated as 'calf' in the RSV means a bull. It may refer to a young bull or to a fully grown one. In Psalm 106.20 the image is called an ox (that is, a grown bull). 'Molten' means made of metal which has been melted. The gold was melted, either to make a solid golden image, or to make thin gold plate for covering a wooden statue.

32.4. These are your gods: or, as in the Jerusalem Bible, 'Here is your God'. With this story in Exodus, compare the story about Jeroboam in 1 Kings 12.25–28. The two stories are similar. Both are about idolatry. In one the idol is a golden bull, in the other there are two golden bulls. Why was this story in Exodus 32 written down? Scholars have suggested several different reasons. Here are some of them:

(a) Because this is what happened, and the writer wrote it down to warn the people of Israel not to take part in idolatry.

(b) Because the descendants of Aaron were high priests, and other families wished to claim the high priesthood. So they invented this story to try and show that Aaron was not worthy to be high priest. This idea is not very easy to accept, because the story in Exodus 32 does not chiefly blame Aaron: it shows that the *people* urged Aaron to make the image.

(c) Because the priests in Bethel in the time of Jeroboam wanted to prove that they were right to use a golden bull for worship: so they wrote or told a story saying that Aaron, the first high-priest, had made one. (If so, their story must have been altered by a later editor, for the story in Exodus

32 does not suggest that Aaron did what was right: it shows clearly that such idolatry is wrong.)

(d) Because the prophets in Israel after the time of Jeroboam I wanted to condemn the worship at Bethel and Dan: so they made up this story about Aaron's idolatry to show that idolatry is always wrong, however important the priest who leads such worship. (We must note, however, that the prophets Amos and Hosea were able to condemn the worship at Bethel and Dan without needing to use any stories about Aaron.)

Reasons (b), (c), and (d) can only be valid if the Book of Exodus was not written, or not completely written, until the eighth century BC or later (see Special Note E, pp. 184–191).

32.10. Of you I will make a great nation: Compare Genesis 12.2–3. Moses had the opportunity to become a new Abraham. But he saw that this would not bring glory to God: people would praise God when they saw that He kept the promise He had made to Abraham (32.11–13).

32.13. Abraham, Isaac, and Israel: The promise of the land of Canaan was repeated to each of them—to Abraham (Gen. 13.14–17); to Isaac (Gen. 26.2–4); and to Jacob (Gen. 28.13–15).

32.14. The LORD repented: We may say, 'God never does what is wrong, so how can He repent?' To answer this question we need to study the difference between the meaning of the English word 'repent', and the meaning of the Hebrew word which is here translated 'repent'. Because repentance is such an important idea in the New Testament, we will also consider its meaning in the New Testament.

The Hebrew word usually includes the ideas of sorrow and compassion; e.g. in Judges 21.6 the RSV translation of it is 'had compassion'. In fact it is used in three different ways, to show, either:

1. that a person (a) feels sorry for someone, and (b) acts to help them (see Judges 21.6); or
2. that a person (a) is thinking of doing something, but (b) out of compassion or sorrow he changes his mind and does not do it (see Joel 2.13 and Jonah 4.2); or
3. that a person (a) says he will do something, but (b) because he is deceitful, does not do it (see 1 Sam. 15.29).

So the Old Testament writers are not saying that God changes His actions because of anything wrong in Himself (1 Sam. 15.29). They are saying that if people listen and respond when God warns them of the punishment He has in mind to bring upon them, then He may spare them because He is loving and merciful (Jonah 4.2; Joel 2.13; Exod. 32.14).

We may find this difficult to understand, because in English the word 'repent' usually shows that: (a) a person has done wrong; (b) he sees that he has done wrong; and so (c) *he feels sorry that he has done wrong.*

In the New Testament the Greek word translated 'repent' (see, for example, Mark 1.14) means that: (a) a person has been wrong, or has done wrong; (b) he sees that this is so; (c) he is sorry; (d) *he turns away from the wrong and has a new attitude of mind.*

So in the New Testament the most important aspect of repentance is that a person *changes* to a new attitude of mind; a new attitude towards himself and towards God. We shall not understand what repentance means in the New Testament if we think it only means feeling sorry for what we have done.

Because words have different meanings in different languages, the task of a Bible translator is often very difficult. It is also easy for people to misunderstand each other. For example, in some of the languages of Uganda the word used for 'repent' means: (a) that someone has done wrong; and (b) *that he makes a public confession* (to the family or clan) *that he has done wrong*. Because of this, sometimes one Christian in Uganda would say to another, 'You have not repented' (meaning 'you have not confessed your sins publicly'), and the other would reply, 'I have repented' (meaning 'I have turned from my sins to God'). So people failed to understand each other, and each considered the other to be wrong.

32.14. Of the evil: The writers of the Old Testament did not believe that God ever does wrong. But when they suffered, they felt that their suffering was 'bad' (evil). When they said that God brought evil upon them, they did not mean that God was doing wrong. If we think about what sometimes happens to boys at school, it may help us to understand this. A boy who has done wrong and has been punished may say, 'I had a bad day at school: I was punished for not doing my work.' The boy experiences the punishment as bad, he does not like it; but he does not mean that the schoolmaster did wrong in punishing him.

32.29. for the service of the Lord: See Numbers 3—4 for the special work which the Levites were to do. Some scholars have suggested that Exodus 32.25–29 was written to show why the Levites were priests. But notice that this verse (32.29) does *not* say the Levites were ordained to serve 'as priests': contrast 28.1, 3, 41 which refers to Aaron and his sons. Because Aaron was a Levite, all the priests descended from him were also members of the tribe of Levi; but there were many other members of the tribe who were not priests. All priests were Levites, but not all the Levites were priests.

32.32. If thou wilt forgive their sins . . . : The sentence is not finished. It means, 'If you will forgive them, that will be good, and I will continue to lead them.'

32.32. blot me . . . out of thy book: that is, let me die.

STUDY SUGGESTIONS AND QUESTIONS

REVIEW OF CONTENT

1. Why did the people of Israel demand that Aaron should make a god for them?
2. Why did Aaron do so?
3. What sort of god did Aaron make, and what did it symbolize?
4. Why did God condemn the action of Aaron and the Israelites?
5. What did Moses pray for?

BIBLE STUDY AND REFLECTION

6. What is the chief difference between the idea of 'repentance' as expressed by the Old Testament writers, and the idea of repentance as expressed in the New Testament? What differences are there between these ideas, and the ideas expressed by the word for 'repentance' in your own language?
7. *Idolatry:* Read Isaiah 40.12–23; 41.1–10, 21–29; 42.8–9, 17; 43.8–13; 44.9–20; 45.16–23; 46.1–11; and 48.3–5.
   Make a list of what is said in these passages:
   (a) about God,
   (b) about idols,
   (c) about those who make idols and trust in them.
8. (a) Do people in your country make idols? If so, how do they make them and how do they use them? Do they think the idol is a god, or that it represents a god? If not, what do they believe?
   (b) What would you reply to someone who said: 'It is sensible to make idols, because they help us in our worship'?
9. *Dancing and worship:* The Israelites danced when they worshipped and thanked God for saving them from Egypt (Exod. 15). They also danced before the golden idol.
   (a) What differences can you find between these two occasions of dancing?
   (b) Why was one dance acceptable to God and the other not?
   (c) How would you decide whether any particular sort of dance is suitable for use in Christian worship?
10. *Prayer:* (a) Moses prayed for the Israelites because he cared for them. Discuss the following statement: 'We can tell how much we care for people by considering how much we pray for them.'
    (b) Read the prayers of Moses in Exodus 32.11–13, and 32.31–32. Compare them with this prayer, 'Lord, please bless me and my family.' What are the main differences you notice? What do you think we can learn from the prayers of Moses, about our own way of praying?

11. *Promises:* 'The making and keeping of promises is an important part of life' (p. 154).
(a) What do you consider are the most important promises people make in their lives?
(b) In what ways do people most often break the promises they have made? Why do you think they do this? How do you think people can be helped to keep their promises?
(c) What would you say to someone who said, 'I only need to keep my promises if it seems useful to me to keep them'?
(d) Have you failed to keep any of the promises you have made? If so, what can you do about it?

33.1—34.35

'God will go with us'

OUTLINE AND CONTEXT

33.1–6: God said that the Israelites had made it impossible for Him to go with them on their journey to Canaan.
33.7–17: Moses prayed. God promised to go with them.
33.18—34.9: Moses saw the glory of God.
34.10–28: The Covenant was renewed.
34.29–35: The face of Moses shone when he had been with God.

INTERPRETATION AND COMMENT

1. THE RENEWAL OF THE COVENANT

When a young man marries a young woman, people are usually glad. They know that this can be the beginning of a long and happy life together. If, a few months later, they hear that the woman has left her husband, they are sad. If the husband truly loves her, he too is sad and lonely. He wants her to come back to him. If we understand this, it will help us to understand the story in Exodus 33—34 about the re-making of the Covenant.

God had taken the Israelites as His people. He had promised them blessing 'to the thousandth generation' if they would be loyal to Him. (20.6). They had promised to be faithful to Him (24.7). After a few weeks they broke their promise (Exod. 32). They were like a wife who leaves her husband. They soon knew that they had done wrong. Then, for a time, it seemed as if God would not be with them any more.

However, Exodus 33—34 tells a happier story. It shows that God does not stop loving people when they do what is wrong. When He punishes them it is not only because they deserve to be punished, but also so that they may come back to Him. When the Israelites came back to God and the Covenant was renewed, it was wonderful for Israel. It was like a marriage being made again.

2. 'WILL GOD GO AHEAD OF HIS PEOPLE OR WITH THEM?'

God had promised to go with the Israelites, (a) to protect them on their journey, and (b) to bring them into Canaan (23.20). Now He said to Moses that He would go ahead of His people to drive out the Canaanites (33.2), but that He would not go with them (33.3). This made Moses and the Israelites sad. They took off their ornaments as a sign of their sorrow.

Then Moses prayed (33.12–13). He wanted to say to God, 'Go with us!' But he said it very politely: 'Let me know whom you will send with us' (33.12). It was not enough for Moses that God would go ahead of them. He wanted to be sure that God would go *with* them.

God gave Moses a promise: 'I will go with you and give you rest' (33.14). Moses wanted to be sure about this, so (a) he repeated: 'We don't want to go without you' (33.15), (b) he asked God to show His presence in a special way (33.17–18), and (c) he reminded God that His promise would mean going with a sinful people and being loving and forgiving (34.9).

To walk in God's ways and to know that He is with us is one of the greatest of all blessings. The Christian life is not a matter of struggling through difficulties alone, hoping that in the end we shall be with God in heaven. It is a life of going forward *with* God now. It is a life in which we experience God's presence and guidance and blessing day by day, and know that in the end we shall have the joy of seeing Him face to face.

3. GOD IS MERCIFUL (34.6–8)

When God revealed Himself to Moses, He spoke to him. First of all He said, 'The LORD, the LORD' (in Hebrew, 'Yahweh, Yahweh'). For God is God. There is nothing and no one else that is really like Him. God is always greater than any of the word-pictures we can use to describe Him. If someone asks us what a rat is like, we may perhaps say, 'It is like a mouse, only it is much bigger.' But if someone asks us what an elephant is like, all we can say is that an elephant is like an elephant! There is no other animal like it, so we cannot easily describe an elephant. God is far greater and more wonderful than anything we know. So it is difficult to describe Him. We may, for example, say that He is like a good father, but this word-picture of a 'good father' can only express a part of God's nature. He is always Himself, and beyond any description we can give.

God went on to reveal more of His nature to Moses (34.6–7):

He is merciful—He loves us tenderly.

He is gracious—He is kind to us although we do not deserve it.

He does not quickly become angry—He is patient with us when we go wrong.

He abounds in steadfast love—He loves us constantly, as a husband who goes on loving his wife, or as a mother who always cares for her children.

He is faithful—He speaks the truth and keeps the promises He has made.

He is forgiving—He accepts us back when we have been unfaithful to Him.

He is also just—He will not say of a guilty person, that he is innocent.

When we read the New Testament we find this revealing of God's nature made more plain in the life and character of Jesus Christ.

4. THE RELIGIONS OF CANAAN (34.11–17)

The people of Israel were warned not to follow any of the religions of Canaan. When they entered any part of the land, they must destroy the Canaanite places of worship. They must avoid any kind of union with the Canaanites which might tempt them to follow Canaanite ways of belief and worship.

Some people, when they read such passages in Exodus, find it difficult to understand why the Israelites were told to have nothing to do with Canaanite worship. Such people believe that all religions are ways to God; and some of them also think that it does not matter what religion a person follows so long as he is sincere.

We can better understand why the Israelites were warned to take no part in Canaanite religion if we know something about the gods which the Canaanites worshipped. For example, in the Canaanite stories about their gods we find that the god El dethroned his father and castrated him. El also killed his favourite son and cut off his daughter's head. Anath, Astarte and Asherah were goddesses of war and sex. Anath was a prostitute among the gods. She also delighted in slaughtering people, and when she waded in blood up to her knees 'her heart was full of joy.' The worship of Anath included prostitution of both men and women. Such a religion was neither true nor good. The writers of both the Old and the New Testament insisted that the people of God must learn to know the difference between what is good and what is bad, and between what is true and what is false in religion. 'Test everything: hold fast what is good' (1 Thess. 5.21).

5. A SHINING FACE

When Moses came down from Mount Sinai, his face shone, 'because he had been talking with God' (34.29). Moses is the only person in the Old Testament of whom this is said. It seems that this kind of radiance of face is not something that God gives to everyone. But sometimes when people draw near to God He gives them an experience similar to that of Moses. For example, a few years ago a pastor was spending a few days of rest and prayer in a Christian community. He was feeling very depressed, and found it difficult to pray. Then one morning he prayed, 'Lord, make this a day of praise for you.' During the service of Holy Communion he felt the heaviness and darkness lifted from him. He felt himself to be in heaven, before the Lord, worshipping and adoring Him. He said, 'My face felt as if it was burning.' Someone sitting near him told him later that it was obvious that something wonderful was happening to him, and he himself said, 'If heaven is as wonderful as that, then I thank God that He has saved me from death through Jesus, and promised me a place in glory with Him for ever.'

Not every Christian has such experiences of God. But all who come to God and begin to find His peace and His joy may expect that this will show in their faces in some way. As the Psalmist said, 'Every face turned to Him grows brighter' (Ps. 34.5 JB).

In 2 Corinthians 3 Paul discussed the glory that was seen on Moses' face. He said that Christians share in a greater glory, because the Spirit of God is at work within them. He is at work to make us like Jesus, and this means being changed 'from one degree of glory to another' (2 Cor. 3.18).

NOTES

33.1–16. I will not go up among you . . . My presence will go with you . . . : In the section Interpretation and Comment we have tried to interpret the text of the Book of Exodus as we find it in our Bibles. Some scholars think this is a wrong way to interpret it. They say something like this: 'There were once two different stories told by people in Israel. In one story God refused to go with His people because of their sinfulness. In the other story He promised to go with them. Later on, a writer or editor joined together parts of both stories, so we now have a story in which at some times God promises to go with His people, and at other times He refuses to do so.'

33.7–11. The tent of meeting: There was a seven-month period before the Tabernacle was ready. It may be that during this waiting period Moses set up an ordinary tent outside the Israelite camp as a place for his communion with God.

There are many scholars who believe that the story of the Tabernacle was not written down until the time of the exile in Babylonia, or even later. They suggest that Exodus 33.7–11 describes a simple tent that was used by Moses in the Wilderness. They think that there was no elaborate Tabernacle such as the writer of Exodus describes in chapters 25—31 and 35—40. For a fuller discussion of this view of the way the Book of Exodus was written, see Special Note E, pp. 184–191.

33.20–33. I will put you in a cleft of the rock . . . : The language of these verses is picture-language: we should not understand it literally. It seems to mean that even Moses could not possibly know God fully, as He is. God is greater than human beings can know. Notice that in 34.5–6 there is no mention of the actions described in 33.20–23.

34.1. Tables of stone: In NEB and JB the translators rightly translate this as 'tablets of stone'. In the time of Moses several different kinds of material were used in Egypt for writing, including papyrus (a kind of paper made from reeds), and parchment (made from animal skins). For inscriptions that were meant to last, stone tablets were used for short passages; longer inscriptions were carved on walls of rock or stone.

34.13. Asherim: These were cultic objects or images. They represented the Canaanite goddess Asherah and her power of fertility.

34.14. Jealous: See note on 20.5, p. 111.

34.16. Play the harlot: i.e., commit adultery or fornication. This refers to the people's unfaithfulness to Yahweh who had chosen Israel as a bride. Such unfaithfulness was chiefly shown when the Israelites worshipped other gods. It may also refer to the sexual rites which were customary in Canaanite worship.

34.17–26: This chapter describes the renewing of the Covenant. In these verses some of the Covenant laws are repeated. Since the Israelites broke the Covenant by idolatry, most of the repeated laws are concerned with worship.

STUDY SUGGESTIONS AND QUESTIONS

REVIEW OF CONTENT

1. What did Moses pray for, and how did God answer each of his prayers?
2. In what ways did God reveal His nature to Moses?
3. What did the other Israelites notice about Moses when he came from the presence of God?

BIBLE STUDY AND REFLECTION

4. 'I will go with you, and I will give you rest' (Exod. 33.14).
   (a) What is the meaning of the word 'rest' in the following verses?
   (i) Deut. 25.19; Josh. 1.13; 1 Kings 5.4
   (ii) Isa. 14.3; 28.12; Ps. 116.7
   (b) Which verses best help you to understand the meaning of the word 'rest' in Exodus 33.14 and in Matthew 11.28–29?
5. 'God is merciful' (Exod. 34.6–7). Make a list of all the descriptions of God in Exod. 34.6–7.
   (a) How many of them are similar to the idea of God which is expressed in the life and words of Jesus?

(b) Compare these ideas with the ideas about God to be found in any other religion that you know of.

6. 'Anath, Astarte, and Asherah were goddesses of war and sex' (p. 164).
(a) What results do you think it has in people's lives, if they believe in gods of this sort?
(b) Do you know of any other religions which have goddesses like Anath, Astarte, and Asherah? If so, what are they, and what is your opinion of them?

7. The English name for the sixth day of the week is 'Friday'. It reminds us that at one time (about 1,000 years ago) some of the inhabitants of England believed in the Norse god Frey, and the goddess Freya. Like the Canaanite Anath, Freya was a prostitute among the gods. She was supposed to have had sexual intercourse with all the gods. The worshippers of Frey and Freya sometimes killed men as a sacrificial offering to them. This cruel aspect of Norse religion is one reason why some people in England were glad when Christians arrived there, bringing the good news of one God who is loving and holy.
(a) What would you say to someone who said, 'There are many people who are not Christians, but they have their own religions. Christians should not try to tell them about Jesus Christ.'
(b) Which do you think is the more important, that a person should have a religion, or that a person should have a true religion? How can we tell whether a religion is true or false?
(c) If a farmer finds a better way of growing his crops, other people are usually pleased if he is willing to teach them this better way. Why do you think people often refuse to listen if someone tries to teach them a better way of religion?

35.1—40.38
Making the Tabernacle

OUTLINE AND CONTEXT

35.1–3: Moses warned the Israelites not to work on the Sabbath.
35.4—36.7: The Israelites gave what was needed to make the Tabernacle.
36.8—38.31: The workmen and women made the Tabernacle.
39.1–31: They made the special clothes for the priests.
39.32—40.33: They put up the Tabernacle.
40.34–38: God's glory filled the Tabernacle.

Exodus 35—40 tells the story of how the Israelites made the Tabernacle. They made it in accordance with the instructions which are recorded in chapters 25—31. The final verses of Exodus, 40.34–38, mention the journeys of the people of Israel, and so prepare the way for the story of the journey to Canaan which is told in the Book of Numbers.

INTERPRETATION AND COMMENT

1. GENEROUS GIVING (35.4—36.7)

Notice in 35.4—36.7:

1. *Who the people were who gave:* Both men and women brought gifts and helped in the work. In the work of God's people, men and women need to work together.

The people who gave the gifts were those who were willing (35.5, 21, 29; 36.2). They were willing to give because they were thankful for all that God had done for them. They were also willing to give because they wanted to obey God and to please Him (compare 2 Cor. 8—9). Christian congregations usually find: (a) that the best way to raise money and to get work done is by asking people to give, and (b) that when people realize how much God has done for them, then they become generous in their own giving.

2. *What they gave:* (a) They gave what they possessed (35.22–24). Some had gold, and they gave that. Some had linen, and they gave that. Some had goatskins, and they gave them. Whatever we have, we may find an opportunity for giving. In Churches in Europe, most people give gifts of money to Churches and charities. In some parts of the world people give what they grow in their gardens. All sorts of gifts are valuable (2 Cor. 8.12).

(b) The Israelites also gave their time and their abilities (35.25–26; 36.2–3). None of the gifts of wealth and possessions would have been of any use unless people had also given their time and ability to do the work. In the world today there are millions of people in need of help. We must be willing to spend time and to use our abilities to help them. In the world today there are millions of people who do not know God or trust Him. God calls us to use our time and ability to help them to come to know Him.

3. *How they gave:* They gave until the work was done (36.2–7; 39.32–43). The sailor, Francis Drake, wrote: 'It is not the beginning of a work but its continuing until it is completed that yields true glory.' The Israelites who worked to make the Tabernacle continued until everything had been completed. Contrast with this the message sent to the Church at Sardis; 'I have not found any work of yours completed' (Rev. 3.2 NEB).

Such giving of money, possessions, time, and abilities brings its own reward. In one part of Africa two different missions were working. One mission brought money from overseas to pay for the building of Churches. The other mission encouraged people to make their own gifts, to work for themselves, and to build their own Churches. Sometimes they complained to the missionaries, saying, 'Why can you not give us money to pay for the building of our Churches?' But as they worked together, the people found the satisfaction of making something that was their own, and of working together for the glory of God. After many years some of the leaders of the other mission said, 'We ought to do as the others have done. When we do work for other people which they could do for themselves, we take away from them the joys of creation and of shared work: we treat them as young children instead of helping them to be responsible men and women.'

2. CAREFUL OBEDIENCE

Notice in chapters 35—40 how many times it is said that the people did 'as the LORD had commanded Moses'. One of the great lessons of the books Exodus—Deuteronomy is that when we obey God we continue to receive His blessing. When people know how good God is, then they are ready to obey Him. And when people obey Him, they find that His will is also the best way for their lives.

Some people believe that nothing can ever happen which is against the will of God. When someone is ill, such people often say, 'It is God's will.' Because they believe that it is God's will for the person to be ill, they often do not take much trouble to seek for medical care to help the person to get better. When people believe that nothing can happen except what God wills, this belief often leads them carelessly or dangerously. For example, on a certain road taxi drivers usually overtook other vehicles as they approached the top of the many hills over which the road went. Because they could not see the road ahead there were many accidents. Someone asked, 'Why do they drive like this?' Someone else answered, 'They believe that if this is the day which God has fixed for them to die, they will die today however carefully they drive; but if today is not the day fixed for them to die, they will not be killed however dangerously they drive.'

But the writers of the books of the Bible did not believe this. They make it clear that a person can either obey God or disobey God. We can do what God wants us to do, or we can refuse to do it. When we disobey God, things happen which are not according to God's will.

3. THE GLORY OF GOD'S PRESENCE

When the Tabernacle was put up (40.17–33) it was filled with the glory of God (40.34). This is the climax of the Book of Exodus. God had promised to be with His people. Now He was showing them that He was with them, and that He would continue to be with them wherever they went. For the Israelites, as they set out from Sinai to travel to Canaan, the appearance of the glory of God in the Tabernacle was like the promise later given to Christians as they set out from Jerusalem on their mission to the world: 'I am with you always, to the close of the age' (Matt. 28.20).

God used a cloud and a shining light to make His presence and glory known to the people of Israel. Perhaps this was the best way to express the truth that God does come to be with us, but that His glory is always greater than we can understand. On the day that I was preparing to write this section I went out for a walk. As I went along the sky was cloudy. Then, across the countryside, I saw a place where the light of the sun was pouring through the clouds. It was a splendid sight against the background of dark clouds. I could not see the sun itself, but I saw something of its splendour. The Israelites could not see God Himself, but they saw something of His splendour.

Sometimes people ask questions about this. For example, they say, 'Was the glory of God in the Tabernacle something that anyone could have seen? Could it have been photographed if the people had had cameras in those days? Or was it a vision in the minds of the Israelites?' Because we were not there, the only answer we can give is, 'We do not know.' And if God, the creator of the universe, is in control of the world He has made, perhaps it is not very important whether at a particular time He chooses to make Himself known through scientifically observable events or through visions in people's minds.

4. THE TABERNACLE AND THE WORSHIP OF ISRAEL

The Tabernacle and the Ark of the Covenant were to help the people of Israel to know that God was with them, and that He had a plan for their lives, a way in which He wanted them to live. In the time of Solomon the Israelites built a temple in Jerusalem, into which they carried the Ark of the Covenant.

The Israelites found that to have such a place as the central shrine for their worship was in some ways helpful, but in other ways unhelpful. We can feel some of the joy of their worship when we read a passage like Psalm 84.1–2, 'How lovely is thy dwelling place, O LORD of hosts! . . . my heart and my flesh sing for joy to the living God.' When we read Psalm 15 we can see that the devout worshippers in the Temple were encouraged to avoid evil and to do good: 'O LORD, who shall sojourn in thy tent? . . . He who walks blamelessly, and does what is right' (Ps. 15.1–2). Christians, when they worship in Church buildings, often find a sense of the presence and peace of God. They too face the challenge to be holy in word and in deed.

But some of the writers of the Old Testament saw that there were dangers to Israel's faith and worship. In the time of Eli, the High Priest, the Israelites were struggling against the Philistines. The Philistines had a strong army. The Israelites believed that if they took the Ark of the Covenant with their army, they would win their battle against the Philistines. They took it, and they lost the battle (1 Sam. 4.1–11). They needed to learn that neither the Tabernacle nor the Ark was a fetish. The

'The Tabernacle and the Ark were to help the people to know that God was with them.' . . . 'Jesus taught that God is not concerned about the place which people use for worship' (pp. 170, 172).

A family of Indian Christians in Malaysia pray together in their home (above). At a church service in Ethiopia, one of the ministers (right) wears brilliant robes and a ceremonial gold crown given to the Church by a past Emperor as a thanksgiving for victory in battle' (see Exod. 39.30).

When and where do you yourself feel closest to God? Are you helped most by private and family prayers, by informal church services, or by splendid ceremonies?

Ark and the Tabernacle could be useful symbols of God's presence, but they could not be used as a magic way of controlling events.

In the eighth century BC the prophet Isaiah warned the people of Jerusalem that God could not be pleased with their worship in the Temple, because in their daily lives they were treating people cruelly and unjustly (Isa. 1.10–17).

About a hundred years later, when the Babylonians were attacking Jerusalem, some of the people in Jerusalem said, 'We shall be kept safe because we have the Temple of the LORD.' The prophet Jeremiah told them that the Temple could not save them, and that God would only save them if they turned away from doing evil (Jer. 7.1–7).

In the time of Jesus some Jews argued that the Temple in Jerusalem was the only proper central shrine for the worship of God. Jesus taught that God is not concerned about the place which people use for worship. He is concerned about whether they worship Him truly and honestly. For God is not physical, and He is not limited to any place: 'God is Spirit, and those who worship Him must worship in spirit and in truth' (John 4.24).

5. THE TABERNACLE AND THE WRITERS OF THE NEW TESTAMENT

We have seen that the Tabernacle had a message for the people of Israel. It showed them: (a) that God was with them, and (b) that God was holy, so that people could only come near to Him through the offering of sacrifice for their sins (see pp. 142, 143). In the New Testament the references to tne Tabernacle are about these two subjects:

(a) *God's presence with His people:* In John 1.14 RSV we read: 'The Word became flesh and *dwelt* among us.' The Greek word for 'dwelt' is literally 'tabernacled'. John meant his readers to understand that in Jesus God was truly present among men. We find the same Greek word used in Rev. 7.15 and Rev. 21.3. The final blessing that God will give to His people is this: He will dwell with them, and they will know Him in all His glory.

(b) *The offering of sacrifice for sin:* The writer of the Epistle to the Hebrews had been a Jew before he became a Christian. He knew the Old Testament account of the Tabernacle, its priests, and its sacrifices. He had thought much about them. He said that the Tabernacle erected by Moses was like a shadow or a picture that represented a spiritual reality (Heb. 8.1–5). It pictured the presence of God. The sacrifices offered in it day by day and year by year pictured the need for people's sin to be taken away if they are to come into God's presence. But what the Tabernacle and its sacrifices only pictured, Jesus Christ performed (Heb. 9.11–14, 23–28).

6. GOING ON WITH GOD

The final verses of Exodus (40.36–38) refer twice to the journey which the Israelities were about to begin. The end of the Book of Exodus is not the end of the story of Israel: it is only the beginning of a much longer story. From Sinai the people of Israel were to travel on to the land which God had promised to give them. They were to go on with God. They were to go on with Him, as people whom He had saved from slavery in Egypt. Because He had saved them they were called to obey Him and to serve Him gladly as their King.

The Christian life also is a journey. God is still at work in the world. He is at work to save people from injustice, from sin, and from death. Christians are called, not to sit still, but to go on with God (Phil. 3.8–14). Christians in the Revival Fellowship in East Africa used to be very ready to tell people how God had saved them from their sins in the past. As time went by this meant that some Christians were constantly repeating the story of how Jesus had saved them ten or fifteen or twenty years earlier. Then many of them began to say, 'We are wrong only to be thinking about the past. We need to tell each other what Jesus is doing for us *now*.' They were learning that the Christian life is a journey, in which God goes with us and gives us new experiences of Himself and of His help. We are called to travel on until our journey ends in the glory of the presence of God.

NOTES

Chapters 35—40. These chapters describe how the instructions given to Moses were carried out. The writer of Exodus repeated much of what he had already written in chapters 25—31. But he did not simply copy the instructions out again. There are differences which show that he wrote carefully. For one example, compare 36.8–38 with 26.1–37. In 26.1–37 we find instructions: (a) for making the curtains and frames, and (b) for erecting them. 36.8–38 tells us only how they were made: the story of their erection comes later, in chapter 40.

Some scholars have suggested that chapters 25—31 were written by one writer, and that chapters 35—40 were written at a later date by a different writer. They suggest this partly because they think that a writer who had written chapters 25—31 would not need to repeat all the details again in chapters 35—40. It would have been enough to say, 'Moses and the Israelites did all the work exactly as the LORD had commanded Moses.'

How can we tell whether this suggestion is likely to be true? Certainly if we look at modern European writing we shall find that writers do not often repeat what they have already written, except in stories for children. But the Book of Exodus is not modern, and it is not European. It will be better for us to compare it with ancient stories written by people in the lands of the Fertile Crescent.

Ancient stories about instructions for the building of a shrine for a god have been found in a number of these countries. One story is from Canaan. It is a poem, in which the writer tells how the god El gave instructions to

King Keret in a dream. These instructions make up about ninety lines of the poem. The following ninety lines are a repetition, with certain small changes, to describe how King Keret did as the god El had commanded him.

When we consider how important such repetition was in other ancient stories, it seems more likely that:

1. Exodus chapters 25—31 and chapters 35—40 are two parts of one story, written by one writer.

2. The idea that they were written by two different writers would perhaps be sensible if Exodus was a modern book, but such an idea does not fit in with the methods and style of ancient writers.

35.10–11. The Tabernacle, its tent and its covering: The whole structure (the holy place, and the most holy place) could be called the *tabernacle* or the *tent* (the tent of meeting). But the words 'tabernacle' and 'tent' were also used with more limited meanings. In these verses '*tabernacle*' is used to mean the ten curtains of fine linen which formed the inner covering of the holy place and the most holy place (compare 36.8–13). The word 'tent' refers to the outer covering of woven goats-hair curtains (36.14–18).

We do not know whether the leather *covering* was to cover the curtains when they were taken down and folded up for travelling (compare Numbers 4.5–12), or an outer covering to be used when the tabernacle was erected. Since there is little rain in Sinai, and an outer covering of leather would be rather heavy, it is perhaps more likely that 'its covering' means covers which were used to protect the curtains when they were packed for travelling.

35.22. Brooches and earrings . . . : In Old Testament times there were no banks to take care of people's money. Even today, families in some countries keep most of their wealth in the form of ornaments and jewellery. The people of Palestine and Arabia have been particularly fond of ornaments, especially for brides at their weddings. In more recent times, brides belonging to wealthy families might wear ornaments valued at as much as £100,000.

38.8. Mirrors: At that time mirrors were always made of polished metal, not of glass. Egyptian women usually used brass mirrors.

38.8. The ministering women: We do not know whether their work was sweeping and cleaning, or singing and dancing (compare Exod. 15.20).

38.24–31. Weights: A *beka* was about 6 grammes, a *shekel* about 12 grammes, and a *talent* about 30 kilogrammes.

38.25. Who were numbered: That is, those whose names were recorded in the census.

39.42–43: Compare this with Genesis 1.31 and 2.3. God's creative work is good and complete. Man's work for God should similarly be good, and should be completed.

40.17. The Tabernacle was erected: For references to the later history of the Tabernacle and the Ark of the Covenant in the period up to the building of Solomon's temple, see Joshua 18.1; 19.51; Judges 18.31; 1 Samuel 1—7 (especially 1 Sam. 2.22); 1 Kings 1.39; 2.28; 8.3–4; and 2 Chronicles 3.6.

The period of Israel's history from the conquest of Canaan to the time of David was one of almost constant struggle, trouble, and wars. It is not surprising that in the brief records that we have of those times there are only a few references to the Tabernacle.

STUDY SUGGESTIONS AND QUESTIONS

REVIEW OF CONTENT

1. Who were the people who contributed gifts for the making of the Tabernacle? What different sorts of gifts did they give?
2. In what way did the writer of Exodus 35—40 show the importance of obeying God?
3. In what ways did God show the Israelites that He was with them?

BIBLE STUDY AND REFLECTION

4. *Giving:* What lessons do you think we most need to learn about our own giving from the story in Exodus 35.4—36.7?
5. *Obedience:* Consider these statements:
   (a) 'We obey God because He has been so good to us.'
   (b) 'We obey God because we hope this will make Him pleased with us.'
   (c) 'We obey God because we are afraid of Him.'
   Which of these statements do you think expresses most clearly:
   (i) The feelings of the Israelites at Sinai?
   (ii) The experience of the Apostle Paul?
   (iii) Your own experience?
6. *God's Presence:* (a) In what ways do you think God makes His presence known to people today?
   (b) Do you think that God makes Himself known to people in some places more than in others? If so, in what places?
7. A Christian in Africa said, 'Once or twice, in my prayers, everything in front of me has become shining, and I knew that I was talking with God.' Do you know anyone who has had a similar experience? Do you think that such experiences are:
   (a) Necessary for everyone who wants to know God?
   (b) Not necessary for everyone, but helpful to people when they happen? or
   (c) Dangerous because they may lead to pride, or to the idea that only

those who have such special experiences can truly know that God is with them?

Give reasons for your answer.

8. *Going on with God:* When the people of Israel had escaped from Egypt and had received the Covenant at Sinai, this was only the beginning of a new life. They were called to go on with God. When a Christian hears the call of Jesus: 'Come to me, and I will give you rest,' this is only a beginning: Jesus also says, 'Follow me', and 'Learn from me.'

Consider the following list of activities. Which of them do you think are important for us if we want to go on with Jesus? Which of them do you think we shall *not* want to do? Give reasons for your answers, and, if possible, discuss them with other people:

Joining a political party.

Doing our daily work well.

Going to services of worship with other Christians.

Joining a small group of Christians to pray together.

Keeping all the traditional customs of our family or tribe.

Working in a community centre, or with some group that is trying to improve the welfare of the community.

Keeping away from people who are not Christians.

Reading the Bible and praying every day.

Visiting people who are lonely.

Telling other people about Jesus.

Keeping away from what is evil.

POSTSCRIPT
LOOKING BACK AT THE BOOK OF EXODUS

The Ideas in Exodus

Now that we have read through the Book of Exodus, we can see that it makes us think about God, about freedom, and about people. Here are some of the main ideas that the Book of Exodus may have brought into our minds as we seek to know God and His will for our lives:

1. GOD IS REAL

He revealed Himself to Moses as 'He who is'. God is real. He exists. He is the creator and cause of everything else that exists. He is not a comfortable idea invented by the minds of men, but a Person who calls people to know Him, to belong to Him, and to serve Him in the world.

2. GOD RESCUES PEOPLE

The Israelites in Egypt were suffering: God heard their prayers and set them free. He is at work still in the world to save people from all kinds of evil, to help them, and to heal them. We do not always know whether the way God will help us will be by setting us free from our troubles, or by giving us strength to bear them; but we know that He loves us and will help us.

The Book of Exodus shows that God set the people of Israel free, and led them out towards Canaan, in fulfilment of His promises made centuries before to Abraham, Isaac, and Jacob. This idea of God as the Lord of time and history, who is at work through the centuries to fulfil what He has promised, is one of the basic ideas of the Old Testament and of the New Testament.

3. GOD RULES

God is able to control the world He has made. The stories in the Book of Exodus show that He used people, and natural events, and supernatural events to bring about His will.

God rules over the people He has set free. In the story of the making of the Covenant we see God speaking to the people of Israel as a great King. Because He loved them, and had rescued them from Egypt, He called them to obey Him. The kingly rule of God meant for the Israelites:

(a) That He was with them, to keep them, to guide them, and to protect them. They knew that they belonged to Him. They were secure in His love.

They did not have to ask anxiously, 'Will God still care for us tomorrow?'

(b) That He demanded that they should live a life of love and loyalty to Him, loving and caring for their fellow men.

When we read the detailed laws in Exodus, we are reminded that God's kingly rule extends to every aspect of the life of His people. He does not only save us so that in the future we may be with Him in the glory of heaven; He saves us first of all so that we may live a new life in this present world. He cares about our family life, our agriculture, our work and wages, our politics, and our freedom.

The kingly rule of God is also shown in contrast to the oppressive rule of Pharaoh. God's power is shown to be far greater and far better than the power of Egypt. Those who trust God and obey Him find blessing. Those who oppose God bring trouble to other people, and in the end find that God punishes those who are determined to resist Him.

4. GOD IS WORTHY OF OUR WORSHIP

Sometimes people read only the earlier chapters of Exodus. They see that God is concerned, (a) to set people free, and (b) that they should treat other people justly. But these readers miss the chapters about the Tabernacle. These later chapters are necessary too, if we are to understand the Book of Exodus as a whole. They show that we cannot be truly free, and cannot find the right ways to live together in the world, unless God is with us and is the centre of our thinking and our action.

God is great and holy. He is worthy of our worship. The light of His glory shines in the world. We can draw near to Him, we can be forgiven, we can know Him as our guide.

5. GOD CALLS PEOPLE TO SERVE HIM, AND HE GIVES THEM ABILITY TO DO SO

The stories of Moses and Aaron, of Bezalel and Oholiab, and of the men and women who made the Tabernacle, make it clear that God calls people to serve Him. When He calls them He gives them the ability to serve Him. When they serve Him they also help and encourage their fellow men.

6. THE PEOPLE WHOM GOD CALLS ARE REAL PEOPLE

In the Book of Exodus we read stories about Moses and how he cared for people, led them, listened to them, prayed for them, and passed on to them the word he received from God. We read how Aaron helped Moses, how Bezalel and his helpers made something beautiful, for the glory and praise of God. We read how the Israelites rejoiced, and worshipped God, and promised to obey Him. But this is only part of the picture of these people. We read also how Moses acted violently, committing murder. We read how he tried to refuse when God called him. We read how Aaron and the

Israelites followed Canaanite ways of worship. We read how the Israelites were afraid, and how they complained against Moses and against God.

Sometimes when people are asked to commit themselves to God they say, 'I am kind and helpful to other people. I do not need anything more.' The stories in the Book of Exodus suggest that such people may be shutting their eyes to part of the truth about themselves. 'If we say that we have no sin, we deceive ourselves' (1 John 1.8).

Other people say, 'I am not good enough for God'. The message of the Book of Exodus, and of the Bible as a whole, is: God calls you as you are. He does not wait until we are good enough for Him. He is the giver of goodness, and, if we come to Him as we are, He will give us the goodness that we lack.

7. GOD WANTS PEOPLE TO BE FREE

God set the people of Israel free from slavery in Egypt: free to worship Him, free to praise Him, free to obey Him; free from oppression and from fear. In the world today freedom is limited. Hundreds of millions of people are not free from poverty and hunger: every year hunger kills more people than were killed in the five years of the Second World War. Millions of people suffer from diseases which could be cured: there are, for example, about 15 million people who suffer from leprosy, but only about 3 million who are being medically treated for it. There are millions of people held in labour camps and prisons because they do not agree with the political ideas and policies of those who rule them. People throughout the world live in fear that we shall destroy ourselves quickly through atomic warfare, or more slowly by polluting the land, the sea, and the air of this planet. The Book of Exodus shows that men, like Pharaoh, are ready to enslave others when they think they may gain some advantage by enslaving them. It shows that God wants people to be free.

The Israelites could not be free until Pharaoh and the Egyptians gave up their control over them. Pharaoh did not wish to give up this control. Like Pharaoh, people who have power seldom wish to give up their power over other people. But people who are oppressed can seldom find freedom unless other people are willing to give up their power, or are forced to do so.

Moses tried to win justice for an oppressed Israelite by murdering an Egyptian officer. He failed to bring real help to his people in this way. In various parts of the world today terror and violence and murder are being used by groups who believe they are right to fight in this way for the freedom or justice which they desire. The Book of Exodus makes us ask whether this is God's way.

The people of Israel were not set free until Moses was willing to face difficulty and death to bring them out of Egypt. People will not be set free from hunger, from disease, from tyranny, and from fear unless we give ourselves to God, unless we fight for freedom by love, by prayer, by giving, by work, by readiness to suffer.

Again and again Pharaoh hardened his heart, and would not let the people of Israel go. When we hear of people who are in need or who are oppressed, it is easy for us to harden our hearts. We can harden our hearts by saying, 'It is not my business', 'I can't risk it', 'I can't afford to help', 'I have no time', 'There is nothing I can do.' But if God is calling us to do something to help other people to be free, then there is something we can do, and God will be with us as we do it.

So the Book of Exodus challenges us to trust in God; to find our freedom, not in doing as we like, but in doing what pleases Him; and to love other people and to work for their welfare.

STUDY SUGGESTIONS

REVIEW OF CONTENT

1. Which parts of the Book of Exodus do you think illustrate most clearly:
   (a) That people fail to live as God intends them to live?
   (b) That God wants people to be free?
   (c) That when God sets people free, He does so in order that they may live a new life, obeying Him as their King?
2. Which parts of the Book of Exodus do you think are most important for:
   (a) People who are suffering?
   (b) People who are leaders and politicians?
   (c) People who think that we are only free if we can do as we like?
   (d) People who think that God will only save those who are good?

BIBLE STUDY AND REFLECTION

3. What do you find in the story of Moses that encourages you to do any of the following?
   (a) To wait patiently;
   (b) To endure loneliness and disappointment;
   (c) To pray;
   (d) To expect God to help the people you pray for;
   (e) To expect God to use you to serve other people.
4. What would you say to someone who said; 'The Book of Exodus was written a long time ago. I do not think we need to read it today'?
5. What do you think are the most important lessons we can learn from the Book of Exodus?
6. What questions and problems do you have in your mind as a result of your study of the Book of Exodus?

7. 'The writer of the Book of Exodus . . . meant the readers . . . to think, to make decisions, and to act (p. 3).' As a result of your study of the Book of Exodus, have you changed any of your ideas about the following, and, if so, in what way?
   (a) God.
   (b) Other people.
   (c) Your country and its leaders.
   (d) Your country and its laws.
   (e) The Church.
   (f) The importance of trust in God.
   (g) The importance of worship.

   As a result of your study of the Book of Exodus, is there anything you have decided that God wants you to do? If so, what?

Exodus and the other books of the Bible

Exodus is part of the Pentateuch and part of the Bible. Together with the Book of Genesis, it forms a foundation for the whole of the rest of the Bible (see pp. 6–8).

EXODUS AND THE OLD TESTAMENT

When we read the other books of the Old Testament, we shall see that their writers believed that there is only one God. They believed in Him as the creator and controller of all that exists. They believed that He had called the people of Israel to live in a special relationship to Him, serving Him as their Lord and King. They believed that God had spoken to them in the past, and that He would go on revealing Himself and leading them on into the future. So their faith rested on God's way of revealing Himself through Abraham and Moses, and on the story that is recorded in Genesis and Exodus.

EXODUS AND THE NEW TESTAMENT

A man once gave a copy of the New Testament to a Chinese student. The student came back after a time to thank him for the book, and said, 'And now may I have Volume One'. As the student read the New Testament, he had been aware that the faith of the writers of the New Testament rested on a foundation which had already been laid. The writers of the New Testament did not need to discuss at length the question of idolatry, or whether there is more than one God. They did not have to argue at length that God speaks and acts within the history of the world He has made. The foundation of faith in God and His kingly rule had already been laid, especially in the Book of Exodus.

EXODUS AND THE PROPHETS OF ISRAEL

The great prophets of Israel, men like Amos, Hosea, Isaiah, and Jeremiah, did not introduce startling new ideas into the religion of Israel. They challenged people to turn back to the God who had *already* called Israel into a Covenant relationship with Himself.

In the kingdom of Israel Hosea said that trouble was coming upon Israel 'because they have broken my covenant and transgressed my law.' Isaiah, in the kingdom of Judah, announced a similar message: 'The land lies polluted under its inhabitants, for they have . . . broken the everlasting covenant.' But they also looked forward to a time when God would again bless and restore His people, as He had done long before when He delivered them from Egypt (Hos. 13.4; 14.4; Isa. 11.16—12.2; 51.9–10). Jeremiah and Ezekiel looked forward to the day when God would re-establish His covenant in a new and better way (Jer. 31.31–34; Ezek. 36.26–27).

EXODUS AND THE MINISTRY OF JESUS

The writers of the New Testament saw Jesus as a new and better Moses (Acts 7, note particularly 7.35, because Stephen was saying to the High Priests, 'you have rejected Jesus whom God sent to be ruler and deliverer, just as the Israelites at first rejected Moses'). They saw Him as the Passover sacrifice (1 Cor. 5.7–8) whose death on the cross brought deliverance from sin and death (Mark 14.24; Heb. 10.11–17). And, just as the story in the Book of Exodus does not come to an end, but leads into a new story of Israel's journey towards and into the Promised Land, so the story of Jesus in the Gospels does not come to an end. It leads into the story of the spreading of the Good News to the furthest parts of the world.

EXODUS AND NEW TESTAMENT THEOLOGY

In the time of our Lord Jesus many Jews believed that if they kept God's laws very carefully they could make themselves good. Then, they thought, God would accept them and help them and bless them. One of the important questions we must try to answer, when we think about God and our lives, is this: 'Do we have to make ourselves good enough for God, or will He accept us as we are?' And another question is, 'Do we have to persuade God to bless us by doing many good deeds?'

The story in the Book of Exodus helps us to think about these questions. The people of Israel were slaves in Egypt. God did not give them His law while they were in Egypt. He did not say to them, 'If you keep my law, I will set you free.' No. He *first* saved them from slavery and oppression. Then, afterwards, He gave them His law to show them how they should live. First

'God first saved the Israelites from slavery and oppression, and afterwards gave them His law.' . . . 'Jesus did not wait for people to make themselves good. He came to bring people a new life' (pp. 182, 184).

The early Christians, including the New Testament writers, looked back to the events of the Exodus and compared them with the saving events of Jesus's life, death, and resurrection (see 1 Cor. 10.1–5, 11).

Carvings on a Christian coffin of about AD 340 from Salonae in Dalmatia show the Egyptians (wearing helmets) with their horses drowning in the Sea of Reeds, while the Israelites (at the right of the picture) hurry their children away to safety—meaning perhaps that the deceased person had already passed from death to life through baptism.

of all they came to know God as the One who had saved them. Then they showed their thankfulness by promising to serve Him. They did not have to serve God first so that afterwards He might save them. They served God *because* He had already saved them.

This is what the writers of the New Testament also say about Christians. Jesus Himself said, 'I did not come to call good people: I came to call sinners' (Mark 2.17). He did not wait for people to make themselves good. He came to bring people a new life and a new power so that they might *become* good.

When we read Paul's letter to the Christians at Ephesus we see that he had the same view. In Ephesians chapters 1—3 Paul showed how God calls and saves and blesses people. Then in chapters 4—6 he showed how people who have been saved ought to live, and that God gives them the power for this new way of life. Note particularly Ephesians 2.8–10: 'God has saved you because He loves you freely, and you are saved as you trust in Him. All this is God's gift; it is not a result of what you were nor of anything you did, so no one can boast about it. We are God's workmanship: He has made us what we are through Jesus Christ so that we may do all those good things that He has already planned for us to do.'

So there is a basic harmony between the theology of the writer of the Book of Exodus and the theology of the writers of the New Testament. But this does not mean that the Book of Exodus is exactly the same as the New Testament. Since the time of the Book of Exodus God has been leading His people forward. When we go forward we always leave something behind. So we need not be surprised if there are some ideas in the Book of Exodus that we have left behind. God's final revelation of Himself was not in Moses but in Jesus (John 1.1–18; Heb. 1.1–3).

Human beings cannot live without changing. As God went on teaching the people of Israel, they had to leave behind some of their earlier ideas and customs. Let us not be unwilling if He wants us to change. Let us be ready to leave behind some of our earlier ideas and our earlier ways. We cannot live without changing; so let us ask God to change us in the ways He wants us to be changed.

Special Note E:
When was Exodus written?

1. WE DO NOT KNOW WHO WROTE THE BOOK OF EXODUS

When you look at this Guide to the Book of Exodus, you can find out the name of the writer and the year in which it was published. But when we read the Book of Exodus itself, we cannot find out who wrote it, nor when it was written. We have to teach our tongues to say, 'We do not know.' None of the books of the Old Testament contain clear statements about who wrote them. We should like to know, but it is more important for us to be able to study what has been written than to know exactly who wrote it, or the date when it was written.

However, there are some clues which enable us to say when we *think* that some of the Old Testament books were written. For example, the Book of Kings (1 Kings and 2 Kings in the RSV) mentions the fall of Jerusalem and the exile in Babylon. But the writer does not mention the return of the Jews from exile in 539–538 BC. So it is likely that the writing of the Book of Kings was finished during the exile in Babylonia. The writer of the Book of Kings refers to earlier written records. These were the 'Book of the acts of Solomon', the 'Book of the Chronicles of the Kings of Judah', and the 'Book of the Chronicles of the Kings of Israel' (1 Kings 11.41; 14.29; 14.19). It is possible that a 'first edition' of the Book of Kings was written before the fall of Jerusalem in 587 BC.

2. SOME CLUES TO THE DATE OF THE BOOK OF EXODUS

1. The latest historical event which is mentioned in the Book of Exodus is the arrival of the Israelites at the border of Canaan (16.35). In the passages which refer to God's promise to be with them, and to lead them into the land He had promised to Abraham, Isaac, and Jacob, there is no mention that He would lead them across Jordan, and no mention of Jericho or any of the towns that were conquered by Joshua. In the story of the Tabernacle there is no mention that it would one day be replaced by the Temple in Jerusalem. This suggests, either (a) that the traditions of the Exodus period were kept very carefully, and told with little change from generation to generation, or (b) that the writing of Exodus itself belongs to an early period in Israel's history, probably before David made Jerusalem the capital city of Israel.

2. In the list of tribes inhabiting Canaan there is no mention of the Philistines (Exod. 3.17). After the Israelites entered Canaan, the Philistines were their chief enemies in the period about 1150–1000 BC.

3. The form of the Sinai Covenant described in Exodus chapters 20—24 is similar to the form of the Hittite treaties (see Special Note D, p. 114). This covenant form seems to belong to the period before 1000 BC.

4. The poetic and grammatical forms found in the song in Exodus 15 are similar to the forms found in Canaanite poems composed before the time of Moses.

5. The closest known parallels to the laws which we find in Exodus chapters 20—23 are laws known in Mesopotamia before the time of Moses. In the Exodus laws there is no reference to kingship. There were changes in the structure of Israelite laws after Saul became king.

6. From about the time of the establishing of the kingship in Israel it seems that the words 'the LORD of hosts' became the most common way of referring to God in the historical and prophetic writings of Israel. In the Book of Exodus there is not even one use of the term 'the LORD of hosts.'

7. There are a number of other words and expressions which seem to belong to the early literature of Israel. Some of them are Hebrew words which were later used with a rather different meaning (see, for example, the note on Exodus 3.6 'The God of your fathers', p. 23). Some appear to be Egyptian phrases, for example, 'a mouth for you', 'the finger of God', 'from the day it was founded' and 'the eye of the land' (see notes on 4.16; 8.19; 9.18; and 10.5).

8. From the time of the Judges until the fall of the kingdoms of Israel and Judah, the people of Israel were again and again involved in the worship of Baal. Prophets preached against this worship and writers condemned it. Exodus contains many warnings against idolatry, false worship, and superstition, but there is not a single mention of Baal.

All of these clues point to the conclusion that the Book of Exodus belongs to the early days of Israel's existence as a nation. But none of these clues can show us certainly when the Book of Exodus was written. It is possible for us to believe either:

(a) that Exodus is one of the earliest books of the Old Testament, and was written before the time when David became king (perhaps a long time before), or

(b) that the people of Israel remembered very carefully the stories their fathers and forefathers had told about the Exodus from Egypt, and that some hundreds of years after the time of the Exodus they wrote these stories down, being careful to use the sort of words and phrases that belonged to an earlier age.

The writer of this Study Guide believes that view (a) is more likely to be correct. He believes that most of the material in the Book of Exodus can now be shown to belong to the very earliest part of Israel's history as a nation, and that it is unlikely to have been written at a late stage in the development of Israel as a kingdom. But most of the scholars who have written books about Exodus in the past hundred years have not taken this view. They have believed that the Book of Exodus was not written in its present form until some time in the period 550–400 BC.

3. SOME REASONS FOR SUGGESTING THAT THE PENTATEUCH WAS WRITTEN IN THE PERIOD 550–400 BC

In the eighteenth and nineteenth centuries AD, a large number of Old Testament scholars put forward a variety of different views about how the Book of Exodus was written. By AD 1900 most Old Testament scholars were agreed that the Books of the Pentateuch were composed in the period

550–400 BC by an editor who used stories that had at one time been written in four separate books. Why did they think this?

They put forward three main arguments:

1. People and places in the Pentateuch often have more than one name, and some stories seem to be told twice. For example, God is most commonly called either Elohim (RSV God) or Yahweh (RSV LORD). The father-in-law of Moses is called Reuel (Exod. 2.18) or Jethro (Exod. 3.1; 4.18; 18.1–12). In Genesis 1.1—2.4a it seemed that there was one story of how the world was made, and then in Genesis 2.4b–25 there was another quite different story. In Exodus 20.1–17 and Exodus 34.10–26, scholars thought, there were two quite different accounts of the Ten Commandments. So they argued, 'A single writer would not have used different names for one person. Probably one writer wrote a story using one name, while another writer wrote the story using a different name for the same person or place. Later on an editor put the two different stories together in a single book.'

2. In different parts of the Pentateuch we find different types or styles of writing. For example, Genesis 1.1—2.4a is rather like poetry: it contains much repetition. But Genesis 2.4b–25 is an ordinary kind of story: it is not poetic but in prose. In some parts of the Pentateuch we find genealogies (lists of ancestors), but in other parts we do not. So scholars argued like this, 'A writer usually has one style of writing. In the books of the Pentateuch we find a mixture of styles of writing. This must be because there were originally a number of different books by different writers. Later on, editors must have joined together parts from these different books to make one new book.'

3. Scholars also thought that in Israel there was a very slow progress towards faith in only one God. Before the time of Moses, they said, the Israelites probably believed in many gods. After the time of Moses and up until the time of the eighth century prophets, they probably believed that there were many gods, but that they themselves were specially called to worship Yahweh. The prophets of Israel who preached in the period 750–540 BC taught the people of Israel that they should believe that there is only one God, the creator of the whole world. Scholars who accept this theory of the slow development of Israelite theology found that some parts of the Pentateuch showed a belief in only one God. So they argued, 'These parts of the Pentateuch must have been written in the eighth century BC or later. Some of them were probably written in the period 600–450 BC.'

4. FOUR MAIN SOURCES: J, E, D, AND P?

Put fairly simply, the most commonly accepted theory of how Exodus and the other books of the Pentateuch were written was this:

(a) About 950 BC, when Solomon was king of all Israel, a writer in Judah began to write down the story, as he had heard it, of Israel's faith and history. He began with the story of Adam, as we find it in Genesis 2—3. He went on to tell stories about Abraham and his descendants, and about Moses.

From the beginning of the story this writer called God by the name Yahweh, or as it used to be written in English: Jehovah. For this reason, the writer has been called the 'Yahwist', or more simply: 'J'.

(b) About 750 BC, when Jeroboam was king of the northern kingdom of Israel, a writer in Israel wrote down the stories he had heard about Israel's early faith and history. He believed that until the time of Moses the Israelites did not know the name Yahweh, so in his stories about the time before Moses he called God 'Elohim' (in English 'God'). For this reason, scholars referred to this writer as the 'Elohist' or 'E'.

(c) About 650 BC, when Manasseh was king of Judah, some of the men of Judah were troubled because people were worshipping other gods. So they wrote a book to encourage people to worship Yahweh, and to offer sacrifices to Him only in Jerusalem. They wrote the book as if it was sermons preached by Moses to the people of Israel. The book which they wrote was hidden in the Temple, and in 621 BC it was discovered and taken to king Josiah; it forms the main part of our present Book of Deuteronomy. For this reason scholars called the writers 'the Deuteronomists', or 'D'.

(d) About 550 BC, when many of the priests and people of Judah were in exile in Babylonia, some of the Jewish priests began to write down stories and laws and details about worship, and about Israel's faith in God. They wrote the story of creation which we can now read in Genesis 1.1—2.4a. They wrote about God's covenants with Noah, with Abraham, and with Israel. They included many genealogies (for example Gen. 5 and Exod. 6.14–25) and many numbers. Because they were priests they wrote many stories about Aaron, the priests, the sacrifices, and the Tabernacle (for example Exod. 25—31 and 35—40). Scholars called them the 'Priestly' writers, or 'P'.

5. EDITORS OR COMPILERS

How were these four main written sources, J, E, D, and P, combined to make the Pentateuch? Most scholars suggest that about 700 BC an editor combined the stories of J and E to make a new book (JE). Later on, perhaps about 600 BC, another editor added on what the Deuteronomists had written. At the same time he made some changes in JE. After the Exile, perhaps about 400 BC, a final editor took the story written by the Priestly writers and added in the stories he found in JED. When he finished this work the Pentateuch was complete.

6. IS THIS THEORY OF J, E, D, AND P ACCEPTED BY SCHOLARS TODAY?

Many scholars still accept some of the ideas that make up the theory of J, E, D, and P. But they believe that this theory was too simple.

Some of them say that instead of thinking of J and E as two writers, we should think of them as being either (a) groups of writers, or (b) groups of people who told stories and passed them down from generation to generation by word of mouth.

Other scholars accept the idea that the Pentateuch is the result of the growth of stories during many centuries, but they believe that these different groups of stories grew up chiefly in the temples and shrines of Israel. Some of them think that the Book of Exodus was written, not so much because the Israelites escaped from Egypt, as because the Israelites had a Passover festival and they wished to explain it.

Other scholars believe that the J, E, D, P theory was basically wrong from the start. They do not think that it fits in with what we know about the literature of the other ancient lands of the Fertile Crescent.

7. SOME REASONS WHY SCHOLARS REJECT THE THEORY OF J, E, D, AND P

Most of the arguments used to support the theory of J, E, D, and P are arguments that we can now see were either doubtful or wrong. Let us look again at the three main arguments (pp. 186, 187):

1. *Two or more names for a person or a place:* Such double names are common in the writings of the ancient Egyptians, Canaanites, and Babylonians. A single writer often gave two or more names to gods, people, and places. The Canaanite god El was sometimes called Latpan. The Babylonian god Enlil is also called Nunamnir. In Merenptah's inscription (see p. 85) the land of Egypt is called both Kemit and Tameri. The same inscription has five names for the Egyptian town of Memphis: Mennefer, Ineb-hedj, Inbu, Inebheqa, and Hatkuptah. In cases like this we know that the inscription was written at one time by one writer. So when we find two names for a person or a place in the Pentateuch we cannot argue that the use of two different names necessarily shows that there were originally two different writings or two different traditions.

2. *Different styles of writing:* Different styles of writing are common in the literature of Egypt, Canaan, and Babylonia. For example, the story of the life of an Egyptian official called Uni was inscribed on stone about 2400 BC shortly after his death. The inscription contains stories of his life, short summaries, and a hymn. We cannot say that there is evidence of a story source (like J and E) and a hymn source (like P?), which were later joined together by an editor because we know that the inscription was written and engraved on stone shortly after his death. So when we look at passages like Genesis 1.1—2.3 and 2.4–25 we are not forced to say, 'There

are two separate styles, therefore there were two different writers.' Perhaps we should say, 'Like many other ancient writers, the writer of Genesis could use more than one style.' (See also note on chapters 35—40, pp. 173, 174).

3. *A slow development of faith in one God:* In the later part of the nineteenth century AD scientists were particularly interested in the idea of the gradual evolution of animals. When Old Testament scholars put forward the idea of a gradual development of belief that there is only one God, this seemed a very easy idea to accept. But we now know enough about the thoughts and beliefs of other thinkers in the lands of the Fertile Crescent, to be able to say that the idea that there is only one God was often expressed before the time of Moses. For example, in an Egyptian hymn to the god Amun the writer said, 'Thou art the only one who created, the unique one who created what exists.' A hymn to the god Aten calls him, 'the only God beside whom there is no other.' Both these hymns belong to the period before Moses (fifteenth and fourteenth centuries BC).

In the following centuries little notice was taken of these ideas; most Egyptians continued to believe in many gods. So we have to say: (a) the people of Israel might have been taught by Moses to believe in only one God, (b) we cannot in other cultures trace a steady development of such ideas, so we cannot assume that in Israel there was a slow development towards faith in one God which did not reach a climax until the eighth century BC or later.

We have now looked briefly at some of the main arguments which scholars have used to support the idea of four sources for the book of Exodus, J, E, D, and P. We have seen that the books of the Pentateuch were written by men in ancient Israel, who shared the general culture of the lands of the Fertile Crescent. Therefore we must consider other ancient writings from these lands when we put forward our ideas concerning the writing of Exodus and the other books of the Pentateuch. Since double names and differences of style are found in inscriptions that we know to have been written by one person in a short time, we cannot rely on such arguments to show that the books of the Pentateuch were written over a long period of time using several different sources. The books of the Pentateuch are not special books so far as their literary style is concerned. We must judge them exactly as we would judge any other ancient documents. So when we look at the theory that the Book of Exodus was compiled from four basic sources, J, E, D, and P, we need to say:

(a) This is a theory, it is not a proved fact.

(b) It might be true, but before we accept it as true, we need better arguments to support it than the arguments many scholars have put forward in the past.

(c) It may be false. The clues to the date of Exodus that we have examined (pp. 185, 186) suggest that the Book of Exodus belongs to an earlier period than 950–450 BC.

CONCLUSIONS

From our discussion about the writing of the Book of Exodus, we can draw the following conclusions:

1. We do not know exactly when the Book of Exodus was written.

2. A careful study of the contents and character of the Book of Exodus suggests that it belongs to the earlier part of Israel's history as a nation, and that it may have been written before David established Jerusalem as the centre of the Israelite kingdom.

3. Many scholars believe that our present Book of Exodus was not written until the time of the Babylonian exile. They believe that the writer of Exodus used either (a) earlier written documents, or (b) oral traditions that had been carefully handed down from generation to generation. The author of this Study Guide believes that these views have not been supported by convincing arguments.

4. Whatever view we hold on this question, we need to keep in mind the following points:

(a) It is more important for us to know *what* is written in the Book of Exodus, than to know *when* it was written.

(b) It is likely that scholars will continue to hold different views about the date of the writing of the Book of Exodus. In our discussion of these views we need continually to consider which points can be supported from our knowledge of the other ancient books and writings from the lands of the Fertile Crescent. If another student disagrees with us, we cannot help to solve the problem by accusing him of being unbelieving or of being simple. What we need is firm evidence, clear reasoning, respect for those who differ from us, and the humility to admit that we may be wrong.

Then perhaps we shall be able to continue to study the Book of Exodus together, in order to discover what it has to say to us about God and our own lives, and so come to trust in God more fully and obey Him more gladly.

STUDY SUGGESTIONS AND QUESTIONS

REVIEW OF CONTENT

1. What evidence can we find in the Book of Exodus which suggests that the stories it contains belong to the early days of Israel's existence as a nation (i.e. that they date from 1300–1000 BC)?
2. We may find evidence of early traditions in the Book of Exodus. Does this enable us to be certain at what period the book was written? If not, why not?
3. (a) Many scholars have believed that the Book of Exodus was compiled by a number of different writers and editors in the period

from about 950 BC to 450 BC. Give three of the chief arguments which they used to support this belief.

(b) Other scholars have rejected these arguments. What are the chief reasons these scholars have put forward for rejecting them?

BIBLE STUDY AND REFLECTION

4. Most of us cannot easily study other ancient literature from Egypt or Canaan or Mesopotamia. So we cannot compare such writings with the book of Exodus in order to assess for ourselves the evidence which scholars put forward for believing that different parts of the Book of Exodus come from different sources. But we can evaluate some of the evidence by studying other books of the Bible.

   Scholars agree that the Book of Jonah was all written at one period of time by one single author. The author may have used a traditional story, but his book is not a combination of several earlier written stories. Read through the Book of Jonah and make a note of all the references to God.

   (a) How many times is He referred to as 'God' (i.e. translated from the Hebrew *Elohim*)?

   (b) How many times is He given the name 'the LORD' (i.e. from the Hebrew *Yahweh*)?

   (c) In which passages does 'God' occur most often?

   (d) In which passages does 'the LORD' occur most often?

   (e) Do you think that we can relate the different parts of the Book of Jonah to different sources by noting whether God is referred to as *Yahweh* or *Elohim* in the original Hebrew?

   (f) Does your study of the Book of Jonah make you more ready or less ready to accept the argument that different parts of the Book of Exodus can be related to different sources, partly by noticing whether God is named as *Yahweh* or referred to as *Elohim*?

5. Read through Luke's Gospel chapters 1—4.

   (a) Which parts of Luke 1—4 are:

   (i) stories of what happened?

   (ii) hymns or poems?

   (iii) genealogies?

   (b) What would you reply to someone who said: I believe that Luke 1—4 was written by a number of different writers at different periods of time, and then combined together by an editor at a later date?

   (c) In Luke 1—4 we find different styles of writing. These styles may have been influenced by the different people from whom Luke gathered his information, and by the different writings he studied (see Luke 1.1–3). But Luke arranged all his material together at one period of time.

   Does your study of Luke make you more ready or less ready to accept the argument that we can relate the Book of Exodus to different writers or sources belonging to different periods of time, by noticing the different styles of writing that are used?

6. In Luke 1—2 notice that Luke says Jesus spent part of His childhood in (i) Bethlehem and (ii) Nazareth. There are two stories about the birth of a baby: (i) the story of Elizabeth and John, and (ii) the story of Mary and Jesus. There are two stories about people in the Temple who spoke about Jesus: (i) the story of Simeon, and (ii) the story of Anna. There are three names or titles given to Mary's son: (i) 'Jesus', (ii) 'The Son of the Highest', (iii) 'the Son of God'. The angel is referred to as (i) 'the angel', (ii) 'an angel of the LORD', (iii) 'the angel Gabriel', (iv) 'Gabriel'.

   How does your study of Luke 1—2 help you to answer someone who says: 'I think the Book of Exodus was written by a number of different writers, because some of the people mentioned in it are given two or more names, and because some of the stories it contains seem to be told twice over'?

7. (a) Which do you consider it is more important to discuss: (i) How and when the Book of Exodus was written, or (ii) What lessons we can learn from the Book of Exodus today, to help us in our faith and in our daily lives?

   (b) What answer do you think St Paul might have given to 7(a)?—see 1 Timothy 1.3–7 and 1 Corinthians 10.1–13.

   (c) In your own study of the Book of Exodus, are you chiefly concerned with the question of when it was written or the question of what we can learn from it?

8. Discuss the following statement: 'It would be interesting to know when the Book of Exodus was written, but it is not important for us to know.'

9. What would you reply to someone who said: 'I cannot read the Book of Exodus, because I am confused by all the different theories about how and when it was written'?

10. What would you reply to someone who said: 'I cannot accept that anyone is a serious scholar unless he agrees with my views about how and when the Book of Exodus was written'?

Key to Study Suggestions and Questions

In the Study Suggestions and Questions there are many questions which ask you to say what you think. This Key cannot do your thinking for you. So there will be many of the questions which are not mentioned at all in this Key. But there are some questions where you may find help, if you have difficulty, by looking at a particular passage in the Bible or by reading a particular part of this Study Guide.

('para.'=paragraph, 'section' refers to a numbered section of the Interpretation and Comment.)

THE CONTENT AND CONTEXT OF EXODUS (pp. 8–9)

1. See p. 4.
2. See p. 6.
3. See p. 4.

EXODUS 1, 1–22: OPPRESSION IN EGYPT

1. See middle of p. 10.
2. See Exod. 1.8–10 and p. 13, note on 1.10.
3. Exod. 1.11 and 1.16.
4. See p. 11, para. 3.
7. God's promise to give the land of Canaan to Abraham and his descendants.

2. 1–25: MOSES BEFORE HIS CALL (p. 18)

1. See Exod. 1.16.
2. See Exod. 2.2.
3. See Exod. 2.11–15.
4. See Exod. 2.16–17.
5. See p. 17–18, note on 2.18.
6. See p. 18, note on 2.24.

3. 1–22: THE CALL OF MOSES (1) (p. 24)

1. See Exod. 3.1 and p. 19, note on 3.1.
2. See Exod. 3.10 and 3.15–16.
3. (a) See Exod. 3.11; 3.13. (c) See Exod. 3.12 and 3.14–15.

4.1–31: THE CALL OF MOSES (2) (pp. 31–32)

1. See Exod. 4.1; 4.10; 4.13; and 4.2–9; 4.11–12; 4.14–16.
2. See Exod. 4.2–4; 4.6–7; 4.9; and 4.1; 4.5.

5.1–23: 'I WILL NOT LET ISRAEL GO' (pp. 35–36)

1. See Exod. 5.6–9.
2. (a) See Exod. 5.20–21; and 5.22–23.
3. See p. 33, para. 1.
4. See p. 33, section 2, second para.

6.1–27: GOD ENCOURAGED MOSES (pp. 42–43)

1. See Exod. 5.6–23.
2. (a) See Exod. 6.1–8 and p. 38, section 2. (b) See pp. 36–38, section 1.
3. See pp. 38–39, section 3.

6.28—8.19: THE FIRST THREE PLAGUES (pp. 49–50)

1. See Exod. 7.17–21; 8.2–6; 8.16–17.
2. See p. 47, section 2.
3. See Exod. 8.1–2; 8.9–13; 8. 30–31 and p. 48, last two paragraphs.
4. (a) See Exod. 8.8 (b) See Exod. 8.15.

8.20—9.12: THE FOURTH, FIFTH AND SIXTH PLAGUES (p. 55)

1. See Exod. 8.21–24 and p. 54, section 3.
2. See Exod. 9.3 and p. 54, section 3.
3. See Exod. 9.9–10 and p. 54, section 3.
4. See p. 51, section 1.

9.13—10.29: THE SEVENTH, EIGHTH AND NINTH PLAGUES (p. 60)

1. See Exod. 9.19–25.
2. See Exod. 10.4–6; 12–15.
3. See Exod. 10.21–23.
4. See p. 58, section 3.
5. See pp. 57–58, sections 1 and 2.

11.1—12.28: THE PASSOVER (pp. 67–68)

1. See Exod. 12.3; 12.6; 12.8.
2. See p. 61, section 1.
3. See p. 61, section 1, and pp. 62–63, sections 3 and 4.
4. See pp. 64–66, section 6.
5. See pp. 63–64, sections 3 and 4.
7. See p. 64, section 6.

12.29—13.22: THE FIRST-BORN SONS (pp. 72–73)

1. See Exod. 12.29–33.
2. See pp. 68–69, section 1.
3. By keeping the festivals of Passover and Unleavened Bread; and by the consecration of their first-born sons.
4. See Exod. 13:17 and map on p. xiv.

14.1–31: 'THE LORD BROUGHT US OUT OF EGYPT' (p. 77)

1. See Exod. 14.5 and 1.11.
2. See Exod. 14.6–9.
3. See Exod. 14.11–12.
4. (a) See Exod. 14.13–14.

15.1–21: SONGS OF VICTORY (p. 83)

1. See p. 79, section 1.
2. See Exod. 15.1–13 and 15.14–17.

15.22—17.7: 'IS THE LORD WITH US?' (p. 93)

1. (a) See Exod. 15.22–23; 16.3; 17.1. (b) See Exod. 15.24; 16.3; 17.2–3, 7. (c) See Exod. 15.25; 17.4.
2. See Exod. 15.25–26; 16.4–15; 17.5–6.
3. See Exod. 15.26 and 16.22–30.

17.8—18–27: 'THE LORD IS WITH US' (pp. 98–99)

2. See Exod. 17.14 and 17.15.
3. (a) See Exod. 18.8. (b) See Exod. 18.9–12. (c) See Exod. 18.13–18. (d) See Exod. 18.19–23.

19.1–25: THE COVENANT—INTRODUCTION (pp. 104–105)

2. See particularly Exod. 19.10–25.
3. See pp. 100–102, section 1.

20.1–17: THE COVENANT: ITS FOUNDATIONS (p. 112)

1. See Exod. 20.2; 20.5; 20.7; 20.11; 20.12.
3. See Exod. 20.8–11.

20.18—22.17: THE COVENANT: ITS LAWS (1) (p. 124)

2. See p. 120 section 3, and notes on Exod. 21.18–27; 21.28–36; 22.1–15.

22.18—23.33: THE COVENANT: ITS LAWS (2) (p. 129)

1. See Exod. 22.21–22; 22.25–26; 23.3–6; 23–9; 23.12.
2. See Exod. 22.21; 22.23; 22.27; 23.9.
3. See Exod. 23.22–31 and 23.33.

24.1–18: ISRAEL ACCEPTS THE COVENANT (p. 134)

1. See Exod. 24.3–8.
2. See Exod. 24.5–7.
3. See Exod. 24.9–11.

25.1—27.21: HOW TO MAKE THE TABERNACLE (p. 140)

1. See pp. 136–138, sections 2–4.
2. See pp. 136–138, section 4, and pp. 139–140, note on Exod. 25.10–22.

28.1—29.47: MAKE AARON THE PRIEST (p. 146)

1. See pp. 141–142, section 1.
2. See pp. 141–142, section 1.

30.1—31.18: THE TABERNACLE—MORE INSTRUCTIONS (p. 151)

1. See pp. 147–148, sections 1 and 2.
2. See p. 148, section 2.
3. See pp. 148–149, section 3.
4. See p. 149, first para.
5. See p. 149, section 5.

32.1–35: THE ISRAELITES BREAK THE COVENANT (p. 161)

1. See Exod. 32.1 and p. 153 section 1.
2. See p. 156, section 2(e).
3. See p. 153, section 1 and p. 158, note on Exod. 32.4.
4. See pp. 153–154, section 2.
5. See Exod. 32.11–13.
6. See pp. 159–160, note on 32.14.

33.1—34.35: GOD WILL GO WITH US (p. 166)

1. See Exod. 33.12–17 and 33.14; 33.17; 34.5–7.
2. See Exod. 32.17–23; 33.5–7.
3. See Exod. 34.29–30.

35.1—40.38: MAKING THE TABERNACLE (p. 175)

1. See Exod. 35.20–29.
2. See p. 169, section 2.
3. See Exod. 40.35–38.

SPECIAL NOTE: (p. 191)

1. See pp. 185–186.
2. See p. 186, para. 4.
3. See p. 187.
4. See pp. 189–190.

Index

INDEX